Owain
Glyn Dŵr

Owain Glyn Dŵr

The War of Independence in the Welsh Borders

by
Geoffrey Hodges

Logaston Press 1995

LOGASTON PRESS
Little Logaston Woonton Almeley
Herefordshire HR3 6QH

First published by Logaston Press 1995

Reprinted 1996, 1998, 2000, 2002

Copyright © Geoffrey Hodges 1994

ISBN 1 873827 24 5

Set in Times 11/13 pt by Logaston Press
and printed in Great Britain by
Antony Rowe Ltd. Chippenham, Wiltshire

*Cover illustration: From a panel at Kentchurch Court, believed
by some to depict Owain Glyn Dŵr, though by most to be Jack of
Kent, a sage or sorcerer, and by others to be one and the same.
(Courtesy of John Scudamore)*

For Nicola and Michael

Geoffrey Hodges

Geoffrey died when this book was in page proofs—he was still completing the footnotes to his satisfaction. Whilst his family and I have worked to try and ensure all his notes and comments have been incorporated, it may be that there was still some new information he would have wished to include, or revisions to make. We have done our best, and I hope I have compiled as extensive an Index as he would have wished. Sadly, he was not around to help guide the final stages.

Andy Johnson
Logaston Press

Contents

		Page
	Preface	*ix*
Chapter 1	Wales in the Fourteenth Century	1
Chapter 2	Owain ap Gruffydd Fychan	11
Chapter 3	Plantagenet, Mortimer, Lancaster and Percy	25
Chapter 4	The Rising	37
Chapter 5	The Battle of Hyddgen	51
Chapter 6	The Battle of Pilleth	63
Chapter 7	The Years of Victory	89
Chapter 8	Owain Glyn Dŵr, Prince of Wales	111
Chapter 9	The French in Wales	129
Chapter 10	Owain Glyn Dŵr at Bay	141
Chapter 11	The Disappearance of Owain Glyn Dŵr	153
Chapter 12	Owain Glyn Dŵr's Place in History	167
Appendix 1	Castles in South Wales and the Marches	175
Appendix 2	Robert Whitney and Thomas Clanvowe	179
Appendix 3	Destruction of Churches in the Diocese of Hereford	181
Appendix 4	Bastard Feudalism	183
Appendix 5	Sir John Clanvowe and Lollard Doctrine	187
Appendix 6	Owain Glyn Dŵr: a Summary	191
Table 1	The Pedigree and Progeny of Owain Glyn Dŵr	193
Table 2	Mortimer of Wigmore; Plantagenet, York and Lancaster	194
	Notes	195
	Bibliography	211
	Index	217

Preface and Acknowledgements

Some fourteen years ago the author, a native of the Wigmore district, began to do some serious work on the Wars of the Roses, beginning with the battle of Mortimer's Cross. These studies grew steadily to include Wales and the Marches in the later middle ages. Occasional lectures to local history societies clearly showed the growing interest in medieval history. Finally the author was asked to give a talk on the battle of Pilleth, but knew too little of Owain Glyn Dŵr, and had first to learn more about one of the most fascinating characters in our history. However, an Englishman who does not know Welsh can never be really qualified to write a book about one of the greatest Welshmen of all time.

This book is not, therefore, a true biography of Owain Glyn Dŵr; in any case, personal circumstances have made it impossible for the author to read nearly as widely as he should have done. It is a study of Owain, his life and times, and his unsuccessful war of independence against England, giving particular attention to events in the central and southern Welsh Marches, as that term is understood today. After the Norman conquest the Marches were those areas of Wales and the English border counties ruled by Marcher lords. Henry VIII's Acts of Union of England and Wales abolished the Marcher lordships and created eight new shires, which together with the five shires of Edward I's Principality of Wales were now represented in Parliament. Wales was ruled by the Council of Wales and the Marches at Ludlow, which also had jurisdiction over Cheshire, Shropshire, and indeed the area between the River Severn and the new Welsh border. Although the Council was finally abolished in 1689, the new meaning which it had given to 'The Welsh Marches' has been in use ever since, but in the text 'the

Marches' mean those lands which were ruled by the medieval Marcher lords.

The situation in fourteenth-century Wales and the upheavals of Richard II's reign are described in outline, in order to explain why and how the Rebellion occurred. As has been said, this study originally began with the battle of Pilleth, perhaps Owain's most spectacular victory, which widened the conflict, gave substance to Owain's claim to be Prince of Wales, and enabled him briefly to play the part of an independent European ruler. This diplomacy reached its climax with the extraordinary and little-known French expedition of 1405, which accompanied Owain and his army to the gates of Worcester; but already that year the Welsh were losing the initiative, as their defeats in Gwent showed only too clearly. These events and the end of the French and Scottish alliances in 1407 forced Owain Glyn Dŵr onto the defensive. He could not hold the strategic fortresses of Aberystwyth and Harlech without French naval support, and defeat was now inevitable.

The dire effects of Glyn Dŵr's revolt included widespread lawlessness in Wales and the border counties, leading to the breakdown of Lancastrian government, and providing a link between Owain Glyn Dŵr's Rising and the Wars of the Roses. Another can be seen in the fact that Walter Devereux of Weobley, killed at Pilleth, was the great grand-father of his namesake who fought at Mortimer's Cross. Some readers will be familiar with an earlier book, *Ludford Bridge and Mortimer's Cross*, published by Logaston Press in 1989.

It is hoped that the notes which follow the text will be helpful to students, without distracting the general reader from a story of tremendous drama and interest. The notes also form a useful depository for interesting and important details, which might otherwise interrupt the narrative. Some of these details are topographical, and may help those who like to visit the sites of historical importance referred to in the text.

The author of any serious historical work must feel a great sense of obligation to all those whose writings have gone into the finished article. This begins with those great and famous people who were actors in the drama described in these pages and whose personalities appear through the letters which they wrote, espe-cially the three Henries: King Henry IV, Prince Henry and Henry Percy, known as Hotspur. Equally interesting are the occasional comments made on them by their contemporaries. This gratitude extends to all authors of secondary sources in the following centu-ries, including Shakespeare himself, and those whose labours have led to the publication of so much of our medieval archives. This material is used to make the story as vivid as possible and is quoted freely. It will be familiar to academic historians, but some of the local material may be less well known. Books by twentieth-century authors must finally be mentioned; the last fifty years have been a golden age in medieval scholarship, but anyone interested in Owain Glyn Dŵr will acknowledge a special debt to Sir John Lloyd.

I owe many debts of gratitude for the very kind help and interest shown by many people. Professor Glanmor Williams very kindly read an early draft, and made many valuable suggestions. My publisher, Mr Andy Johnson, took much trouble over the later drafts, pointing out places where clarification was needed; thanks to his care, all Logaston books are excellently designed and produced. Professor Ralph Griffiths and Professor Rees Davies have both helped me with sources. Professor Joan Rees and the late Mr Christopher Morris, my Director of Studies at King's College, Cambridge, both gave me wise advice on Shakespeare's historical plays. The late Mr G.D. Lockett and his grandson William kindly lent me the six volumes of *Powys Fadog* for as long as I wanted them. Mr Richard Williams has generously shared his wide docu-mentary and topographical knowledge of Owain Glyn Dŵr and his movements with me. Mr C.O.M. Bedingfield, Q.C., supplied very useful details about medieval legal training. Mr Peter Hood of Pilleth Court has given me much useful information about the immediate vicinity of the battle. Mrs Oddie Harrison kindly lent me some papers of the Blount family, of which she is a member. Mr Roger Worsley and Mr Charles Hopkinson have also given me useful advice. I am also much indebted to library staffs: at Croft Castle, where Mrs Diana Uhlman always makes me welcome; at Hereford, to the Record Office (Miss Sue Hubbard), the City Reference Library (Mr Robin Hill), and the Cathedral Library

(Miss Joan Williams); at Leominster, to the Public Library and its mobile service, whose driver is Mrs Sue Morris, for finding me many important books; to the National Library of Wales, where Mr Vernon Jones was exceedingly helpful; to Cambridge University Library (Photographic Department, Linda Unchered); to the Special Collections, Edinburgh University Library (Jean Archibald); and to the Institute of Historical Research (Mr Robert Lyons). Mr Tony Bolton of BWCL and his staff have kindly given me vital technical help with computers.

Finally, my love and thanks go to my wife and daughters, especially Nicola and Joanna, who have advised me over word-processing problems. They have all given me much encouragement, and have been very tolerant of the unsociable habits inevitably resulting from my having been fascinated for some years by Owain Glyn Dŵr and his adventures.

Aymestrey,
Herefordshire.   October, 1994.

CHAPTER ONE

Wales in the Fourteenth Century

On St. Alban's Day, 22 June 1402, a small, savage battle was fought at Pilleth, a little church on a hillside above the River Lugg, five miles upstream from Presteigne in Radnorshire. Pilleth, the anglicised form of the Welsh Pyllalai, is the usual name of the battle referred to in the opening scene of Shakespeare's historical play, *The First Part of King Henry IV*. Led by Owain Glyn Dŵr, the Welsh inflicted a bloody defeat on a Herefordshire army, whose commander, Edmund Mortimer, was taken prisoner. The broad hillside overlooking the church has given the battle its other name of Bryn Glas (green hill).

The Rising of Owain Glyn Dŵr followed hard on the events of 1399, in which Duke Henry of Lancaster deposed his cousin Richard II and seized the throne. King Henry IV very well knew that many people believed the Mortimer claim to the throne to be stronger than that of Lancaster; they thought that he was a usurper, and that the rightful king was the Earl of March, only eleven years old, whose uncle Edmund was now Glyn Dŵr's prisoner. Henry therefore refused to ransom Edmund Mortimer, who could only secure his release by becoming Owain's ally and marrying his daughter. Until his nephew came of age Edmund was the leader of the most powerful of all the Marcher families; his defection gravely weakened English control of Herefordshire and Shropshire, and greatly increased the military and diplomatic power of Owain Glyn Dŵr.

1

The Roman army which the emperor Claudius had sent to Britain in 43 AD had conquered Wales in only forty years, despite the heroic resistance of Caradog, the revolt in 61 of Boudicca (Queen of the Iceni in Norfolk), and distant imperial distractions: the Jewish War of 66-70 and the civil-war which followed Nero's death in 68.[1] By contrast with the Roman achievement the conquest of Wales was quite beyond the military capacity of the Anglo-Saxon kings. King Offa had carved his Dyke as a visible and indelible boundary between the English and Welsh. Earl Harold Godwinson, later King Harold II, was the author of a more aggressive policy, continued by the Norman and Angevin kings and their Marcher lords, whose efforts to conquer Wales all failed until Edward I's victory in 1283. The military system of Rome with her far-flung empire had been much more sophisticated even than that of the best organised kingdom in feudal Europe twelve centuries later.

Edward I understood the lesson learned by his Roman predecessors, that if Anglesey, the granary of north Wales, was taken, resistance on the mainland would collapse. Edward had been on crusade in the Mediterranean, where he had gained wide experience of the use of seapower in war. Like the Romans, he based himself on Chester, which was a seaport till it began to silt up during the fifteenth century. He employed the eminent Savoyard engineer, Master James of St. Georges, to build seven new coastal castles in north-west Wales, which could be supplied by sea; Aberystwyth, Rhuddlan and Flint during the war of 1277 (also the inland fortress of Builth), and with the war of 1282 work began on Conwy, Caernarfon, and Harlech. Beaumaris was added as a result of the rebellion of 1293. Like Edward's conquest of Wales, this castle-building was accomplished in an incredibly short time. Edward's castles have left a permanent mark of his formidable personality on Wales, but he also gave charters to new boroughs, to which English settlers were lured on easy terms. His military and political settlement survived the supreme test to which it was subjected by Owain Glyn Dŵr, and there can be little doubt that the castles played a decisive part in the war which followed his rebellion.[2]

As usually happens after a conquest, there ensued for the victors a golden age, during which they were able to enjoy the fruits of success, and ruthlessly to exploit the vanquished. After the rebellion of Llywelyn Bren in south Wales in 1316 the Welsh offered virtually no resistance, realising that co-existence was the best policy. It is easy to see why the English medieval kings were more successful in Wales than in Scotland. The geography of Wales prevents that country from having any natural centre, such as the Scottish lowland plain between the Clyde and the Forth. It is only half as far from London to Wales as it is to the Scottish border, and Scotland was less easy for medieval armies to penetrate than Wales. In the eastern half of Wales, river valleys run from west to east, making access easy in both directions. The main rivers are the Dee, Severn, Wye and Usk, which rise in Wales, and high roads run along their valleys deep into Wales from England; but the mountain ranges which separate them have always hindered communication between north and south Wales. Between Wye and Severn is the land of small rivers (the Onny, Clun, Teme, Lugg and Arrow) for which the English have no name, but which the Welsh used to call *Rhwng Gwy a Hafren* between the Wye and the Severn. Castles abound in this area, especially along the rivers, though perhaps no more than in other parts of the borderlands.

Campaigning in Wales was often rendered difficult if not impossible by the weather. In any season, heavy rain could reduce the primitive roads to impassable mud. In winter, never a favourite campaigning season in the middle ages, rain may alternate with bitter cold and blizzards. Even in summer, torrential rain and floods might thwart the best-laid plans, and never at any time was there enough grain and fodder to supply a large army of men and horses. Edward I's conquest of Wales was a remarkable logistical achievement, but he was able to bring in both supplies and manpower from the adjacent English shires of the west midlands.

Scotland was to be closely involved in the Glyn Dŵr Rebellion. She had retained her independence because she was (apart from the Gaelic Highlands) a cohesive feudal kingdom with a king and nobility of Anglo-Norman origin, many of whom held lands in England of the English king. Whereas in Wales the English Marcher lords dominated large areas of the country, they did not do so in Scotland, whose independence was finally recognised by the

3

English in 1328. On the other hand, until the thirteenth century Wales contained several different native dynasties, who warred with each other, the Marcher lords and the English king, making alliances where they could. There was therefore no tradition of political unity in Wales, either before or after the conquest by Edward I.

The principality of Wales was first granted to the future Edward II. It consisted of the shires of Carmarthen, Cardigan, Caernarfon, Anglesey and Merioneth. The March of Wales consisted of about forty lordships. Flint was partofthe Prince of Wales's earldom of Chester; Powys and Builth were royal lordships within the gift of the king. Brecon, Abergavenny, Caerleon, Usk, Monmouth, Chepstow, Glamorgan, Kidwelly and Pembroke were the main Marcher lordships in south Wales; Denbigh, Chirk, Montgomery and Radnor are examples in east Wales. Finally there were those lordships adjacent to the border counties of Shropshire and Herefordshire: Oswestry, Bishop's Castle, Ludlow and Clun; Wigmore, Ewyas Lacy, Clifford, Hay and Huntington.[3]

The Marcher lords were descended from the Norman nobility of William the Conqueror. These powerful magnates effectively owned the English lands which they held of the king as tenants-in-chief. Still more was this true of their Marcher lordships, in which they were virtually sovereign princes. The Marcher lordships formed larger and more compact areas than the widely scattered lordships and manors which the Norman magnates and their descendants held in different shires all over England. In a Marcher lordship the king's writ did not run; the lord's court executed justice, raised taxes and generally ruled in the lord's interest. A felon prosecuted in Brecon could slip into Carmarthen or Glamorgan or England, where he would be safe from pursuit. Consequently a permanent state of disorder prevailed in Wales and the bordering English shires. Most important of all, Marcher lordships were valuable as military recruiting grounds, and it is no wonder that they were so greatly prized by their fortunate owners.[4] It must be added that though Edward I recognised the privileges of the Marcher lords, he lost no opportunity of making them all realise who was master if the occasion arose. He did not hesitate to imprison the Earls of Hereford and Gloucester for waging a private war.[5]

4

Wales in the days of Owain Glyn Dŵr

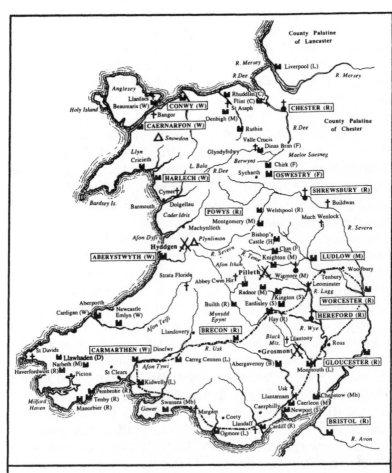

Castles: Royal (R)   Duke of Lancaster (L)   Prince of Wales (W)
Mortimer (M)   Earl of Chester (C)   Audley (A)   Stafford (S)
Fitzalan (F)   Mowbray (Mb)   Beauchamp (Be)   Despenser (De)
Bishop of Hereford (H)   Bishop of St David's (D)
Franco-Welsh route, 1405 - · · · · · ·

5

The Mortimers, Barons of Wigmore, were the outstanding Marcher dynasty. In the first place, no other family of comparable importance had held land in the Marches continuously since the Norman Conquest without a break in the male line. They could show an unmatched record of military prowess and political acumen, and their contribution to the conquest of Wales had been outstanding. They had nearly always been steadfast in their support of the crown, the only serious exception being the treason of Roger, first Earl of March, who deposed Edward II. Thanks to the generosity of Edward III they had recovered the estates lost in that disaster by the time of Richard II (1377-99). These lands included Denbigh, Montgomery and Cedewain in the north, Ludlow, Wigmore, Radnor, Maelienydd, Ceri, Cwmwd Deuddwr and Gwrtheyrnion in the middle Marches, Usk, Crickhowell and Caerleon in the Usk valley, and Narberth in Pembrokeshire. There were also many individual manors in Herefordshire, Shropshire, and other counties further afield.

Secondly, the Mortimers had a much larger proportion of their lands in the Marches than other Marcher lords. Early in the fourteenth century they acquired the Lacy/Geneville inheritance, which gave them Ludlow and many other manors in Shropshire and north-west Herefordshire. This marriage, together with an earlier one to an heiress of the de Braose family, also made the Mortimers very large landowners in Ireland, although the nucleus of their power continued to be the area centred on Wigmore and Ludlow.

Thirdly, Edmund Mortimer, third Earl of March, had married Philippa, heiress to Lionel, Duke of Clarence and second son of Edward III, whose English lands were mostly in East Anglia; the dukedom took its name from the Honour of Clare in Suffolk. This marriage brought yet more Irish lands, including the earldom of Ulster. The Mortimer Earls of March had therefore enormously increased their wealth and power, and had also won a claim to the throne which was to be of national importance in the future, and a vital element in the story of Owain Glyn Dŵr; but all this good fortune was an illusion. The responsibilities imposed by their Irish lands proved to be a fatal burden, and the last three earls all died prematurely in Ireland.

The great inheritance of the Bohun earls of Hereford had passed, at the death of the last earl in 1373, to his two daughters. Edward III's youngest son, Thomas Duke of Gloucester, thus became a Marcher lord through his wife, Eleanor Bohun, who held Huntington in the west of Herefordshire. Her younger sister Mary was married to Henry of Bolingbroke, John of Gaunt's heir; the exceptionally rich lordship of Brecon, together with Hay, thus came to him as well as the duchy of Lancaster, greatest of all English magnate empires of he late middle ages, which included seven Welsh castles: Monmouth, White Castle, Skenfrith, Grosmont, Ogmore, Carreg Cennen and Kidwelly.[6]

The Fitzalans, earls of Arundel, were lords of Yale, Bromfield, Chirk, Oswestry and Clun, the foremost magnates in north-east Wales, where their neighbours included Owain Glyn Dŵr's family. Other leading Marcher lords were the Beauchamp earls of Warwick who held Elfael (the southern part of Radnorshire) and Gower, the Despensers who held Glamorgan, and the Mowbray dukes of Norfolk who held Chepstow and Gower. As time passed, the picture constantly changed, as one family after another failed in the male line. In 1625 Sir Ranulfe Crewe, Chief Justice, when speaking of the extinction of the de Vere earldom of Oxford, described this natural tendency in a memorable judgment:

> 'There must be a period and stop to all temporal things, an end to realms and territories and whatsoever is terrain. For look and ask. Where is Bohun? Where is Mowbray? Where is Mortimer? Nay, what is more and most of all, where is Plantagenet? They are intombed in the urns and sepulchres of mortality.'[7]

In describing the death of Prince Llywelyn, known as 'the Last', as a national calamity, the Welsh bards were reflecting the national mood; it marked the beginning of 'the Saxon yoke'. The English princes of Wales and Marcher lords comprised the heaviest part of this yoke, and for them the fourteenth century was a time of plenty, as they mulcted the conquered land through the exaction of rents and judicial fines and fees. They lived mostly as absentees in

7

London or on their English estates, but tended to retire to their Welsh lordships at times of disturbance, when they needed to drum up military support, especially during the troubled reign of Edward II. John of Gaunt is believed never to have visited his Welsh castles and lordships.[8] No doubt such neglect helped to convey to several generations of Welshmen the feeling that they were nothing to their English masters but a source of profit.

A few examples will show how much the Marcher lordships could yield to their owners. The great grassy hills of Mynydd Epynt carried such enormous flocks of sheep that Henry of Bolingbroke received £1,600 from Brecon and Hay alone in the year preceding Owain's rebellion. Denbigh, the richest of the Mortimer lordships, provided about half of the £2,000 or so which was their total value. The principality of Wales was worth over £5,000 a year. The chronicler Adam of Usk reckoned that the sum exacted from Wales by all the English lords was about £60,000. When the total revenue of the King of England himself during the fourteenth century was about £80,000 a year, it seems incredible that such huge sums could be extorted from a land as poor as Wales. It is not surprising that well before Owain Glyn Dŵr's rebellion began there was a decline in the Welsh revenues, to which the Black Death and the economic difficulties of the period must also have contributed.[9]

Wales was not an English colony in any modern sense, although English settlers did have a monopoly of trade in the boroughs which grew up around the new castles. They were jealous of their rights, but tended to cower under the protecting walls of the fortresses: Caernarfon and Harlech, Conwy and Cricieth, Rhuddlan and Ruthin, Denbigh and Flint, Aberystwyth and Builth. None of these towns really flourished, but they were an extra source of grievance to the Welsh who were largely excluded from benefiting in trade.[10]

Consequently, there was a smouldering sense of anger, exacerbated by the rigour of the administrative and judicial machine which extorted so much money. It is remarkable that the sense of grievance very seldom boiled over into violence despite the oppressive rule of the English lords; the murder in 1345 of the newly appointed attorney of the Prince of Wales on his way to Caernarfon was exceptional. The century was, curiously enough, a great age for Welsh literature. The bards, by recording the national mood of anger and frustration, helped to keep the pot of discontent simmering.[11]

'Good lordship' was very important in the medieval world, in Wales like anywhere else. After the Edwardian conquest of Wales the native ruling class, the *uchelwyr*, did not disappear as did the Saxon nobility and gentry during the generation following the Norman conquest of England. However much they might exploit the conquered land, the new rulers of Wales needed the help of dependable Welshmen in the delicate task of government, though the top administrative jobs inevitably tended to be given to the English retainers of the Prince of Wales and the Marcher lords. A gentleman depended for advancement on the protection and patronage of a great lord, and the opportunities available were usually military. Large contingents of Welsh archers, spearmen and dagsmen (light infantry with short swords) used to serve in the retinues of the English lords in the Scottish and French wars, under Welsh officers. Gentlemen such as Sir Gruffydd Llwyd and Sir Rhys ap Gruffydd were loyal to Edward II throughout his troubled reign. The earls of Hereford, with their lordship of Brecon, received equally constant service from their Welsh retainers. During the Hundred Years War, Marcher lords who formed retinues to serve in France relied heavily on their Welsh tenantry, and on Welsh captains to lead them. Notable captains who fought under the Prince of Wales were Sir Degory Sais and Sir Hywel *y Fwyall* (of the Axe). These captains were members of the *uchelwyr*, the natural leaders of the Welsh people, on whom the English rulers relied for administrative as well as for military service. The English had every reason to persuade the uchelwyr that co-operation was in their interest. If they were to think otherwise, their experience of war would make them dangerous.[12]

The Welsh clergy were equally important to the English rulers. Wales was divided into four dioceses: Bangor and St. Asaph in the north, and St. David's and Llandaff covering south Wales. Prudence might have suggested that these bishoprics were best reserved for Welshmen, but here was another irresistibly tempting field of patronage. The Black Prince himself set an especially bad example by appointing his own men to St. Asaph and Bangor. Before the Reformation, English and even foreign absentees were allowed to enjoy the revenues of Welsh sees and other benefices. Senior appointments were nominally in the gift of the Pope, in both England and Wales, but in practice they went to civil servants and others whom the king wished to favour. Consequently the Welsh clergy as well asthe laity were left with a sense of grievance. Exceptions were John Trefnant, a Welshman who was Bishop of Hereford (1389-1404), and John Trefor, the only Welshman in the late fourteenth century to hold a Welsh see, who was Bishop of St. Asaph from 1395 to 1410. Trefor was one of many eminent Welshmen who eventually joined Owain Glyn Dŵr.[13]

There was another side to English extortion and oppression in Wales. Leadership ultimately depends upon mutual loyalty, respect and support; a 'good lord' needed to be generous, and also sensitive to the feelings of his tenants, servants or retainers. All imperial rulers must in their own interests cultivate good relations with the conquered. Local administration is impossible without native advisers to find out what is going on, though interpreters can easily mislead rulers, especially those who are totally ignorant of the language. Whatever misgivings there may have been about possible unrest in late fourteenth-century Wales, the English magnates were much more concerned with the upheavals in England during King Richard II's troubled reign.

Meanwhile Owain Glyn Dŵr had been advancing his career, at the Inns of Court, through his father-in-law, Sir David Hanmer, and as a retainer of the principal Marcher lord of his area, the Earl of Arundel. After 1397 both were dead, which may well help to explain what we shall never know for certain: exactly why Owain rebelled. In 1400 Owain was over forty years old, with a sound position in life, and apparently everything to lose by rebellion. Substantial, middle-aged men do not take so drastic a step without very serious reasons. It is therefore certain that Owain Glyn Dŵr, and those who followed him, considered that 'the Saxon yoke' had become intolerable to a proud people; the arrogance and contemptuous insolence of the English could no longer be borne.[14]

CHAPTER TWO

Owain ap Gruffyd Fychan (1359?-1415?)

The name of Owen Glendower, as the English spell him, is imperishably connected with the last attempt of the Welsh to throw off the English yoke by force, at the beginning of the fifteenth century. The Welsh spelling of his name is Owain Glyn Dyfrdwy, meaning Owain of the Glen of the Waters of Dee—Glyn Dŵr for short; his patronymic is Owain ap Gruffydd Fychan. Many readers may have first encountered the story of Owain and his rebellion in *The First Part of King Henry IV*, which shows clearly that here was a man of exceptional personality, power and charisma. More can be said: Owain Glyn Dŵr exploded on the scene like some violent cloudburst, one of those devastating summer deluges which send great floods down the rivers flowing into England, and are talked of for many a year afterwards. Like such a storm, Owain interrupted the course of history; but while a river may change its course for a short distance, and after a few years resume its normal flow, Wales was never the same again after Owain Glyn Dŵr's Rising. Owain remains to this day a man of mystery, whose birth was attended by strange portents, according to traditions known to Shakespeare. Owain's argument with Harry Hotspur includes these memorable lines:

Give me leave
To tell you once again, that at my birth

The front of heaven was full of fiery shapes;
The goats ran from the mountains, and the herds
Were strangely clamorous to the frighted fields.
These signs have mark'd me extraordinary;
And all the courses of my life do show
I am not in the roll of common men.[1]

It was also said that at his birth the horses in his father's stable
were found to be bathed in blood to their knees. Unfortunately, this
fearsome sign, which seems to fit Owain so well, is attributed by
the earliest chroniclers to Edmund Mortimer, a much more prosaic
person. When Edmund was defeated and captured by Owain at
Pilleth, the carnage there was considered by two chroniclers to be
the fulfilment of this ghastly omen. Later writers report it of Owain
through, apparently, nothing more exciting or romantic than the
misreading of a Latin text.[2] It is a common disappointment to find
that a good medieval story is contradicted by some other authority,
or by modern research.

Like Arthur, the greatest of all Celtic heroes, Owain seemed to
vanish into the mists whence he came; there was no certain news of
his end. In this he was more fortunate than other Celtic warriors.
Vercingetorix was murdered on Julius Caesar's orders. Caradog,
whose guerilla warfare against the Romans in Wales might have
served as a model for Owain's resistance to the English, died some-
what ingloriously in Italy as a pensioner of the Emperor Claudius.
Boudicca poisoned herself amid the bloody ruin of her rebellion
against Rome. In 1282 the last Prince of Wales, Llywelyn ap
Gruffydd, was slain in battle by Mortimer and other Marcher lords
near Builth; the spot is marked by a modern monument on the
Llandovery road.[3]

We have no reliable portrait of Owain, a disadvantage which is
true of most medieval people, though we know more of his personality than we do of many important figures of the fifteenth century,
for example Warwick the Kingmaker. Historical biographers, dram-
atists and novelists, when writing of people who are long dead,
should strive to be objective if they are to get anywhere near the
truth. In his preface to his life of Augustus, John Buchan reflects on

'the fallibility of all historical reconstruction'; he quotes a German classical scholar, who despairs of rebuilding history from the ruins of tradition, but recalls the incident of Odysseus offering blood to the spirits of the dead in these haunting words:

> Tradition is dead; our task is to revivify life that has passed away. We know that ghosts cannot speak until they have drunk blood, and the spirits which we would evoke demand the blood of our hearts. We give it to them gladly, and if they then abide our question something of us has entered into them.[4]

Among the books which influenced Shakespeare was the Tudor compilation, *The Mirror for Magistrates*, which is full of moral reflections on some of the great people of the past. Perhaps something of Shakespeare entered into them when he brought them into his history plays, especially when he indulged in poetic licence; if this is so, lesser mortals may be excused. Certainly he was misled by errors in the chronicle record repeated by the Tudor writers Edward Hall and Raphael Holinshed; but he had an extensive knowledge of tradition, and a profound understanding of humanity. Though we cannot be certain how much oral tradition he picked up, many of the events in his plays were recent enough to have occurred within a century of his birth. It is fair to suppose that Shakespeare, so deeply interested in people both as individuals and in groups, listened eagerly to stories about great people and events of history. Modern historians gain much valuable evidence from archaeologists; in a rather similar way they sift through the ruins of the past in their search for clues. They have to discover which traditions are inaccurate, erroneous or even spurious, and to recognise those which are dormant rather than dead: embers in which there is warmth, wells from which water can be drawn. Many examples of all can be found in the study of Owain Glyn Dŵr.

Shakespeare was first and foremost a writer of plays and a poet. In his day history was not studied in the modern manner; it was read in the classics and in the late medieval chronicles, which tended to have a very strong political bias. Like others of his time,

Shakespeare was fascinated by government and politics. In Tudor days people were concerned with law and order. So was Shakespeare, but he also demonstrated that it depended on just government: kings, princes, nobles and their servants must obey the rules. Modern research proves that, whatever their apologists may have said, in this respect the Tudors were little better than their Lancastrian or Yorkist predecessors. Moreover, Shakespeare wrote a play primarily to be to be seen on the stage. An actor may recite speeches which are great poetry, but are placed in the mouth of a weak, neurotic character like Richard II; we may get the wrong impression if we only *read* the play. 'Shakespeare was not only a playwright but a great one,' wrote Christopher Morris, whose subject was the history of political thought. 'Therefore he does not always show his hand. He can and does get inside and sympathize with all, or almost all, his characters even the villains.' Shakespeare presents us with the evidence, and lets us form our own conclusions. He does not hold Owain Glyn Dŵr's claim to be Prince of Wales against him, although Owain was decidedly out of favour in an age when any defiance of royal authority seemed to threaten the very survival of the nation. *King Richard II* was for this reason considered a seditious play; in 1601 the rebellious faction of the Earl of Essex bribed the players to revive it.[5]

Shakespeare's depiction of Owain Glyn Dŵr is typical of his method in the portrayal of a character; he also probably brings us as close as we are ever likely to get to this great Welshman. His first mention of Owain is when Westmorland calls him 'the irregular and wild Glendower', but this idea of an uncouth guerilla leader is corrected by Owain himself. We are shown a second facet of his character, that of a gracious gentleman whose courtesy makes Hotspur, the flower of chivalry, seem boorish by comparison. Perhaps this is an example of Shakespeare being guided by oral tradition; Professor Joan Rees suggests that he could well have heard this view of Owain's character from Welshmen whom he may have met in Stratford or London. The famous meeting at which Owain plans the partition of England with Hotspur and Mortimer gets off to a bad start. Hotspur has forgotten the map but Owain, the trained lawyer, has thought of this and has one ready. Hotspur loses his temper and tries to provoke Owain, who politely reproves him, and gets the best of the argument in the following lines:

> I can speak English, lord, as well as you;
> For I was train'd up in the English court;
> Where, being but young, I framed to the harp
> Many an English ditty lovely well,
> And gave the tongue a helpful ornament,
> A virtue that was never seen in you.

Mortimer also testifies to his father-in-law's courtesy:

> In faith, he is a worthy gentleman;
> Exceedingly well read, and profited
> In strange concealments; valiant as a lion,
> And wondrous affable, and as bountiful
> As mines of India.

Hotspur was reproved by Mortimer and his uncle Worcester for his rudeness; but it is difficult not to sympathise with his irritation at Owain's often bombastic mode of speech, which goes with yet another side to this amazing man: the Celtic culture which was natural to him. To Owain's boast that 'I can call spirits from the vasty deep!' Hotspur's scornful reply is:

> Why, so can I, or so can any man;
> But will they come when you do call for them?

However, many would find this the most fascinating side of Owain: the ease with which, in his close association with the bards, he moved in the arcane world of Celtic mystery, and the fact that his mastery of strategy appeared positively uncanny to the bewildered English.[6]

In this scene Shakespeare introduces an important event in Owain's life, the sealing of the Tripartite Indenture, which in fact took place after Hotspur's death at the battle of Shrewsbury. Nevertheless the unrealistic idea of partitioning England and Wales was shared by both Mortimer and the Earl of Northumberland, Hotspur's father, a very subtle politician.

Owain Glyn Dŵr came of very distinguished ancestry. He could, first of all, claim descent from Cadwaladr Fendigaid, reputed to be the last King of Wales, who lived in the seventh century AD, the 'illustrious Cadwallader' cited on the Mortimer's Cross Monument at Kingsland, Herefordshire, as an ancestor of the Tudors. Cadwaladr was supposed to be of the ancient but mythical line descended from Brutus, Prince of Troy, with whom Geoffrey of Monmouth begins his *History of the Kings of Britain.* This great romantic work was written during the reign of Henry I (1100-1135), who is plainly referred to in Merlin's prophecy as 'The Lion of Justice'. It tells of the descendants of Brutus, who include King Lear and Cymbeline, but also Ambrosius and Uthr Pendragon, Merlin, and Arthur. It attracted severe criticism from twelfth-century chroniclers, and has been in disfavour with succeeding historians ever since. But scholarly disapproval did not prevent its acceptance in the later middle ages as reliable history; in an age of dynastic monarchy the immense propaganda value of Geoffrey's *History* and its fanciful genealogies was realised by Henry II, Edward I and Edward III. Its literary influence has been profound, both as the source for two of Shakespeare's tragedies and as the main quarry for writers of Arthurian romances ever since. It plays its part in the story of Owain Glyn Dŵr. It also encouraged the Welsh to think that, if they were descended from the Trojans, they must be one of the most ancient nations of Europe. 'Base Trojan, thou shalt die!', says that 'scurvy, lousy knave' Pistol to Fluellen, who in one of Shakespeare's famous comic scenes beats Pistol for his insolence and forces him to eat a leek. This incident underlines the main lesson to be learned from Owain Glyn Dŵr's Rebellion, that a proud people would no longer submit to English insolence.[7]

In fact, as opposed to fiction, Owain Glyn Dŵr was descended from all the three great royal dynasties of medieval Wales, which was of much more immediate relevance since, in Welsh eyes, it fully justified his claim to be the rightful Prince of Wales, as opposed to the English king's heir, wrongfully raised to that position. Owain was descended from the princes of Powys Fadog, which lay roughly between the Dee and the Severn; two of their lordships had passed to his father Gruffydd Fychan II, so-called by Welsh custom because he had his own father's name. His mother Elen was a member of a Cardiganshire family descended from Llywelyn ap Iorwerth (The Great), Prince of Gwynedd, also from the Lord Rhys, the last Prince of Deheubarth, which included Brecon, Carmarthen and Cardigan. Elen's father was Owain ap Thomas ap Llywelyn; her sister, or cousin, married Maredudd ap Tudur of Anglesey; their son Owen changed the spelling of the name to Tudor, and was the ancestor of the Tudor dynasty.[8]

The last male of the house of Gwynedd was Owain ap Thomas, not to be confused with the descendant of the Deheubarth princes. He was great-nephew of Llywelyn the Last, and died in 1378. Owain was known as Lawgoch (The Red Hand), also as Owain of Wales, a mercenary captain of great experience in the French service. His dynastic claims made him a very grave threat to the English, and aroused great alarm, especially when in 1372 the French king Charles V gave him a fleet and army to invade Wales; but the expedition was called off. Owain Lawgoch was finally murdered by a spy in English pay.[9]

By the end of the fourteenth century the *uchelwyr* (the Welsh gentry) were ripe for revolt, and sufficiently experienced in war to defy the English. Owain Glyn Dŵr's lineage made him pre-eminent among them. He was the last of seven generations of the Powys Fadog dynasty: Owain ap Gruffydd Fychan II ap Gruffydd ap Madog ap Gruffydd Fychan I ap Gruffydd ap Madog. In 1269 the elder Gruffydd ap Madog died; his lands were divided between his sons, according to the Welsh custom of *gavelkind*. Gwynedd was then conquered in 1282 by Edward I, who took the lands of the Welsh princes for the new principality, except for Powys Fadog which he kept in hand; but Gruffydd Fychan I managed to save two lordships which were finally entailed on his grandson, the younger Gruffydd ap Madog, and his heirs, who were from now on tenants-in-chief, as they held their land direct from the king; an heir who was a minor at the death of a tenant-in-chief became a royal ward. One of these lordships was Dyfrdwy, part of Edeirnion in the Dee valley between Llangollen and Corwen, which offered good hunting; but the other, Cynllaith Owain, with its manor house of Sycharth a few miles west of Oswestry, was richer. Owain was almost unique among Welsh landowners, in holding from the crown lands which had once belonged to his ancestors; the only other was his cousin William of Mawddwy, in western Powys. The entail was an Anglo-Norman custom, by which large estates could pass undivided to the heir; *gavelkind* was the main cause of the endemic political weakness of Welsh landowners. Owain Glyn Dŵr's grandfather, Gruffydd ap Madog, was born in 1298. He was six years old when he married Elizabeth, daughter of Sir John L'Estrange, of Knockin near Oswestry, a member of one of the numerous Anglo-Welsh families in the Marches. Madog knew that he would not live long and arranged that when he died the wardship of his young son should be held by Sir John. In this way Gruffydd came safely into his estates. Owain Glyn Dŵr ap Gruffydd Fychan II was a native of a part of Wales which is adjacent to England; he was heir of Powys Fadog, but also had some English blood.[10]

One tradition dates Owain's birth to 20 September 1349, the year of the Black Death, at Carrog, the chief residence of the lordship of Glyn Dyfrdwy. Thomas Pennant, the eighteenth-century historian, saw a document giving 28 May 1354, but a later date is probable. In 1386 the famous case of Scrope and Grosvenor, when Owain appeared as a witness before the Court of Chivalry, provided evidence that he was then 'twenty-seven years old and more'. It can be safely said that he was born between 1354 and 1359. In the middle ages a man's birthplace was often used as a surname. Owain Glyn Dŵr got his name from Glyn Dyfrdwy, but his home was Sycharth in Cynllaith Owain, where his happiest days were passed. His love for Sycharth suggests that it is more likely to have been his birthplace, but the Cynllaith landscape is softer than Glyn Dyfrdwy, a more attractive setting for a permanent home.[11]

Dr. R. Ian Jack has shown that Owain's father, Gruffydd Fychan II, was dead by 1370; he cites a roll dated 1370-71 with the names of twenty-six people who had been given loans by Richard Fitzalan, Earl of Arundel, one of Edward III's principal war-captains. Arundel's war service and Marcher lordships had made him so wealthy that he lent cash to the great and good. His debtors included the king himself and the Black Prince, various nobles, knights and ladies, the Abbot of Wigmore, and John Trefnant (later Bishop of Hereford), all of whom he would have known personally. Another was Elen, 'formerly the wife of Gruff. Glindorde', who was a near neighbour; Arundel had ordered his receiver at Oswestry to lend her 30 marks, which she now repaid. By now Owain was presumably a royal ward; he was not more than sixteen, but he may have been only eleven. He had a younger brother named Tudur, but there is no record of any other. A royal wardship was a valuable item of patronage, bestowed by the king on any specially favoured person. The Earl of Arundel seems the likeliest candidate for Owain's wardship; his castle of Dinas Brân is near Glyn Dyfrdwy, while Oswestry is a few miles from Sycharth. Owain's mother sounds a capable woman, but she would have welcomed the patronage of the earl, whose household was the obvious place for Owain to serve as a page, and learn gentle behaviour, heraldry and the use of arms. Gruffydd Fychan II had been the earl's steward of Oswestry, and may have arranged that his son should become Arundel's page. After the old earl's death in 1376 his son, also named Richard, would probably have assumed the wardship, unless Owain had already come of age. When Owain came into his estates he became a minor Marcher lord, drawing about £200 a year from his paternal lands. He inherited from his mother two manors, Iscoed Uch Hirwen and Gwynionydd, in Cardiganshire. In wealth Owain ranked high among the *uchelwyr*, and compared well with most English gentry.[12]

Owain's family connections enhanced his prospects for advancement in English society. If Owain spent a few years in Arundel's household as a page, as he very likely did, he would have travelled about England, because noblemen often moved between their various estates; they also spent much of their time in London, especially when Parliament was sitting. By 1376, when the old Earl of Arundel died, Owain would have commenced the next stage in the education of a man of rank: seven or eight years in the study of law at the Inns of Court in London. At twenty-one he could become an apprentice-at-law or barrister. He would then have to practise at lesser courts for three years, until the King's judges would grant him the right of audience at Westminster. Thomas Walsingham, the St. Albans chronicler, said that he 'was apprentice-at-law at Westminster'. This term included all barristers except the privileged class of serjeants-at-law. About 1383 Owain married Margaret, daughter of Sir David Hanmer, chief justice of the king's bench, who must have helped him in his legal career. The Hanmers were an important Anglo-Welsh family in north-east Wales. If the date of his marriage is right, it gives a reason for dating his birth nearer to 1359; twenty-four seems quite old enough for such an eligible bachelor to marry, in times when it was not unusual to do so at seventeen.[13]

The Inns of Court were a sort of public school or university for the sons of landowners. A knowledge of law helped a gentleman to administer his estates, to draw up indentures and entails, and to carry on the litigation about landownership which was endemic during the middle ages; he might also earn valuable fees by carrying out such services for a nobleman. He could more readily serve as a justice of the peace, coroner, sheriff or Member of Parliament. Young men could also sow their wild oats, and participate in riots and other exciting activities, like students in any age. Falstaff and Justice Shallow boasted about the wildness of their salad days at Clement's Inn: 'Lord, Lord, how subject we old men are to this vice of lying!'[14]

Military service, like legal studies, was a natural pursuit for a man of rank, unless he took holy orders. His training as a man-at-arms began in his boyhood, and could continue while he was studying for the Bar. Magnates relied heavily on gentlemen who were skilled at law and estate management as well as at soldiering; a man retained for life by one lord might be paid by another as a councillor, receiver or steward on his estates. Owain could therefore have combined the law with the military career which he began in his early twenties, and which could well have augmented his landed income.

Owain's upbringing therefore made him a full member of the polite and chivalric society of late fourteenth century England; he fulfilled the Elizabethan idea of the complete gentleman. His first military service was in 1384 with Sir Degory Sais, perhaps the most celebrated Welsh captain of the age, who was in command at Berwick-on-Tweed. His retinue includes the names of Owain and his brother Tudur Glyn Dŵr among the men-at-arms; they joined Richard II's expedition to Scotland in August 1385. In a well-known *cywydd* (praise poem) the bard Gruffydd Llwyd exults in his prowess as a warrior, how he excelled at the tournament, how in a fierce fight, with a scarlet flamingo feather in his helmet, and a broken lance as a dagger, he drove the Scots before him like wild goats.[15]

Owain's new reputation for courage and leadership established him as a respected member of the world of chivalry. So did the legal case which has indicated the year of his birth, and which was very much a *cause célèbre* in its day. Richard Lord Scrope and Sir Robert Grosvenor contested the right to bear the arms *azure a bend or;* almost as much importance was attached to heraldic devices as to the ownership of land. In 1386 a court of chivalry convened under the Duke of Gloucester, Constable of England, which sat on and off for five years. Owain and his brother Tudur had both seen Robert Grosvenor bearing the device during the Scottish campaign; moreover, both testified that 'in the counties of Chester and Flint ... the public voice and fame is that the said arms have belonged as above to the said Monsieur Robert and his ancestors.' Another witness was the poet Geoffrey Chaucer. The solid local evidence did not, however, avail against the opinion of the magnates; Scrope won the case, but Grosvenor could use the arms if a white border was added to the shield. Here is clear evidence that Owain had served in the recent Scottish campaign, and was at home in the chivalric society of his day. It also gives a reliable pointer to the ages of Owain and Tudur, who was said to be the younger by about two years.[16]

In 1387 Owain became a retainer of Richard Fitzalan, the new Earl of Arundel, and was eighth among his twenty-five esquires, Tudur twentieth. While describing Owain's military service, D. Goodman suggests that Owain was probably retained by Arundel for life in peace and war, not for only a few months at a time, as with Degory Sais. To be retained for life was a very different matter, for you were then a member of your lord's affinity, on his permanent staff, drawing an annuity or fee, and enjoying his protection. Arundel was admiral that year, and Owain was fortunate to have participated in the first major naval victory since war was resumed in 1369, off Cadzand, on the Flanders coast. The enemy were mostly Flemish, and their cargoes of wine were taken by the English, making it a lucrative as well as honourable exploit. Arundel seems to have been pleased with Owain, whose name headed the list of the esquires indented for service in France in 1388; but for some reason he was crossed off. He did not miss much, as in fact the expedition achieved nothing. In 1387 Arundel was one of the Lords Appellant, who opposed the king's peace policy and rebelled against him. It is not known whether Owain and Tudur were with Arundel when the Appellants, under the future Henry IV, defeated Richard II's favourite, Robert de Vere, at Radcot Bridge. Owain is said to have been with the king's expedition to Ireland in 1394, and that he also fought in France, but nothing is known of this.[17]

Owain seems to have received no honours for this honourable service, certainly no knighthood, and may have been left with a sense of grievance. It must be said, however, that many esquires preferred to retain that rank, rather than take on the greater expenses and responsibilities incurred by knighthood. There was also a tendency for the English to regard Scotsmen as their equals and worthy of honours, but not Welshmen or Irishmen. Very few Welshmen achieved knighthood in the fourteenth century.

According to a story current at the end of the sixteenth century, and repeated by later writers, Owain was esquire to Richard II. This seems improbable when Owain had been a retainer of Arundel, and may therefore have been in his retinue during the rebellion of 1387. It is possible that Owain had left Arundel's service before 1397, when the earl was disgraced and executed. When Walsingham first mentions Owain, he explains that he had first practised law and then, 'a worthy esquire to the present king [Henry IV], before he took the realm, laudably performed his military duties'. If this is true it looks as though Owain was in Henry's retinue during the events leading to Richard's deposition. It is therefore most unlikely that Owain was ever esquire to Richard II. During his exile Henry's entourage included two Fitzalans: Thomas, Earl of Arundel and heir of Owain's late master, and his uncle Thomas, called Archbishop Arundel, both of whom were shortly restored to their dignities.[18]

These details about Owain's early life established by Thomas Walsingham and his contemporaries were accepted by their successors. Walsingham was a monk of St. Albans Abbey, the great Benedictine house on the road to the north, with many important people constantly coming and going, so that all the latest news was readily available. St. Albans also had a long tradition of chronicle writing, and Walsingham was then its foremost historian. He wrote several books, of which his *Historia Anglicana* is often quoted. In his latter years he was responsible for the work of the Scriptorium, where the abbey chronicle was composed. The *Annals of Henry IV* were largely his work, but are clearly based on the earlier history, with more detail. He is considered a reliable witness, but was not free from bias; for instance he loathed John of Gaunt.[19]

For two centuries Owain Glyn Dŵr was dismissed as a sort of brigand or warlord by most writers, Welsh as well as English, until Shakespeare painted a more kindly portrait. In the seventeenth century Welsh historians began to take Owain Glyn Dŵr more seriously. The first biography, the *Memoirs of Owen Glendowr*, was based on fifteenth-century sources, and was probably written by Robert Vaughan of Hengwrt (d.1667). His friend Thomas Ellis (d.1673), is believed to have revised his work, but it was only published a century later in an anonymous history of Anglesey. It was an important source for Thomas Pennant in the first full account of Glyn Dŵr's Rising ever written, which formed part of his famous work, *A Tour in Wales* (1778). Pennant took from Ellis the error that Owain had been esquire to Richard II, but he was a careful scholar, and the first writer to portray Owain as a genius and a national hero, a verdict which has become generally accepted by posterity.[20]

Owain may have been at home in English society, but he always remained a Welshman at heart. Glyn Dyfrdwy, the deep wooded glen, was a paradise for the sportsman: the river abounded with salmon, the forests and moors with game, but Sycharth was the place for gracious living. This was where Owain and his delightful lady made their home, of which such idyllic descriptions have been given by the bards. Here Owain and Margaret raised their large family. There are said to have been at least six sons and five daughters, but Owain is also thought to have had several illegitimate offspring. Not long before the Rising the bard Iolo Goch wrote a *cywydd* on Sycharth, describing Margaret as:

> The best of wives. Eminent woman of a knightly family,
> Her children come in pairs, A beautiful nest of chieftains.

Iolo Goch, Gruffydd Llwyd and other bards were prominent among the many people who were welcome to Owain's hospitable board, where the fare was all of the best: white bread, meat, wine, and Shrewsbury beer. The high mound was encircled with a gleaming moat. A bridge and lordly gatehouse led to a timber hall, as high as the cloisters of Westminster. Four wooden columns stood at the corners, each supporting a loft in which the minstrels slept. The hall had all the latest amenities: slate roof, chimneys and stained glass windows as fine as those in St. Patrick's Church in Dublin. There one could also see nine wardrobes, each well furnished with rich garments, like fine shops in Cheapside. The bards describe the church, the mill on Afon Cynllaith, a tall stone pigeon house, deerpark, stables, heronry, fishpond and rabbit warren, the trim meadows, hayfields, corn fields and orchards. There were no locks or bolts on the doors, everyone was welcome, and hunger and thirst were unknown there. Owain emerges as the model country squire, Welsh or English, a truly chivalrous gentleman, open-handed and generous, kind to the weak, stern towards the proud and violent; the very qualities which drove him into armed resistance in defence of his rights and those of his people. Perhaps nothing is more notable than the close rapport of Owain with the bards, guardians of the culture, and prophets of the destiny of Wales. It is impossible to contemplate this picture of peace and enjoyment without thinking with foreboding of the horrors to come, the destruction of this happy home, and dispersal of those who had loved it so much.[21]

CHAPTER THREE

Plantagenet, Lancaster, Mortimer, & Percy

The dynastic turmoil in England, which reached a climax in the deposition of Richard II in 1399, was an immediate cause of Owain Glyn Dŵr's revolt, and a fatal influence on its course. Richard II was only ten when he came to the throne, at a time when discontent and revolt were erupting in both France and England. Edward III's glorious reign ended in disillusionment and gloom as he became prematurely senile; his heir, the Black Prince, was already dead. The strains, stresses and costs of a long and futile war led to the Peasants' Revolt of 1381. It was suspected that Wales also might be near breaking point. Richard had none of the warlike tastes of his grandfather Edward III and father the Black Prince. He was intelligent, charming, generous to a fault, handsome and courageousbut he had inherited from his father an arrogant, violent and irrational trend. Probably spoilt as a child, he grew up to have inflated ideas of his position as king, and to behave in a more and more arbitrary manner. He was only ten at his accession in 1377, only a year after his father's death, and at a time of rising unrest.

Richard's eldest uncle was John of Gaunt, Duke of Lancaster. Gaunt's father-in-law Henry, the first duke, was master of the greatest inheritance and affinity in England; his great military talents, wealth and retinue had all been devoted to the royal service. Gaunt was equally loyal and not without ability, but he was both arrogant and unscrupulous. He quarrelled bitterly with the Church and the City of London, and presumably treated the populace with contempt and disdain, judging by the bitter hatred with which they responded: he, the richest magnate in the realm, paid no more poll tax than they did. Gaunt was also much disliked by his nephew the king, whose preference for the advice of his own friends had unfortunate results.[1]

When the rebellious peasants broke into London in 1381, almost their first act was to burn the Savoy, John of Gaunt's splendid palace. Richard's courtiers fled from the Tower, taking the king with them but abandoning the hated ministers Archbishop Sudbury and Sir Robert Hales the treasurer, also Richard's fifteen-year-old cousin, Henry of Bolingbroke, Gaunt's heir. When the rebels took the Tower they beheaded Sudbury and Hales, and were only with some difficulty dissuaded from murdering young Henry also. This may help to explain some of Henry's subsequent coolness towards Richard and his courtiers, despite the notable courage shown by Richard when facing the rebels at Smithfield and Mile End. The cousins were the same age, and were both admitted to the Order of the Garter on St. George's Day, 1377.[2]

Richard II presided over a cultured and civilised court. It was an age of great intellectual brilliance, which produced Geoffrey Chaucer, William Langland, John Wyclif, and the first English Bible. At such times people tend to question traditional authority. Wyclif and the Lollards, with the connivance of John of Gaunt, protested against the corruption within the Church, while the peasants challenged the social order. There were yet more violent upheavals in France. It was typical of this turbulent age that the Welsh should attempt to overthrow the English yoke.

It has to be said in Gaunt's favour that he never used his great power against the crown. He had a strong sense of duty and loyalty towards his difficult nephew, but he was absent at a critical time, vainly attempting to secure the throne of Castile to which his Spanish second wife Constance had a claim. There were two other royal uncles. Edmund the first Duke of York was a nonentity, but important as the ancestor of the House of York. The youngest, Thomas Duke of Gloucester, was a dangerous and violent man, like his close associate the Earl of Arundel, Owain Glyn Dŵr's patron. They and the less forceful Earl of Warwick favoured an aggressive policy towards France, for which they had some reason, as in 1386 a large French fleet and army had been massing to invade England, though eventually nothing came of this threat. Gloucester and his friends resented the king's preference for such favourites as Robert de Vere, Earl of Oxford, whom Richard made Duke of Ireland. They 'appealed' Richard's favourites of treason, so were known as the Lords Appellant. In 1388, during Gaunt's absence, they seized power with the support of the 'Merciless Parliament', and executed Richard's ministers. They were only dissuaded from deposing and killing the king by his cousin Henry of Bolingbroke, who had led them to victory over de Vere at Radcot Bridge. Despite what had happened in 1381 Henry took advantage of this golden opportunity to heap coals of fire on Richard's head. His magnanimity was much to his credit, but the signs are that as the years passed Richard envied, feared and hated Henry more rather than less. Only Gaunt himself, chasing crowns and castles far away in Spain, could have prevented these disasters. He would certainly never have allowed his son to support the Appellants in their treasonable activities.

In spite of his humiliation, Richard showed remarkable skill when he announced the following year that he was now of age to rule, and dismissed the Appellants. For the next eight years he ruled the country peacefully, but probably with the aim of taking revenge when the time was ripe. He made Cheshire his power base, recruiting there a bodyguard of archers who wore his livery of the white hart. His principal retainers wore livery collars of suns and broom pods (*Planta genista*), said to be the original device of Plantagenet. But anxiety about the succession was increasing. In 1396, after a childless first marriage, Richard made peace with France and took as his second queen a French princess aged seven. Her nationality made the match unpopular. Her age cast doubts on the willingness or ability of the king, now aged twenty-nine, to beget an heir. In Shakespeare's scene where Richard's favourites are condemned to death, Bolingbroke accuses them of seducing the king into homosexual practices.[3]

Henry of Bolingbroke, Earl of Derby, was the man of destiny of those years. He had been brought up as heir to the Duchy of Lancaster, and would inherit the greatest accumulation of estates of any English magnate in the middle ages, and the largest affinity. Members of Henry's household wore the famous livery collar of linked SSes. His wealth eventually gave him the power to seize the throne, a status for which he had not been trained; he also lacked the political and financial acumen essential for a king. Unlike John of Gaunt, Henry was loyal to the Church and pious to the point of superstition. He had four sons and two daughters by his first wife, Mary de Bohun, who died in 1394. He was well educated, and fond of music and literature, like so many of the nobles and wealthier gentry. His skill at jousting was immense, so that he was the idol of the London crowds. After a great international tournament in the Calais marches in 1390 Henry was admired in France as well as England as outstanding among English knights, the very paragon of chivalry. Like many European nobles, he joined the Teutonic Knights on a Baltic crusade. In 1390 with a small retinue of 150 knights, esquires and soldiers he helped the Teutonic Knights to defeat the Lithuanians and besiege Vilna, but he and his men had to depart owing to sickness and to disputes with their hosts. Henry returned next year only to find that he was unwelcome. Sending most of his retinue home, he visited Prague, Vienna and Venice, and then made his pilgrimage to Jerusalem. These travels and the ensuing publicity made Henry something of a celebrity in Europe, the best-travelled prince of his day. Though Henry was a superb knight, he was not a hardened soldier in the class of Hotspur or other veterans of the French or Scottish campaigns. Possibly he did not find military life to his taste in the siege lines before Vilna.[4]

The Appellants were lulled into thinking that the events of 1388 were forgiven and forgotten, but in 1397, for reasons which have never been made clear unless Richard's sole aim was revenge, he suddenly arrested the three whom he especially loathed. Arundel was executed. Thomas Duke of Gloucester was imprisoned at Calais, where he was murdered. Few doubted that the king had ordered Thomas Mowbray Earl of Nottingham, now his chief favourite, to do the deed. The Earl of Warwick was imprisoned for life. Richard now ruled like a tyrant, placing himself above the law. He created a record number of new peers and titles. Henry of Bolingbroke and Mowbray were made Dukes of Hereford and Norfolk respectively, but Richard did not forget that they had been Appellants. Mowbray voiced his fear to Bolingbroke that the king might still take his revenge on them. Gaunt advised his son to tell the king of this treasonable statement. Mowbray and Bolingbroke exchanged challenges, and a trial by battle was arranged, but before it began Richard II forbade it and exiled both dukes.

There can be little doubt about Richard's real feelings for Henry, who outshone him with his feats of chivalry, scattering knightly largesse among the people and winning their hearts as Gaunt had never done. Gaunt died in 1399, and Richard made Henry's exile permanent, seizing the opportunity to get rid of his glamorous but overmighty cousin for good. Funds were needed urgently to pay for an expedition, which Richard intended to lead, in order to suppress the Irish rebellion in which his lieutenant, Mortimer, had just been killed. The king therefore seized the whole Lancastrian inheritance. This act of expropriation threatened all landowners, so when Henry returned to claim his lands he won almost universal support. He deposed Richard and made himself King Henry IV. He had saved Richard's life and throne in 1388, but in his ingratitude and folly Richard provoked his mighty subject to rebellion. Henry's coup was followed by many violent deaths, more than in the purges of 1388 and 1397 together. Richard himself died mysteriously in Pontefract Castle; many of his friends suffered more publicly, as did also some nobles who had remained loyal to him and were rash enough to dispute Henry's usurpation of the crown.[5]

In the famous though fictitious speech made by the Bishop of Carlisle Shakespeare, admittedly aided by hindsight, shows his deep understanding of how Henry had irreparably damaged the delicate mechanism of monarchy by his usurpation. He shows it again in the scene where Hotspur in rage and fury splutters out his hatred of Henry to his father and uncle; in speaking of 'this vile politician, Bolingbroke' he hits the nail on the head. A king should be above politics, a fact which Henry failed to understand. This underlies the disasters of his reign; he never fully raised himself above the level of a party leader. By taking the crown by force with an uncertain title Henry destroyed the hierarchical relationship which a king ought to enjoy with his nobles. Richard II had also become a faction leader, and the same was later true of the rival claimants during the Wars of the Roses. A usurper inevitably felt insecure; in fact very few of the monarchs for the next two centuries, Lancastrian, Yorkist or Tudor, enjoyed an undisputed title to the throne.[6]

The Mortimer claim was at this time the only rival to Lancaster's. The Earl of March was the greatest Welsh Marcher lord, but his Irish lands were too great a burden on his power. Roger Mortimer, fourth Earl of March, was lieutenant in Ireland and not involved in the troubles of 1397. He was the last effective head of the House of Mortimer, and also heir presumptive to the throne, but historians have rejected the view that this status had been formally recognised by Richard II. The chronicler Adam of Usk knew the third and fourth Earls of March personally, and says that Richard disliked and distrusted his cousin. Earl Roger's Plantagenet blood gave him a more substantial claim to the throne than his descent from Llywelyn ap Iowerth, Prince of Gwynedd, and so from the mythical Kings of Britain. His untimely death in 1398 at the early age of twenty-four was indeed a disaster for the House of Mortimer. Although Roger was brave, personable and energetic, the Wigmore Abbey chronicler admitted that he was also 'licentious and, alas! remiss in matters of religion'.[7]

The Earl of March was 'heir general' to the throne since his claim was through a woman, his mother Philippa; her father the Duke of Clarence was second son of Edward III, and elder brother of John of Gaunt. Henry IV could simply have argued that his claim to the throne was superior to Mortimer's because his descent from Edward III through John of Gaunt made him 'heir male'. Because Henry was also descended through his mother from Edmund, first Earl of Lancaster and second son of Henry III (1216-72), he thought that he could strengthen his claim by reviving the hoary fable that Edmund was really older than his brother Edward I. If this was true the three Edwards and Richard II were usurpers, which Henry's supporters found too much to swallow. No one could deny that Henry's claim was doubtful, and that he had taken the crown by force.[8]

Roger's death caused Richard to lead his army over to Ireland, giving Henry of Lancaster that chance to invade England which he promptly seized. Had he lived, Earl Roger might have challenged Henry's bid for the throne, but his retinue could not have matched the great army which Henry commanded as Duke of Lancaster, unless he had been supported by most of the nobility. Roger's younger brother Edmund was not forceful enough to take his place. His heir, Edmund the last Earl of March, was only eight when Richard II was deposed, after which he and his brother were kept in custody by Henry IV. He was never to show much ability; Henry of Lancaster was more fitted to be king because of his personality and the sheer size of his retinue. What made resistance still more dangerous, as several noblemen discovered to their cost, was Henry's suspicious mind. He could not understand that the Mortimers were in no position to threaten him.

Earl Roger was the most powerful Marcher lord, but was only one of many who were removed by death or exile in the late 1390s. Gloucester, Arundel, and Warwick, for example, were all victims of the 1397 coup. Mowbray and Bolingbroke were exiled. Gaunt died. Richard's favourites partook freely of the spoils, but lost them when he himself was deposed, which widened the power vacuum in Wales still further, since he had been popular there. 'The seismic impact of these changes', as Professor Rees Davies describes it, perilously weakenened English control.[9]

At this point the most powerful family in the north country comes into the story. Henry Percy the elder was born in 1341, and had been made first Earl of Northumberland at Richard II's coronation in 1377. He had been on Gaunt's first expedition to Castile in 1366-67, and had also served as governor of Calais. He was warden of the Marches toward Scotland, and as sheriff for life of Northumberland had resented Gaunt's interference in the area after the Peasants' Revolt. In 1399 his experience and ability, together with the military power of the Percies, had been decisive in deposing Richard II and enthroning Henry IV. His brother Thomas had been created Earl of Worcester by Richard II, and was the best soldier in the family; he had been admiral on Gaunt's second venture to Castile in 1387-89. The younger Henry Percy, Northumberland's son and heir, was known as Hotspur because of his warlike ardour and chivalry; he was not the same generation as the Prince of Wales, as Shakespeare makes out, but was in fact two years older than Henry IV. Hotspur was married to Elizabeth (Shakespeare's Kate),whose brothers were Edmund Mortimer and the late Earl of March. Three of the chief actors in this drama were close contemporaries: Richard II, Henry IV and Henry 'Hotspur'.[10]

The Percies combined political and military power with great ability and restless ambition. All had been retainers of John of Gaunt. Hotspur worked hard to suppress the Welsh revolt; he and his father tried to give Henry what they thought was good advice. As wardens of the Scottish March they had heavy responsibilities. Historians disagree as to whether Henry IV repaid their costs fully, or rewarded them properly for their services. Some think that he treated them as generously as he could afford, while others argue that had he used his great powers of patronage as king and as Duke of Lancaster more wisely and generously, he might well have satisfied them. Thomas Percy, a bachelor, could easily have been given lands and annuities to make up his income to the £1,000 a year needed to support the dignity of an earl.[11]

In 1399 three men achieved advancement of a kind likely to offend the Welsh. Henry of Lancaster had displaced a king for whom the Welsh felt some regard, and imposed the heavy payments which a new king usually demanded. Many Welshmen as well as Englishmen though that he was a usurper; they felt the same towards his son, Henry of Monmouth, raised to be Prince of Wales as one of Henry IV's first acts on becoming king. The third, Hotspur, one of Henry IV's chief allies, was made Justiciar of Chester, which meant in effect chief councillor and military adviser to Prince Henry, and virtually ruler of north Wales. The grants of Anglesey and Beaumaris Castle from the principality of Wales, and Denbigh Castle from the earldom of March, added sinews to this appointment. The ambitious Percy family were not welcome so far from their usual haunts, and this attempt to fill the power vacuum in Wales was widely resented, however necessary it was. This was compounded in 1401 when Hotspur's uncle Thomas Earl of Worcester was made governor of the Prince of Wales. Other former retainers of John of Gaunt who were to have a formative influence on the young prince, and finally to be among his future companions at Agincourt were Ralph Neville, Earl of Westmorland, Sir Thomas Erpingham and Sir John Cornewall.[12]

The Welsh revolt was to make King Henry IV even more dependent on the goodwill and support of the Percies, and on the loyalty of Edmund Mortimer, the acting head of his family while his nephew the young Earl of March was a minor and a royal ward. When Edmund went over to Owain Glyn Dŵr in 1402, the result was an alliance between Owain, Percy and Mortimer which shook Henry IV's throne to its foundations, but which Henry might have prevented had he been more astute, more magnanimous, and less suspicious.

Medieval noblemen tended to see little of their children as they grew up, and Henry of Bolingbroke never became close to his eldest son Henry of Monmouth; indeed there are historical grounds for the antipathy depicted by Shakespeare. There can be no doubt that Prince Henry was an abler and more intelligent man than his father. His maternal grandmother, Joan de Bohun, relict of the last Earl of Hereford, had a strong influence on him. He was very fond of her; she was noted for her forceful character and good works. She was sister both of the Archbishop of Canterbury and of the late Earl of Arundel. There are signs that the young Henry also liked King Richard II, who was his godfather, and who took him and other young noblemen to Ireland in 1399, perhaps as hostages for the good conduct of their fathers. The prince was profoundly disturbed at his father's usurpation. All that Henry IV did to make amends was to have Richard buried in the Blackfriars Church at Langley in Hertfordshire. During the first year of Henry V's reign he reburied the murdered king beside his first wife in Westminster Abbey.[13]

There was too little joy in the life of Prince Henry for the playboy Hal, one of Shakespeare's best-loved characters, to be entirely credible. Probably he whooped it up in the taverns of Cheapside during his visits to London, like any right-minded young soldier on leave from the wars, thus falling into the low company which tradition says that he kept. It is also said that he was imprisoned by the chief justice, William Gascoigne, for interfering with the trial of a servant for some breach of the peace. This need not be very surprising, when so often the nobility showed contempt for the law, like Grey of Ruthin in his dispute with Owain Glyn Dŵr. Nor had his own father been particularly squeamish when he seized the throne. It is quite possible that with some of his fellow bravos Henry may have waylaid his own receivers on Gadshill a mad prank indeed. Chief Justice Gascoigne was retired when Henry came to the throne. Unfortunately, Falstaff must be dismissed as pure fiction; he began as Sir John Oldcastle, Henry's comrade-in-arms who turned Lollard, and then, via Sir John Fastolfe the successful soldier who was a friend of the Pastons of Norfolk, became the fat rogue who still delights us. Some chronicles say that when Henry succeeded his father he underwent a sort of conversion, dropping his wild ways and boon companions, becoming more pious, serious-minded, and formidable than ever. Shakespeare understood that what he called 'the cease of majesty' must be prevented, responsibility accepted, and 'Falstaff' (the low companions) coldly abandoned.[14]

In the words of Henry V's most recent biographer, Professor Allmand, 'as Prince and later as king, Henry spent much of his time in conflict with those who opposed him.' Henry had no sooner become Prince of Wales than he had to fight the war, which for ten years consumed his revenues and energies as Prince and as Earl of Chester. After five years he was able to take the offensive against Owain Glyn Dŵr; it was another five before victory was complete. The war trained a prince who would become probably the most brilliant soldier of all English kings since Richard Coeur de Lion, as well as the new generation of captains who were to command the English armies under him in France. He gained practical experience of all aspects of war, of sieges more than of battles in the field, and of supplying, paying and leading men in remote areas of a land whose brave and tenacious inhabitants used its physical difficulties to the full. All this formed the character of the king whom we see in the familiar portrait. Shakespeare's charismatic war-leader was also a relentless and meticulous administrator who kept tight control of everyone and everything in his kingdom, even when fighting in France.[15]

Shakespeare has been blamed for making a hero of a king whom many see as merely a chauvinistic warmonger. There was certainly a ruthless side to Henry, but his order to kill the prisoners at Agincourt was in accordance with the rules of medieval warfare. Shakespeare would not have agreed that Henry was cold-blooded; he may again be tapping a spring of true tradition in some remarks made by Falstaff in his splendid and revealing soliloquy on 'sherris-sack'. Of Prince John, Hal's younger brother, the fat knight says: 'this same young sober-blooded boy doth not love me; nor a man cannot make him laugh; but that's no marvel, he drinks no wine.' It is sherris-sack which makes a man:

> Hereof comes it, that Prince Harry is valiant; for the cold blood he did naturally inherit from his father, he hath, like lean, sterile and bare land, manured, husbanded, and till'd, with excellent endeavour of drinking good and good store of fertile sherris, that he is become very hot and valiant.

Here are some rare shafts of light on three of the Lancastrian princes, in which Hal is favourably compared with his father as well as his brother (later the famous Duke of Bedford).[16]

A contemporary letter demonstrates that the future Henry V had a warmer side to his nature, and that he genuinely cared for the men whom he led so successfully. In it he sent a personal request to the abbot of an unnamed monastery. William de Ferriby, his chancellor, suffered badly from chronic sciatica, and was always in great pain. One of the monks was reported to be skilled in relieving this malady. The prince prayed most heartily 'that you would give him in your Abbey all the ease, disport and comfort which you possibly can, out of reverence to us and consideration for our present prayer'. This partly explains that genius for leadership which made Henry so exceptional among our monarchs, and why his friends and retainers were ready to follow him to the death. John of Gaunt and

Henry IV had never shown any sympathy with the Welsh, but the younger Henry built up a notable rapport with them; his birth at Monmouth was an undoubted asset. Victory over Glyn Dŵr would have been impossible without Henry's Welsh retainers. He regarded them highly for their courage, especially Dafydd Gam, one of those who died in his defence at Agincourt, and perhaps Shakespeare's model for the fiery and valiant Captain Fluellen.[17]

It is understandable that a prince who valued loyalty so highly was hard on those who betrayed him. Henry felt treachery and treason very deeply and personally. He showed no mercy to former friends who rebelled against him, like those involved in the Southampton Plot on the very eve of the army's embarkation for France in 1415; it was centred on the Earl of March, who saved his own skin by betraying his confederates. Henry, Lord Scrope of Masham, Knight of the Garter, had been treasurer of England and a trusted servant of both Lancastrian kings; it is not known why he turned traitor, but Henry could not forgive him, the Earl of Cambridge or Sir Thomas Grey, the other conspirators:

> What shall I say to thee, Lord Scroop? Thou cruel,
> Ingrateful, savage, and inhuman creature! Thou, that
> didst bear the key of all my counsels, That knew'st the
> very bottom of my soul, ... For this revolt of thine,
> methinks, is like Another fall of man. ... ...

Nor was there any mercy for his old and trusted comrade-in-arms, Sir John Oldcastle, who died on a gallows with a fire beneath him, as a traitor and heretic. Like all great leaders, Henry asked no more of anyone than he was ready to do himself; he set everyone high standards, not least himself. His desire was to rule in harmony with his people. The unity of the realm was sacrosanct, and treason was thus a crime against both king and people.[18]

CHAPTER FOUR

The Rising, 1400 to 1402

If a medieval rebellion did not succeed, it would usually peter out within weeks or months. The Rising of Owain Glyn Dŵr deserves rather to be called an unsuccessful war of Welsh independence, because it went on for about twelve years. Owain's claim to be Prince of Wales was based on his descent from the three most important of ancient Welsh dynasties; in Welsh eyes it was stronger than that of Henry of Monmouth, whose father had usurped the throne, and whose claim it challenged. This was also a war of succession, like the one in Brittany which the English had exploited to their advantage in the reign of Edward III. The French were soon to do the same in Wales for Owain's claim to the princely crown of Wales was as valid as that of the Plantagenets to the throne of France.

The situation in Wales was probably so explosive that only a king with exceptional gifts of statesmanship could have prevented the calamity, which was sparked off by a quarrel between Owain and Lord Grey of Ruthin. A king with a reputation for fairness and strict impartiality could have settled the affair, but Henry IV did not have the authority or tact to do so. Owain was the king's esquire, but Henry was in too weak a position to offend a powerful magnate who had helped him to seize the throne. Nor was there at hand any unprejudiced or well-informed Englishman to warn the king that Owain was a very influential man who could make a lot of trouble if he was wronged; but no one, not even Owain himself, could have foreseen at that time just how powerful he could become.

From now on an important Welsh witness makes a vital contribution to the saga. Adam of Usk's book is as much an autobiography as a chronicle, not infallible but always interesting. Adam came from the Mortimer lordship of that name in Gwent: he was a sort of choric character in the tremendous drama about to unfold, commenting on it, hovering around its periphery, and affording some light relief. He had previously enjoyed the patronage of Edmund, the third Earl of March, who had given him 'an exhibition at the schools', so that he was able to study at Oxford. He had both ability and ambition, one of those Welshmen who made use of the opportunities offered by the English, and became by profession an ecclesiastical lawyer. But in November 1400, with his two servants and others, he had 'lain in ambush at Westminster to rob the king's lieges and there stolen a black horse of Walter Jakes with a saddle and bridle worth 100s, and 14 marks in money'. This was an indiscretion unbecoming an aspiring cleric, and Adam found it advisable to exercise his talents in some safer place. In February 1402 he set out for Rome. The culprits responsible for this highway robbery at the very seat of majesty were tried but escaped with a pardon. As Adam was absent he did not receive one, which made life difficult for him when he tried to return home in 1409. Adam was disdainful towards Owain and his followers, but he was a skilful fence-sitter with a hopeful disposition, always on the look-out for any preferment which might come his way. Self-imposed exile in Rome, however, did not encourage accurate reporting on events at home.[1]

The great, rich Benedictine abbey of Evesham was a favourite port of call for the king, his court, and magnates going to and from Worcester and Wales. Like Thomas Walsingham at St. Albans, an anonymous monk enriched his chronicle with valuable information gleaned from the important visitors whom he met passing through. The Monk of Evesham's work was the basis of another collection, known from its Victorian editor as Giles's Chronicle.[2]

The chronicles give two reasons for the outbreak of the Rising. The first of these was that Lord Grey of Ruthin, a Marcher magnate whose lands included Dyffryn Clwyd, near Glyn Dyfrdwy, had seized Croesau, a common to which Owain, a trained lawyer, thought he could prove his hereditary right. Grey held estates in several English shires, and was a baron of Parliament, the kind of man, experienced in war and peace, whose support the king badly needed. It is not surprising that he became a councillor to Henry IV. Owain's influential father-in-law, Sir David Hanmer, and the old Earl of Arundel were both dead. The young earl lacked Grey's political influence. He could not risk offending Henry IV, who had restored his earldom to him, by supporting Owain against Grey. Nor could he offer his 'good lordship' to Owain, because Owain was the king's esquire, and because King Henry was not even prepared to support his own retainer against an important magnate. The *Eulogium*, another monastic chronicle, says:

> Owen de Glendour, a Welshman who had been esquire of the Earl of Arundel, came to Parliament complaining that Lord de Gray Ruthin had usurped certain lands of his in Wales, but no argument helped against Lord de Gray. The Bishop of St. Asaph [John Trefor] gave counsel in Parliament that they should not entirely despise Owen, as the Welsh might perhaps revolt. But those in Parliament said that they cared nothing for the bare-footed clowns.[3]

The Monk of Evesham's version of events has been doubted, but it in no way contradicts the story that Owain and Grey quarrelled over the ownership of a piece of land:

> When the king was preparing to hurry off to Scotland, amongst other things he sent letters, sealed with his own seal, to the said Owyn, for he was himself thought those days to be a fine esquire, that he should go with the king who would in no way excuse him. Lord Grey of Ruthin was appointed to carry these letters, but having accepted them he put off delivering them until the king's departure, and only handed them over the third day before the king left. Owain was completely taken aback, saying that it was much too late, too sudden and too unexpected a warning for such a

39

journey, and briefly excused himself, as it was quite impossible to go to Scotland. Lord Grey left him in Wales, and went to the king in Scotland as fast as he could, and made the worst of it in telling him that the said Owyn despised his letters and held his commands in contempt.[4]

This story puts Grey and the king in an extremely unfavourable light; the fact that it is told by an Englishman makes it all the more damning. It also bears out Walsingham's statement that Owain was a king's esquire; as a royal retainer, he disobeyed the king's command 'at his peril'. The rolls of the Parliament before which Owain laid his complaint are lost, and we have no further details. The king, who was already ill-disposed towards Owain, was apparently deceived by Grey's lies and malice. Owain received no redress and returned home enraged at English insolence and injustice.[5]

It is easy to understand that in September 1400 Owain, his relations and friends felt that they could take no more, and decided to throw down the gauntlet. Owain was not a man to let the grass grow under his feet, and he probably saw the absence in Scotland of King Henry IV with most of his power as an opportunity not to be missed. This was the opinion of Gruffydd Hiraethog, a poet whose name comes from a hill in Denbighshire. About 1550 he wrote a short chronicle, based on a text, now lost, compiled about 1422. The first Welsh account of Owain Glyn Dŵr is therefore almost contemporary with the events of 1400:

Henry went to Scotland and with him a great host. While he was unoccupied there, one of his lords told him he had better have faithful men in Wales, for he said that Owen ap Gruffydd would wage war against him. Therefore Lord Talbot and Lord Grey were sent to make sure of Owen and they undertook the task. But the man escaped into the woods; the time was the feast of St. Matthew in autumn [Sept. 21].[6]

In fact, Owain and his fellow conspirators had met in Glyn Dyfrdwy only five days earlier. The others included his brother Tudur, his son Gruffydd, and his brothers-in-law Gruffydd and Philip Hanmer. A significant member of the higher Welsh clergy was present: Hywel Cyffin, Dean of St. Asaph, with his two nephews. Finally, the company included their prophet or sooth-sayer, the bard named Crach Ffinnant. Adam of Usk and the Monk of Evesham say that Owain's supporters 'raised him up to be their prince', though he did not use the title of Prince of Wales until he opened diplomatic relations with Scotland and France.[7]

'Followed with a company of stout, resolute men, [Owain] fell upon the town of Ruthin whilst they kept their fair, sacked and burned it to the ground', writes Ellis. The same fate befell the other English boroughs in north-east Wales: Denbigh and Rhuddlan, Flint, Harwarden and Holt. Finally, the rebels attacked Oswestry and Welshpool, and burned both towns to the ground, but they lacked the siege equipment needed to attack the castles. They were then severely defeated by Hugh Burnell, a Shropshire landowner, in a battle placed by Welsh chroniclers on the banks of the River Vyrnwy, north of Welshpool. It seemed as if the rebels had shot their bolt.[8]

The Monk of Evesham was not the only Englishman who blamed Henry IV; there seems to have been a good deal of sympathy for Owain Glyn Dŵr. John Hardynge, a soldier whose verse chronicle was published at the end of his long life and was even presented to Henry VI, wrote:

> The king came home and to London went
> At Michaelmas, wher then he had message,
> That Owen Glendoure then fully blent
> In England sore, and did full great damage,
> For cause the lorde Graye held his herytage;
> And to the kyng of it full sore had playned,
> No remedye gate, so was he then demeaned.[9]

The king was at Northampton on his way home from Scotland when the news of the rebellion reached him. Keenly aware of the strategic importance of Shrewsbury, he at once ordered the burgesses to look to their defences, and to beware of their Welsh residents. He then came to Shrewsbury in person. At first the revolt seemed to be over, but then news came of the seizure of Anglesey by the brothers Gwilym and Rhys ap Tudur, cousins of Owain, who were in fact acting very much in their own interest. Henry decided to show the flag with a punitive march through north Wales. Passing though Bangor, he looted and burned the Franciscan house at Llanfaes, to punish the friars for supporting Owain. The adherence of both Welsh and English Franciscans to Richard II was well known, and reports that King Richard was still alive encouraged his many sympathisers among both Welsh and English. The general devastation roused a hornet's nest. The Tudur brothers attacked the king near Beaumaris Castle, driving him to take refuge inside its walls, an action which brought fresh life to Owain Glyn Dŵr's faltering rebellion.[10]

Riding through enemy territory and plundering it had become known as a *chevauchée* during the Hundred Years' War, though such military terrorism had been used by William the Conqueror, and was as old as war itself. Wide, fair regions of France had been devastated by this crude medieval method of financing warfare, which even the richest lands in Europe could not sustain indefinitely. It was still worse for poor regions like Wales, the north of England and Scotland, where cattle and sheep represented the chief wealth of their owners. Both sides probably saw captured enemy livestock as the main way of feeding their troops, as well as a financial asset. The looting of monasteries, churches, castles and farms could be profitable too; their destruction also satisfied the desire for vengeance and demoralised the enemy. In the English border counties the visits of small gangs of stock thieves now gave way to raids by well-armed war parties who spread terror far and wide. The Welsh, with their country ravaged and the tide of war rising, needed to rustle as many English sheep and cattle as possible. The English were hampered as usual in their military operations by the chronic shortage of supplies in Wales, although this could be overcome by careful logistic planning like that used successfully by Edward I.

King Henry returned to Shrewsbury through Caernarfon and Mawddwy, the mountainous area east of Cader Idris. Although various clergy submitted to the king, this royal *chevauchée* achieved little, and its three successors proved equally futile. The estates of Owain himself and of the Hanmers were confiscated; Owain's lands in both north and south Wales were given to John Beaufort Earl of Somerset, Henry's half-brother, the eldest son of John of Gaunt and Katherine Swynford. The king was taking advantage of a useful opportunity to enlarge the estates of the Beauforts, who having originally been illegitimate were something of an embarrassment to him, but as members of the Lancastrian royal family they had to be provided for.[11]

Parliament met in January 1401, and those members who understood Welsh affairs, especially John Trefor, the Welsh bishop of St. Asaph, explained to the king and his council that the Welsh were in a very dangerous mood. This advice might have been given more profitably in the last meeting of Parliament in 1399, but then the main business had been the deposition of Richard II. The king was told how 'the Welsh scholars who have been living at the Universities of Oxford and Cambridge have departed for their own country; and also the Welsh labourers, who have been living at various places in the Realm of England, have suddenly retreated from the said realm to their own land of Wales, and have provided themselves with armour, bows and swords'. At home the people were selling sheep and cattle to buy arms. There was an atmosphere of secret gatherings; bards, friars and vagrants of every kind were disseminating the latest news.[12]

Oxford, so much nearer to Wales than Cambridge, was the natural centre for the Welsh supporters of Owain. Professor Griffiths has revealed details of their activities. A year after the warning in Parliament about Welsh unrest in England, rumours of treason at Oxford were investigated. Thirteen men and a woman were indicted. One of the men was Hywel Cyffin, Dean of St. Asaph, who had been with Owain at the outbreak of the Rising. There can be no reasonable doubt that he had been sent by Owain to Oxford on a political mission, perhaps indicating plans already forming in Owain's mind or those of his advisers, for training the future leaders of a free Wales at a Welsh university. What rather took the steam out of the investigation was the interference of an 'approver', a person usually with a criminal record, who 'appealed' one of the men of treason. The accused, Owen Coneway, demanded a judicial duel, but before battle commenced the approver's courage failed him, and he was hanged at Tyburn for making a false accusation. After that the case was quietly dropped. Welsh students at Oxford were conscious and proud of their nationality, no doubt partly the result of mixing with English, Scottish and Irish students. When he was at Oxford in 1387, Adam of Usk took a leading part in student riots.[13]

One wonders how far Owain's Rising might have been planned in advance, with agents moving to and fro, or whether it was entirely spontaneous. It is apparent that the conditions were right for a general conflagration. The military situation in Wales could not have been more favourable. The Prince of Wales and the surviving Marcher lords lacked experience. The castles had been neglected for nearly a century; they were delapidated, badly equipped and undermanned. This was shown during the 1370s, when the danger of an invasion by Owain Lawgoch with French support caused a short-lived panic, compelling John of Gaunt to order the restocking and repairing of his neglected Welsh castles.[14]

During the fourteenth century the English had tended to allow Welshmen, who were ready to make themselves useful, to take over many posts in local government. Welshmen had also been able to infiltrate many of the English-occupied boroughs by taking advantage of the equally *laissez-faire* English attitude towards their own laws. Recent events in north-east Wales had shown how vulnerable the English boroughs were. It is not surprising that there were frequent agitated cries from the English at the threat to their language and way of life by the Welsh.[15]

After Parliament had met, the king and prince attempted conciliation, issuing a pardon for all except Owain and the Tudur brothers. During these months Owain remained hidden, to the despair of the bard Iolo Goch; but in the spring of 1401 events began to move at such a speed that it is hard to be certain of their exact sequence. English records give us some idea of chronological order. Welsh accounts do not, but they are the only sources for certain important incidents.[16]

Gwilym and Rhys ap Tudur opened the campaign of 1401 on their own account, with a victory which severely dented English pride. On Good Friday (1 April) with only forty followers, they achieved the amazing feat of taking Conwy Castle, one of Edward I's most powerful fortresses, when the garrison were in church for the service called *Tenebrae*; Adam of Usk says that two warders guarding it were killed 'by the craftiness of a certain carpenter who feigned to come for his accustomed work.' A survey of Welsh castles at the beginning of the revolt says that the garrison of Conwy numbered fifty men-at-arms and sixty archers, none too many for such a huge castle, but enough to have prevented the disaster of April Fool's Day, 1401, if the constable, John de Massy, had shown the faintest spark of military talent. Edward I's castles had been built for larger garrisons, and were very expensive to maintain, but the war was to demonstrate that even such vast castles as these could be defended by remarkably small numbers of determined men. It also proved that command of the sea was vital for the English if they were to hold Aberystwyth and Harlech, or to recover them after their capture in 1404 by the Welsh with the help of a French fleet. The Welsh benefited from English incompetence, but to capture three Edwardian castles was truly remarkable; they even held a fourth, Beaumaris, for a few months in 1404 and 1405.[17]

Henry IV's promotion of Hotspur, a northern lord, to command in Wales shows all too clearly how short of able captains he was; the late Earl of Arundel would have been the natural choice. In due course new leaders would arise among the Marcher lords. Soon after the fall of Conwy Castle, Hotspur was ordered to treat with the Tudur brothers for its surrender. A month later he was no nearer to recovering it, as the Tudurs and their forty men were well able to hold it. The king had been advised to pardon the Tudur brothers and had reluctantly agreed, but an undated letter to Prince Henry shows that he had changed his mind. This was the first time that the prince was on active service in Wales. In this letter his father approved of the way in which he and Hotspur were conducting the siege, with a hundred and twenty men-at-arms and three hundred archers, and agreed that the siege could continue till Michaelmas or even All Saints' Day,

> that the rebels might be punished according to their deserts, or that we should have at least some other treaty which should be agreeable to us and more honourable than was any one of the offers of our afore-said rebels; the which, as seems to your sage counsel and that of our said cousin, are not at all honourable to us, but a matter of most evil precedent.

King Henry was glad that the prince was resolved on a military solution, and he would have a grant towards his costs. But resources for a long siege were lacking, and the negotiations dragged on for nearly three months.[18]

Hotspur told the council on 4 May that the people of north Wales were submissive except for those of the Conwy area. Traces of Percy discontent appear in this letter, pointedly signed as 'Warden of the East March of England towards Scotland', and bidding the council remember 'how several times I have asked you for payment for the soldiers of the King in the town of Berwick and his east march of England, who are now in such great poverty that they cannot bear or endure it'. This may have strengthened the argument that it was not a good time for expensive siege operations, and that the distasteful negotiations at Conwy would have to be resumed.[19]

Hotspur had been growing increasingly discontented at the shortage of cash to pay his troops. He said so again, with emphasis, to the council on 17 May; he could not endure such great labour and costs much beyond the end of the month. In his letter of 4 June he did not mention Conwy, presumably as he had still not retaken it, and perhaps also because of the continuing loss of face. He may have suspected that the king wanted him to pay his costs from his own pocket. Magnates serving kings as war captains naturally became disgruntled if they were not repaid for their expenses. Henry IV was always very short of cash, which was a principal reason for his inability to defeat Owain Glyn Dŵr, though with the huge Lancastrian resources at his disposal he could dispense more patronage than any English king for a very long time. Perhaps Hotspur was less short of money than he pretended, and wanted to make it an excuse to leave the service of a king whom the Percies regarded with deep suspicion and resentment. It may have been at about this time that Hotspur began to discuss with Owain the possibility of peace, but there is no positive evidence on this important point.[20]

We have to remember, whenever the shortage of money is mentioned, that like any king of England in the late middle ages Henry IV had heavy defence expenses, apart from those caused by the Welsh revolt. Calais and the duchy of Aquitaine (also called Gascony or Guyenne) were constantly threatened by the French. The coasts and shipping had to be guarded against piratical attacks by the French, Flemings, Hanseatic League, Scots, Bretons and Castilians, though the English were well able to return the compliment. The Scottish marches were a constant source of expense. There was frequent warfare in Ireland. Henry IV had much to worry him.

Hotspur's negotiations for the surrender of Conwy were completed on 24 June (St. John Baptist's Day). Dr. Rhidian Griffiths says that after Prince Henry returned to London, his governor, Sir Hugh le Despencer, took over from Hotspur and recaptured it. The exact circumstances are not known, but apparently the Tudur brothers had no alternative but to accept very severe terms, whereby they were able to save their own skins only at a price which shamed both parties and shocked men even in that far from squeamish age, to judge by Adam of Usk's comments. They had to arrest and surrender nine of their men, who were executed with extreme barbarity as traitors. Hotspur finally left Wales in August for a more congenial task on his home ground, which was to negotiate with the Scots for a truce.[21]

Meanwhile on 26 May Henry IV had issued a commission of array, which summoned the sheriffs of fourteen shires and their troops to meet him at Worcester:

> News has been brought to us at our castle of
> Wallingford that Oweyn Glendourdy and other rebels

47

of our country of Wales have risen and are again
assembling on the marches of Carmarthen with the
purpose of invading our realm with main force in order
to destroy our English tongue and all our faithful
lieges.

The king arrived with his retinue at Evesham Abbey for the Feast
of Corpus Christi, which fell on 1 June that year; the Monk heard
many interesting details of what followed. The commission of array
was an ancient form of conscription, last used when the Civil War
began in 1642. 'Fencible' [able-bodied] men might be arrayed to
meet a threat of foreign invasion, but 'service was unpaid and
unpopular, and every effort was made to secure exemption.' Some
of the fencible men who were called up might in fact be the sort of
pitiful rogues whom Justice Shallow produced for Falstaff.[22]

When the king arrived at Worcester on 5 June, he was handed a
letter from Owain to Henry Dwnn of Kidwelly, calling for popular
support as 'Owain ap Gruffydd, lord of Glyn Dyfrdwy', not as
Prince of Wales. The letter implied that an invasion of south Wales
was imminent. The reference to Kidwelly was especially alarming
to Henry of Lancaster, because Kidwelly was a Lancastrian lordship with a great castle on the south coast of Carmarthenshire; the
consequences of its falling into rebel hands would be most serious.
The king would also have heard of Henry Dwnn, even if he had not
actually met this impressive member of the *uchelwyr*. In his youth
Henry Dwnn had followed John of Gaunt to the wars in Gascony,
and had more recently been in Ireland with Richard II. Professor
Rees Davies has given us a portrait of him. In Welsh he was 'Harri
Hen' Henry the Elder. He was indeed a most formidable man:
fierce, brave, skilled in war, a born leader, and dominant in the
affairs of his country. A man after Owain's heart and also a
personal friend, he was the natural choice to lead the rebellion in
those parts. The qualities which made Henry Dwnn great were
typical of the *uchelwyr*. It is not surprising that the rising rapidly
gained impetus under leaders of such calibre.[23]

The historian trying to reconcile the English and Welsh accounts
of these events faces a quandary at this point. Henry IV's order to

array the shires seems to have been fully justified by the intercepted letter, which if genuine could only mean that Owain had either started a new campaign in south-central Wales, or was about do so. We do not know if the news which reached the king at Wallingford meant that Owain had actually begun this campaign. Owain's whereabouts were so shrouded in mystery that in the minds of his contemporaries he was a magician; to us he was a strategic genius. Never were his movements more baffling than in May and June 1401. Hotspur told the king on 4 June that five days earlier he had beaten a Welsh force near Cader Idris, and had recently heard from John Charlton, lord of Powys, of a combat with Owain Glyn Dŵr, several of whose men had been wounded.[24]

Charlton wrote at the same time to the Prince of Wales:

> last Monday I was on *chevauchée* with my men on the mountains of my country of Powys and sent some of them into various parts of M. with 400 archers. When they were approaching that area they had seen Owain and his people in the mountains, where my spies had reported their presence beforehand.

By M. Charlton seems to indicate a district, probably the mountainous country of Mawddwy. He advanced with his men-at-arms and archers, hoping to engage the Welsh, but as soon as Owain and his men saw the English coming on fast, they hastily retreated into the mountains. They were chased all night, and dispersed in various directions,

> where I do not certainly know at present, but some say towards K. In this chase were taken some armour of the said Owain, some horses and lances, and a drape of cloth, painted with maidens with red hands, also his henchman, whom I intend to send to our lord the King, your father. That night I lodged with my other troops at M., in order to govern that area and to prevent the aforesaid rebels from returning.

49

We do not know the name of the unlucky henchman, nor what his fate was. We get only a vague idea as to the site of this encounter, but if it was in western Powys, which Charlton seems to be implying, M. now suggests a place, probably Machynlleth. If K. meant Kermerdyn (the English speling of Carmarthen), it implied that Owain was going south, which agrees with his later movements. It may be inferred from the date of the letter that the affair occurred in late May or in early June. John Charlton's letter gives the impression of a commander who was well in control of his troops, and had a reliable network of spies; as English military intelligence seems on the whole to have been poor, this point is of special interest. So is Charlton's account of Welsh guerilla tactics in the face of a superior English army, even though his meaning is not quite clear. The strange cloth was divided by its proud but loyal owner; one portion went to the prince, 'the remnant to the King, your father.' That monarch seems to have believed, in view of the Welsh defeats, that the crisis, and the threat to Carmarthen in particular, was over. Perhaps he found it hard to take Owain Glyn Dŵr seriously if he would not risk a battle with a small English force. Whatever the reason, King Henry IV dismissed his army and on 14 June left Worcester for Wallingford.[25]

What exactly was behind the news which had alarmed the king so much? The answer hangs on the problem of where Owain was then, which leads us to the wider question of his movements throughout April, May and June. Owain's brush with Charlton seems to have coincided with Percy's 'journey to Cader Idris', both of which were after Henry IV's call to arms at Wallingford. Charlton's adversary may not have been Owain but his brother Tudur, who was said to resemble him closely. We do not know why the All Clear was sounded at Worcester, any more than we know the cause of the Alert at Wallingford, or the chronology of the stirring events which must now be recounted.

CHAPTER FIVE

The Battle of Hyddgen, Summer 1401

Only the Welsh annalists mention a battle which Owain Glyn Dŵr now won and which, though only a minor encounter as battles go, immensely increased his prestige. It gave Owain an impetus which led to a year of almost unbroken successes, and finally to two resounding triumphs in the summer of 1402.

It appears probable that John Charlton's encounter with Owain took place at the end of May 1401, as Owain and his men were on their way to the base which Owain had selected for his summer campaign, and of which we learn nothing from English sources. The central position of Plynlimon made it a good choice for raiding far and wide in central and south Wales. Its remote valleys were ideal defensive ground, where the Welsh guerilla fighters could defend themselves against any attack. From here they made several forays, the first of which was probably to the south. The story is told by Gruffydd Hiraethog:

> Owen rose with 120 reckless men and robbers and he brought them in warlike fashion to the uplands of Ceredigion [Cardigan]; and 1,500 men of the lowlands of Ceredigion and of Rhos and Penfro [Pembroke] assembled there and came to the mountain with the intent to seize Owen. The encounter with them was on Hyddgant Mountain, and no sooner did the English troops turn their backs than 200 of them were slain.

Owen now won great fame, and a great number of
youths and fighting men from every part of Wales rose
and joined him, until he had a great host at his back.'[1]

Thomas Ellis enhances Gruffydd's statement with details from
other early sources. He says that in the summer of 1401 Owain led
his band of 120 men to Plynlimon, where he made his
headquarters;

from thence he did much hurt, sending parties to
pillage the country round about. The Flemings of
Rhos, Pembroke and Cardigan, whom Owain
distressed most of all, raised 1500 men and went
against him, being full of confidence that they would
either kill or take him. They hemmed him in on all
sides at a place called Mynyddhyddgant, so that he
could not possibly get off without fighting at a great
disadvantage. He and his men fought manfully a great
while, in their own defence, against them. Finding
themselves surrounded and hard put to it, they resolved
at length to make their way through or perish in the
attempt: so falling on furiously with courage whetted
by despair, they put the enemy, after sharp dispute, to
confusion; and they pursued so eagerly their advantage, that they made them give ground, and in the end
to fly outright, leaving two hundred of their men dead
on the spot of engagement.[2]

These two Welsh accounts tell us all that is known of the battle;
all other accounts depend on them. Nant Hyddgen is a glen north of
Plynlimon, overlooked by Carn Hyddgen, on which is a large cairn
plainly visible from below. There are two boulders of white quartz
near the right bank of Afon Hyddgen on a gentle slope of grass and
short rushes, which are called *Cerrig Cyfamod Owain Glyn Dŵr*,
Owain's Covenant Stones. There is no doubt that the stones were
set there by hand, perhaps to commemorate both the place where
Owain called his men to battle, and the victory which ensued.[3]

Afon Hyddgen is a headwater of Afon Rheidol, above and north of the modern Nant-y-Moch reservoir; on the map its valley looks a very remote place for a battle. In 1307 Robert Bruce, King of Scots, lured an English force into a similar cul de sac at the head of Glen Trool in the highlands of Galloway, and routed it; a monument marks the site of that battle. The age-old tactic of guerilla fighters is, if possible, to engage the enemy on ground which they have chosen themselves. A force of cavalry and ordinary infantry, attacked by resolute men used to mountain warfare on rough ground covered with heather, rocks and tussocky peat bog, would be at a hopeless disadvantage. Although evidence is lacking, Owain Glyn Dŵr could well have deliberately emulated Robert Bruce, one of the great medieval commanders, whose tactics were doubtless known to soldiers of Owain's day. Hyddgen was a small battle, but it was undoubtedly a decisive event which much enhanced Owain's reputation and the morale of his followers. It also encouraged the men of Carmarthenshire to join the rebellion.

Welsh tradition also says that Owain's operations in the summer of 1401 included a raid into Radnorshire. The monks of Abbey Cwm Hir had sent word of his movements to the English, for there was little love lost between the monks and the bards, whom Owain favoured. He took revenge. 'Al the Howse was spoilid and defaced by Owen Glindour', wrote John Leland, the famous antiquary who visited Wales during the late 1530s. His chilling description of what then happened at New Radnor Castle has echoed down the centuries, and has been repeated by several historians including Pennant:

> Radenor [was] partely destroied by Owen Glindour, and the voice is there that, an he wonne the Castel, he took a iii score men that had the Garde of the Castel, and causid them to be heddid on the brinke of the Castel Yarde, and that there sins a certen Bloodworth growith there wher the Bloode was shedde.

In 1845, when the old church at New Radnor was demolished and a new one built, it was reported in the *Illustrated London News* that 'proofs of the sad story of the garrison were found in a mass of human bones in one spot; in another, of a corresponding collection of skulls only'. This verdict has usually been accepted without question. It would certainly be a strange coincidence if the remains are not those of the slaughtered garrison, but it cannot be proved. There could have been a massacre at some earlier time, perhaps of captured Welshmen. The word 'corresponding' might be taken to imply that the number of skulls and skeletons was similar; but the task of sorting out and counting so many bones would have taxed even an expert archaeological team, which would not have been available in 1845.[4]

English chronicles do not mention this raid into Radnorshire, but the story is too emphatic to dismiss. We do not know whether it was before or after the battle of Hyddgen. John Leland's statement that Radnor was only 'partely destroied' agrees with the evidence that it was still defensible in 1403. Yet it is strange that Edmund Mortimer seems not to have responded to this invasion of Mortimer lands, as he did in 1402 before the battle of Pilleth; perhaps the intruders had gone before any counter-measures could be undertaken. The Welsh tradition is supported, however, by a small but significant piece of evidence that a devastating raid was made into eastern Radnorshire as early as 1401, when it was recorded that in the lordship of Presteigne, 'the tenements were destroyed and burnt by rebel' to such an extent that the rents had fallen to £3 7s.0d.[5]

A final but unanswerable question is why, if the story is true, Owain Glyn Dŵr ordered this atrocious massacre at New Radnor. Was it designed to scare English soldiers out of Wales, and Welshmen in the service of Marcher lords into making terms with him? Cruelty tends, in any age, to be counter-productive, and a man of Owain's intelligence must have realised that it would reduce the chances of reconciliation, towards which he was apparently working in November of that same year. Perhaps he was not actually present when the slaughter at New Radnor occurred.

An entry of 1406 in the *Register of Robert Mascall* (Bishop of Hereford 1404-1416) says that fifty-two churches had been wrecked in the deaneries of Archenfield, Weobley, Leominster, Clun and Pontesbury, including Old and New Radnor, Presteigne, Titley, Lyonshall and Kington. In Clun Deanery, few churches west of the Long Mynd were intact. Welsh raids reached the suburbs of Hereford and Shrewsbury. It provides a stark testimony to the widespread devastation in the west of the diocese during the first six years of the war, not only of churches but presumably also of lay property.[6]

The Latin *destruitur* 'was destroyed' implies that the churches were gutted by fire rather than levelled to the ground. Most of these massive medieval buildings still stand today. The mobile Welsh raiding parties were probably too lightly equipped to storm or destroy castles; they had time to strip and set fire to churches, but not to demolish them. Their main aim was to retreat to the hills as quickly as possible with the stolen flocks, herds and articles of value, also any captives who might be worth a ransom, all of which made a very important contribution to Welsh war finance.

With his greatly augmented forces Owain could now attack Aberystwyth and Harlech. His men were now besieging both of these remote castles, whose security was causing anxiety both to the king and to the prince. On 10 July the king granted Prince Henry £1,000 'from the issues and profits of the lands and lordships of the earldom of March', with the fatherly prayer that he would go by the advice of his council in 'the good governance of your country of Wales and resistance to the said rebels', especially towards relieving the siege of Harlech. 'It would cost less and be easier to guard it rather than to gain and recover it from the hands of our rebels.' No doubt the recent lesson of Conwy concentrated all minds.[7]

By the autumn it seems that Owain had left Plynlimon. Adam of Usk says that he gathered troops from north and central Wales and attacked Welshpool and Montgomery. This castle was defended by Brian Harley, who held Brampton Bryan of the Earl of March. Owain probably failed to take Montgomery, but some accounts say that he was successful. Leland says that 'Montgomericke [was] deflorischid by Owen Glindour', though this might mean the suburbs only. The suburbs of Welshpool were devastated, but the assault on the castle was beaten off by the Charltons.[8]

These events made it painfully apparent that Owain was not only still in the field, but also that support for the revolt was growing in central Wales. The king's response was to issue a commission of array for an army to assemble at Worcester on 1 October. The ensuing *chevauchée* penetrated south Wales as far as Carmarthen. The king showed no mercy to those who fell into his hands, venting his spleen particularly on the abbey of Strata Florida, which was occupied by his troops and its lands pillaged. Owain Glyn Dŵr had probably left Plynlimon by this time, and Henry IV seems to have made no contact at all with the enemy during his second invasion of Wales, which was perhaps even more futile than its predecessor. Information reaching Adam of Usk was that south-east Wales, especially the diocese of Llandaff, was at peace. A crop of executions may have consoled the king; he informed the prince of two which took place at Hereford.[9]

Two of these executions in particular attracted attention. Llywelyn ap Gruffydd Fychan of Caeo in Carmarthenshire was, according to Adam of Usk, 'a man of gentle birth and beautiful, who yearly used sixteen tuns of wine in his household'. He suffered death in the king's presence at Llandovery, because of his loyalty to Owain Glyn Dŵr. Another man who is not named refused to betray Glyn Dŵr, and willingly stretched out his neck for the fatal stroke, preferring death to treachery. The Monk of Evesham, who tells this story, thought that 'we Englishmen should follow his example, and depart this life faithful unto death, keeping our counsel and secrets'.[10]

Shortly after the royal *chevauchée* had ended, the council named Thomas Percy, Earl of Worcester, as lieutenant in south Wales, and produced a plan giving the number of troops in the garrison of each castle held by the English, and the name of the person responsible for paying the costs. To the south were Cardigan, Aberystwyth, Carmarthen, Llandovery, Painscastle, Brecon and Builth, and to the north Welshpool, Montgomery and three other Mortimer castles. A surveyor was needed for the castles and garrisons, and since most of them were in the diocese of St. David's, the task fell to the bishop; it was an age when senior clergymen were very often trained civil servants. A sad event which affected these appointments was the unexplained death on 19 October of John Charlton, Lord Powys; perhaps he was with the king and was killed in action. His equally able brother Edward succeeded him and, as he was the husband of the widowed Countess of March, he was responsible for the Mortimer castles of Caerleon and Usk.Welshpool Castle was now held by the king. Hugh Burnell was in charge of the defence of that area, and of the Mortimer castles, the costs of which were charged to the revenues of the Earl of March. Thomas Percy was captain of Cardigan, belonging to the Prince, who was to pay the costs of his own castles.[11]

After his repulse at Welshpool Owain's movements are again obscure, but somewhere in the north his followers humiliated Prince Henry by looting his baggage train. It is not certain whether either of the rival Princes of Wales were in the south during the royal rampage in those parts; Henry may have been at Harlech. On 2 November Owain displayed his standard with the golden dragon of Uthr Pendragon on a white field at Caernarfon. He attacked the castle, the garrison of which (on paper) comprised twenty men-at-arms and eighty archers, who put up a stout resistance. Owain lost three hundred men. Two years were to pass before the next attack on Caernarfon Castle.[12]

In November 1401 there was still time for a peaceful settlement. Owain had declared himself Prince of Wales, but he had not yet formally renounced his allegiance to the English crown. The king stated his wish that a treaty be made with Owain to draw him back into 'the royal obedience', since Owain had expressed his good intent. Owain had also said that he held the Earl of Northumberland in 'great affection and trust'; that he was not the cause of the pillaging, kidnapping and killing, but that he most earnestly wanted peace. He would willingly come to the Marches to treat and parley, but for the hostile clamour of those who said that he wished to drive out the English, or people who spoke English. He pointed out to Northumberland that the commons had sometimes killed great lords against the king's wish; maybe he was thinking of the murder of the Earl of Salisbury at Cirencester in 1400. Northumberland told Prince Henry of this request for a parley. He had promised that he would plead for Owain's life as hard as he could, if he submitted to the king's grace. The opinion of the Percies seems to have been that to conciliate Owain by restoring his lands would be a small price to pay for honourably ending such a dangerous and costly rebellion.[13]

Henry preferred, however, to listen to Grey of Ruthin and other biased advisers who recommended that the revolt be crushed at all costs. No doubt they included the king's half-brother, John Beaufort, Earl of Somerset, who wished to keep Owain's confiscated lands. Although he had told the prince of Owain's desire for talks, Northumberland knew that a military solution would probably be preferred; in the same letter he advised a triple advance into north Wales. Sir Edmund Mortimer and the other Marchers in the border counties could form a large army based on Welshpool. The prince's garrisons would advance from C. and H. (Conwy or Caernarfon, and Harlech). The Percy contingent would enter North Wales via M., probably Mon (Anglesey), which the king had granted to Hotspur in the first year of his reign. The idea was probably to land a seaborne force there. It was pointed out that castle garrisons were not strong enough to venture upon sallies individually, but Northumberland's idea of combining them for offensive operations was to be put into practice by Prince Henry in 1405 with decisive results.[14]

The Prince of Wales was now fifteen years old. Sir Hugh le Despenser was his governor, so perhaps it indicates the prince's maturity that he had recently appointed Despenser to hold judicial sessions after Christmas, in view of fresh unrest following the king's expedition. When Despenser died four men were suggested as his successor, including two of Gaunt's former retainers, Worcester and Erpingham; Worcester was appointed. The Percies had now reached their zenith in the service of the new dynasty.[15]

At about this time Owain took a momentous step in opening diplomatic relations with Robert III, King of Scotland. In 1400 Henry IV had invade Scotland; the expedition was the one which Owain had failed to join, possibly because of Grey's treachery. Henry had wished to force Robert to observe the Anglo-French treaty of 1396, which Robert was bound to do because he was an ally of the French king. Henry had also obtained a valuable ally in George Dunbar, Earl of the Scottish March, who had quarrelled with the famous Earl of Douglas. The question was whether Dunbar's daughter or Douglas's should marry the heir to the Scottish throne. Dunbar lost the argument, and as a result came over to the English. In 1401 some of the Irish princes were in rebellion, and the king sent his second son Thomas, later Duke of Clarence, as lieutenant to Ireland to suppress them; Owain countered by sending them dispatches, offering an alliance against the common enemy.[16]

By establishing his own foreign policy, Owain was in effect claiming the rights of an independent sovereign. For the war of independence to succeed Owain had to win active foreign allies and prevent the English from massing all their military power against him. There were historical precedents for a Welsh prince to make such alliances. In Edward the Confessor's reign Gruffydd ap Llywelyn had won the support of Vikings from Dublin, the Hebrides and Norway against the English. In 1212 Llywelyn ap Iorwerth had made a treaty with Philip II, the powerful King of France who had wrested Normandy from King John. The 'Auld Alliance' of Scotland and France had a natural tendency to revive when either king was threatened by England. If a hostile Prince of Wales joined it as well, the prospect for any English king would be very dangerous indeed, especially if he was a usurper.[17]

Owain's diplomatic dispatches have been preserved by Adam of Usk. He explains to the King of Scots their descent from two sons of Brutus, the mythical Prince of Troy; again we see the extraordinary importance attached to Geoffrey's *History* by aspiring dynasts in the middle ages. Unfortunately Owain's emissaries were caught in Ireland and beheaded, which may explain our good luck in having these letters. Adam also tells us that

> a certain knight, called Sir David ap Jevan Goz, of the county of Cardigan, who for full twenty years had fought against the Saracens with the King of Cyprus and other Christians, being sent by the King of France to the King of Scotland on Owen's behalf, was taken captive by English sailors and imprisoned in the Tower of London.

The Welsh cause was gaining foreign support. Though nothing came of Owain's overtures to the Irish, the Scots chronicler Walter

Bower, abbot of Incholm or Columba's Island, expresses strong Scottish sympathy for the Welsh in language redolent of Geoffrey of Monmouth and the *Matter of Britain*, meaning the lore of Brut, music in the ears of Owain and the Welsh bards:

> The Britons shall flourish, in alliance with the Alban people;
> The whole island will bear its ancient name.
> As the eagle proclaims, speaking from the ancient tower,
> The Britons with the Scots rule their fatherland.
> They will rule in harmony and quiet prosperity,
> Their enemies expelled, until the day of judgement.[18]

Lord Grey of Ruthin persistently tried to prevent any reconciliation between Owain and the king, a policy he lived to regret. Adam of Usk says:

> Owen and his men cruelly harried the lordship of Ruthin in North Wales, and the countryside with fire and sword on the last day but one of January [1402], carrying off the spoil of the land and specially the cattle to the mountains of Snowdon; yet did he spare the lordship of Denbigh and others of the Earl of March, having at his back the counties of Cardigan and Merioneth which were favourable to him both for government and war.

Denbigh, then under the control of Hotspur, with whom Owain was on friendly terms, was the richest of the Mortimer lordships. Owain may have thought it prudent not to harm the interests of a great Marcher family who might even become his allies, even though the young Earl of March was in effect the king's hostage.[19]

The appearance of a comet in the spring of 1402 seemed to foreshadow great events, and is mentioned by all the chronicles. Adam of Usk saw the comet on his way to Rome, 'First at Cologne and thence up to Pisa'. In Italy it was thought to have presaged the death of Gian Galeazzo Visconti, Duke of Milan: 'his dreaded arms too, a serpent azure swallowing a naked man gules, on a field argent, were then oftentimes seen in the sky.' The Welsh bards, burning with enthusiasm, called it the third great star of history; its predecessors were the Star of Bethlehem and Geoffrey of Monmouth's comet, which preceded the coming of Uthr Pendragon and Arthur to save the Britons from the Saxons. Iolo Goch had already been firing Welsh enthusiasm with his verses, and now wrote a poem foretelling Owain's triumph; in the short run he was to prove right.[20]

To the Welsh the comet could only be an omen of victory, and there now came a dramatic stroke of fortune which seemed to bear this out. In April Grey was at Ruthin Castle when Owain was ravaging his lands. The account of Gruffyd Hiraethog is as usual short and to the point:

> Owain and his host went and attacked in the neigh-
> bourhood of Ruthin and Dyffryn Clwyd, and Reginald
> Grey, lord of that region, took the field against him.
> And Lord Grey was there captured and long held a
> prisoner by Owain in wild and rocky places: at last he
> was ransomed for 1,000 marks.

According to Walsingham and the Monk of Evesham Lord Grey thought that he had an opportunity of crushing his insolent enemy and that it would be easy to defeat Owain or even to capture him. But by means which the chroniclers do not explain, this master of guerilla warfare somehow outwitted Grey when he emerged from his castle, and presumably lured him into some kind of ambush. A fierce fight ensued in which very many of Grey's men were killed and he himself was taken alive. By this brilliant coup Owain changed the whole posture of the Welsh Rebellion. He had caught his greatest enemy, who was a hostage of incalculable value, offering prospects of an enormous ransom. Since Grey was so high in royal favour, Owain might well be in a position to name his price, but meanwhile he was taking no chances. Lord Grey was securely manacled and carried off into the fastnesses of Snowdonia, beyond the reach of English pursuit. John Hardyng had little sympathy for Grey:

The lorde Gray Ruthin did hym great wrong,
Destroyed his lande, and he did hym the same ... ...
So on a daye the lorde Graye and he met
With great power vpon eyther syde,
Where then they faught in batayle sore bet,
And toke hym then his prysoner that tyde,
And there the felde he had with mikyll pryde,
Greate people toke and slewe, & home he went,
The lorde Graye he raunsomed at his entent.[21]

CHAPTER SIX

The Battle of Pilleth
Saint Alban's Day, 22nd June 1402

In addition to the comet which caused such excitement during the winter of 1402, other fearful portents were reported in the early summer. There was a terrible storm at the Feast of Corpus Christi. Even more alarming was the appearance of the Devil at the village of Danbury in Essex. He was dressed as a Friar Minor, one of the principal *bêtes noires* of King Henry IV, and he caused a great commotion by entering the church at the hour of Vespers, and 'rampaging about in a most insolent manner'. He seriously injured a member of the congregation; on leaving the church 'he left an intolerable stench' and extensive damage, especially to the tower.[1] The Friars Minor were members of a reformed branch of the Franciscan Order, ardent champions of Richard II. Perhaps a severe lightning strike drove the congregation to seek alcoholic remedies for their shattered nerves; an inventive pothouse comedian made up a good story, showing that King Henry IV's obsessions were well known to his rustic subjects.

The king was much worried by ill-coordinated plots against his life by enemies who alleged that King Richard II still lived. They included Walter de Baldock, Prior of Launde in Leicestershire, Sir Roger of Clarendon (a bastard son of the Black Prince and half-brother of Richard II), a secular priest, and about eight Friars Minor from houses at Canterbury, Aylesbury and Leicester. One friar was brought before Henry and had the courage to accuse him to his face of usurping the crown, and of deposing the rightful king. All were executed as traitors. During his unhappy reign Henry IV suffered a conflict between a troubled conscience, already burdened by the death of his deposed predecessor, and a readiness to use violence against his opponents, of whom an unusual number were executed, even an Archbishop of York. It was the bishops rather than the king who were responsible for the legislation against heresy, and for the burning of a few minor Lollards during his reign. The followers of John Wyclif were now seen as politically and socially disruptive, but they were not a serious threat to Henry IV; the few nobles and knights who supported the movement worried the bishops more than him. It would be wrong to accuse Henry IV of being exceptional for cruelty among English monarchs, but the chronicles of this reign contain many grim descriptions of executions for political offences. Other rulers who seized or held power by force during the next two centuries treated their opponents in an equally merciless manner.[2]

The fact that King Henry had so much to worry him in the early summer of 1402 may help to explain his ineffective response to Owain Glyn Dŵr's latest outrage, the seizure of Lord Grey of Ruthin, one of his most valued supporters. The king had, however, at least succeeded in persuading Hotspur to return to his post as lieutenant in north Wales on 31 March. Hotspur at once ordered the constable of Denbigh, William Curteys, to send help to Ruthin Castle. King Henry gave similar instructions to the chamberlain at Chester on 18 April. Hotspur made an indenture with Sir John de Pulle and Sir William Stanley to serve at sea from Chester for two weeks, no doubt to support the castles on the coast of north Wales. On 4 June Hotspur went to Ruthin to see things for himself. Probably he was too short of money to do more.[3] Seapower had been a vital part of the strategy used in the past by conquerors of north Wales; it was to prove equally important to the English in their suppression of Glyn Dŵr's rebellion.

These defensive measures were much too late in the day to produce any decisive results, and show up the English reaction to the capture of Lord Grey as spineless and ineffectual. With the benefit of hindsight, one may suspect some half-heartedness on the part of Hotspur, who may already have been in correspondence with Owain Glyn Dŵr, not with any treasonable intent but to see whether a peaceful settlement might be made. Alternatively, the Percies may simply have been reluctant to pull Henry's chestnuts out of the fire for him. The initiative remained firmly in the hands of Owain and his men, demonstrating again how swiftly they could move from one part of Wales to another. The English were always kept guessing as to when or where they would strike next. The king was, however, also impeded by the permanent, paralysing shortage of money, with so many military commitments to be met in the British Isles and in France.

The storm now broke on Hotspur's brother-in-law, Sir Edmund Mortimer, younger brother of Roger the late Earl of March, and now twenty-six years old. Sir Edmund was in effect the acting head of the family, though he was only a knight of modest personal means; his father, the third earl, had bequeathed to him land to the annual value of 300 marks. In 1399 he and John Trevenant, Bishop of Hereford, had submitted to Duke Henry of Lancaster at Hereford and had accompanied him on his march north to capture Richard II. Edmund was not apparently a particularly able man, but he was heir to a great military tradition, and there is no reason to think that he and his captains were not competent soldiers. His distinguished brother-in-law Hotspur seems to have held him in high esteem, and stood loyally by him in the misfortunes which were soon to overwhelm him. Sir Edmund's eleven-year-old nephew, Earl Edmund, was a royal ward, kept in custody by the king along with his brother Roger, aged nine. This confinement of a boy with a claim to the throne by a usurping king provides an interesting parallel with the situation in 1483. When King Edward IV died his brother Richard Duke of Gloucester, who was the greatest magnate in the realm, deposed the boy king Edward V, confined him and his brother in the Tower of London, and took the throne himself; but while the fate of the Princes of York remains a mystery, the Mortimer children both outlived Henry IV.[4]

Grim omens were said to have occurred when Edmund Mortimer was born; the chronicles open a window for us on the mind of the medieval world. In the account of the Monk of Evesham: 'On the day when he came out of his mother's womb, his horses were found in the stables standing in blood nearly to their knees.' The writer of the *Eulogium* confirmed this omen and supplied others: 'The sheath of every sword and dagger was full of blood. The axes were red with blood. When put to sleep in his cradle the young lord could not stop crying unless a sword was shown to him. And even in the lap of his nurse he could not be quiet unless other weapons were brought to him.' Despite these ghastly portents, Edmund Mortimer does not seem to have grown up as a notably warlike man.[5]

Gruffydd Hiraethog unfortunately gives the wrong date (1403); otherwise he provides an excellent introduction of almost telegraphic brevity:

> Owen arose with a great host from Gwynedd, Powys, and the South, and made for Maelienydd; where the knights of Herefordshire gathered against him. The battle between them was fought near Pilleth.[6]

There is no doubt that in June 1402 Owain Glyn Dŵr invaded Radnorshire, but tradition seems to gone further than Gruffydd to assume that Owain aimed to bring Mortimer to battle, and that his plan was a brilliant success. Yet it is dangerous to oversimplify this very complex situation. Despite his previous attack on their lands Owain had no personal grudge against the Mortimers; their claim to the throne made them potential allies against Henry IV. Owain had ravaged Lord Grey's Ruthin lands, but had spared the Mortimer lordship of Denbigh. It would also be unsafe to imagine that Owain's success in capturing Grey led him to plan and execute a similar but even more brilliant coup against Mortimer. But his more truculent followers may well have been burning for revenge against the Mortimers, for centuries the most ruthless oppressors of the Welsh, so that he had to defer to their wishes. Perhaps Owain wanted to remind the English that he could strike as and when he liked. Perhaps his victory at Hyddgen and his capture of Grey had increased Owain's confidence in his ability to defeat an attack by a stronger army in hilly country; another triumph like Hyddgen would greatly enhance Owain's prestige, if such a chance arose.

The outcome of Owain's second invasion of Radnorshire could, however, have been the result of brilliant opportunism. Only Welsh sources describe Owain's attack on Glamorgan and Gwent in August 1402, which was surely his most daring plan yet, and was probably intended to be the main exploit of the Welsh army for that summer. Alongside the traditional theory appears an alternative possibility, that the Welsh were passing through Maelienydd on their way to south Wales, looting as they went, were intercepted by Mortimer, and by good fortune were able to give him battle at Pilleth, a most favourable position from their point of view. A small army prefers to avoid a battle with a larger one unless it has no alternative, and Owain may have decided that the chance of winning a smashing victory was too good to miss. If this is how it happened, the priority for the victors would surely have been to take their prisoners and plunder back to north Wales first, even if it meant postponing their *chevauchée* into the south.

Owain showed yet again how fast he and his men could ride across Wales on the sturdy ponies whose descendants we know today, suddenly appearing like the demon king in the pantomime, taking his enemies by surprise. The starting point of the Welsh army was probably the stronghold in Snowdonia where Lord Grey was held captive. Then they may have taken the mountain road via Staylittle to Llanidloes, which may have had military advantages over Glyndŵr's Way, the modern walker's path linking Machynlleth, Llanidloes and Knighton, which traverses the same country. Whatever their exact route it would have led them into the valley of the River Ithon and the lordship of Maelienydd. As with Owain's Plynlimon operations the previous summer we do not know the course of events. The Welsh probably plundered the Mortimer castles in Maelienydd (Cefnllys, Cwm-Aran, Bleddfa and Knucklas) or the various churches which they are supposed to have burnt, now or in later raids. Excavations at Bleddfa Church have revealed evidence that it was burned down at about this time, as other churches in the danger area could have been. Presteigne was one of those in Bishop Mascall's list.[7]

Gruffydd says that Maelienydd was Owain's objective, but with such a large army his plans could have been to advance from

Maelienydd into south Wales. The Monk of Evesham and Giles say that Sir Edmund Mortimer was at Ludlow, when he heard the news that Owain Glyn Dŵr had invaded Maelienydd and ensconced himself on a hilltop at Pilleth, where the church was well known for its shrine and image of the Blessed Virgin Mary. If this is true, Owain would have had to wait several days for Mortimer's arrival. Perhaps this accounts for an idea that Owain lured Mortimer into a trap with a rumour that he was making a pilgrimage to Pilleth. Walsingham does not mention Pilleth, but says that 'Owen Glendor with a rabble [*turba*] of Welshmen suddenly advanced to the attack'; in the *Annals of Henry IV*, written under his supervision where it was not actually his own work, the more polite word *comitiva* was used, meaning 'company' or 'retinue'. The most emphatic statement of all, however, is made in *The Brut*, the earliest English vernacular chronicle: 'Owen brent a towne of the Erles of March in Wales, that hight Kinghton', which can only mean Knighton. Kington, ten miles south, was in the Stafford lordship of Huntington. Adam of Usk and the Monk of Wigmore both place Pilleth near Knighton, but go no further.[8]

The Monk of Evesham and Giles seem to support the view that Owain's plan was to entice Sir Edmund Mortimer into attacking the Welsh on ground of his choice, but *The Brut* seems to speak with greater authority than the other chronicles about what actually happened, suggesting a more complex sequence of events. As will be seen later, the attack on Knighton may in fact have drawn Mortimer that way rather than to Pilleth. Perhaps Owain kept his options open to the very last moment. He would fight only if he felt sure of victory, or if Mortimer made a false move; otherwise he would avoid battle. We are unlikely ever to know for certain if the battle was fought at Pilleth by deliberate design, by a last-minute decision, or by chance.

Pilleth seems a modest setting for the climax to such a drama. There is only the Church of Saint Mary, and the house and farm buildings of Pilleth Court. Domesday Book names it Pelelei (close to the Welsh Pyllalai), one of four small manors in the Lugg and Hindwell valleys totalling nine hides, or about 1,000 acres, held by Edmund's ancestor Ralph de Mortimer; Welsh raids during Edward the Confessor's reign had reduced them to waste. The spelling of the name varies in different chronicles from Pilale and Pylale to errors like Pilate and Pymaren. Pilleth Church has a nave and low tower of rough local stone, which the Welsh burnt, together with the churches at Casgob and Bleddfa. There was another severe fire in 1894, which destroyed a fine roof and rood-screen. To the north of the church there is an ancient well, a relic of pagan times dedicated to a Christian saint.[9]

Edmund Mortimer responded promptly, forcefully and decisively to this challenge which seemed to threaten the very heartland of his family and its power. Walsingham says that he immediately summoned 'almost all the militia of Herefordshire', which is borne out by a report that he was able to do so under a statute of Edward the Confessor:

> If the sheriff goes to war, the able-bodied men among
> the inhabitants are obliged to go with him. If anyone
> who is called does not go, he is to pay eleven shillings
> or one ox to the king.

In a really grave emergency like the present one, the sheriff of Hereford apparently had powers to act as if he had a commission of array, which was normally only issued by the king himself.[10]

On the other hand, the Mortimer tenants were under a feudal obligation to come at the bidding of their lord, and would probably have been easier to call up; with the Welsh ravaging Maelienydd, there was every reason to muster troops as fast as possible. Long experience would have taught the Mortimers that small forces, which were more mobile and easier to supply, were best for warfare in the Welsh hills. Though Edmund may have ordered the sheriff to array the militia, he may in fact have relied on the family retainers. According to Giles's Chronicle: 'The said Edmund sent therefore to his own tenants and adherents in Wales that they would help him in this hard necessity, and they did not omit to come to him at once.' Marcher lordships like Wigmore and Ludlow, now the western fringe of the English border counties, were then considered to be in Wales, and it is clear that Herefordshire tenants also responded to the call.[11]

We do not know how big this army was, but probably not more than two thousand including followers: maybe only a thousand or even fewer. In this period the House of Mortimer could not field a retinue remotely comparable to that of the dukes of Lancaster, but Edmund Mortimer could call on men of proven military experience, whose families had long traditions of service to his. Four knights are named in the records. Sir Walter Devereux was a member of an old Herefordshire family who held Weobley and Lyonshall from the Earl of March. Little is left today of either of these castles, but the family rose to national prominence during the fifteenth and sixteenth centuries. Sir Walter's great-grandson, also Walter Devereux, was a staunch Yorkist who fought at Mortimer's Cross in 1461, and as Lord Ferrers of Chartley died at Bosworth fighting for Richard III.

Sir Robert Whitney had served as sheriff in 1377, and was knight-marshal to the king. He was accompanied by his brother and other relations. He held the castle of Whitney-on-Wye which was soon afterwards destroyed by the Welsh. Its site was totally erased in 1730 by a change in the course of the Wye. The family were prominent in Herefordshire but died out after the civil war in the seventeenth century.

Sir Kinaird de la Bere was lord of Kinnersley Castle, near Weobley; the present beautiful house is of late Elizabethan date. Kinardsley, to use its old name, was part of the Honour of Wigmore, and its lord was bound to go with his retainers to the aid of Mortimer in time of war.

Sir Thomas Clanvowe was another Mortimer tenant and a former sheriff. His family held Ocle Pychard and Cusop of the Earl of March, also Hergest and Yazor. The name is also spelt Clanvow, Clanowe or Clavenogh; the family were of Welsh descent. An ancestor was fortunate enough to be pardoned for supporting the rebellion of the Earls of Lancaster and Hereford against Edward II. Sir Thomas was the heir of Sir John Clanvowe, who was either his father or his uncle; oddly enough we do not know which. Sir John was a man of many parts, a successful soldier, courtier and poet who eventually became a Lollard.[12]

Devereux, Whitney, Clanvowe and others of their rank would have led modest numbers of fighting men and camp followers from their households and estates, but the local Mortimer lordships of Ludlow and Wigmore together with Herefordshire seem to have supplied the bulk of the army. Radnor could have sent a few, but following Owain's invasion of Maelienydd it is likely that only men from the eastern part of that lordship could have come. Some of Mortimer's archers, however, were Welshmen. There may have been no time to get men from further afield.[13]

Since the days of Edward I the greatest strength of English armies had been a combination of dismounted men-at-arms and longbowmen. Men-at-arms varied from armoured cavalry (knights, esquires and sergeants) to footmen carrying bills, halberds, axes or lead clubs, and wearing much less body armour. Heavy cavalrymen had long been used to fighting on foot alongside the ordinary infantry, in support of the archers who had made the English so formidable in their wars against the Scots and French. As the Hundred Years War dragged on, English armies became smaller and more mobile, with men-at-arms and archers mounted for the march.

We know much less about Owain's army than about Mortimer's, but it was probably smaller. His chief captain was perhaps Rhys Gethin ('the Fierce') of Cwm Llannerch in the Conwy Valley who, according to some modern writers, was in command, though contemporary evidence shows that Owain was there in person. The weapons carried by Owain Glyn Dŵr's men would have been similar to those of the English, but the Welsh were more lightly armoured and had smaller horses, both because they were less wealthy than the English, and also on account of their guerilla traditions.[14]

Western Herefordshire is mostly an undulating plain. Today it is noted for its half-timbered buildings. The numerous place names ending in -ley: a settlement in a forest clearing, show that it was once covered with oak forest. It is bordered on the south by the River Wye, and to the south-west the great wall of the Black Mountains. The gently sloping hills to the west and north are deeply cut by steep-sided, glaciated river valleys: the Arrow, the Gilwern, the Hindwell and the Lugg. Long before, Saxon settlers had crossed Offa's Dyke, pushed up the valleys and colonised the

Hindwell basin (south of Radnor Forest) and the Lugg valley as far as Whitton, which is shown both by the numerous English place names, and by the fact that these manors are recorded in the Domesday Book. In those days the hillsides were mostly clad in oak woods. The valley floors were not neatly drained, as they have been since the eighteenth century, but probably swampy, so that the rivers were much more difficult to cross. It was good country for Owain and his guerillas, but very dangerous for a heavily equipped English army unless it was very well led, with plenty of archers and light troops. The roads were only cart tracks, which soon became impassable in heavy Welsh rain.

A grim reality must be faced. This countryside, so peaceful today, was for over two thousand years a land of war. Centuries of oppression by waves of invaders left glowing embers of hatred; the most savage ethnic passions could soon be fanned to a flame on both sides. Even in relatively peaceful times the hill folk had always raided the lowlands, tempted by the superior fatness of the valley sheep or cattle. Guerilla leaders like Caradog and Owain Glyn Dŵr had made brilliant use of the ruggedness of Wales against Roman, Saxon and Norman invaders; but leaving the natural protection of the hill country invited risks which they were very slow to incur, unless as sometimes happened they felt themselves stronger than the opposing English.

The Monk of Evesham and Giles's Chronicle say that Owain went straight to Pilleth. *The Brut*, Adam of Usk and the Monk of Wigmore all suggest that Knighton was his first objective. Knighton lies in the Teme valley, but Pilleth is in the upper Lugg valley above Presteigne. Each town is about seventeen miles from Ludlow, Mortimer's base. Two castles guarded the point where the narrow upper valley of the Lugg ends: Presteigne was on the site called The Warden; Stapleton, now a crumbling ruin, crowned a small, steep hill half a mile north. The town of Presteigne was at the northern end of the lordship of Huntington, belonging to the Earl of Stafford, later killed at the battle of Shrewsbury fighting for the king, but its castle was built in the late twelfth century by the Mortimers, who acquired the manors further up the Lugg about the same time. Stapleton, an older castle which may have predated the

Norman Conquest, belonged to the Lancastrian knight Sir John Cornewall, known as 'Grenecornewayle', whose elder brother Richard was lord of Burford, near Tenbury. He married Henry IV's sister Elizabeth, and was created Lord Fanhope by Henry V for his services in the French wars. Elizabeth's effigy can be seen in Burford Church.[15]

Which route did Edmund Mortimer and his army take? If he decided to make for the upper Lugg valley, he had a choice of two possible routes from Ludlow. The medieval road system was very different from ours, which is based on the turnpikes of the eighteenth century. Today's country lane, farm track or bridle path may have been a medieval main road. Medieval man very sensibly followed the contours above flood plains like the Wigmore basin, across which the Roman engineers had built their road. Mortimer may have gone first to Wigmore, his other great castle, where he could have collected more supplies, and where more troops might have awaited his arrival. He may then have marched over the hills to Lingen, and along the lanes from Kinsham on the north bank of the Lugg to Whitton, passing Stapleton, Norton and Ackhill.

The alternative route from Ludlow was through Richard's Castle, joining the old Manor Road at Shobdon, reaching the south side of the Lugg valley at Byton Hand, and via Combe and Rodd to Presteigne.[16] This route would have involved crossing the River Lugg, a potentially dangerous operation. We have no idea of the weather, though as it was midsummer the level of the river may have been low. If the English came this way, they could still have crossed to the north bank at Presteigne without being ambushed, if the enemy had not advanced further east than Pilleth. (Rock Bridge, a mile west of Presteigne, was built later). Otherwise they would have taken the old road from Presteigne towards Casgob and bivouacked, with the prospect of fording the Lugg next day at the point guarded by an old motte-and-bailey fort on the north bank called Castell Foel-allt. The valley floor is still marshy here, and was probably very much more so in the middle ages, since when there has been extensive drainage.[17]

If Mortimer advanced straight up the Lugg valley, the route from Wigmore along the north bank to Norton and Ackhill seems to be

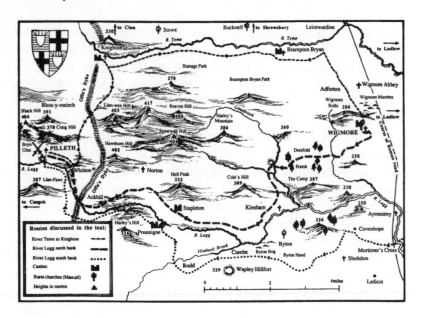

Edmund Mortimer's march to Pilleth
and the area between the Rivers Teme and Lugg

the likelier choice. Whichever way the English were coming, Owain's scouts may have been able to keep him informed about their progress, giving him a fair idea of what they were likely to do. It may have been less easy for Mortimer's scouts to locate the Welsh, but he and his captains would have wanted to avoid unnecessary risks. They would have been well aware of the dangers of an attack when crossing the river in the face of the enemy, who were probably known to be somewhere between the Lugg and the Teme. The north bank route would have avoided this danger, a good reason for thinking that Mortimer would have preferred it. The English would have had enough military and local knowledge to have bypassed such a hazardous obstacle as the Foel-allt ford when they had the chance, before entering territory likely, or perhaps known, to be held by the enemy.

There is, however, a third possibility, arising from the fact that three chronicles mention Knighton, in the Teme valley. If the statement in *The Brut* was correct, and if this was the news which reached Edmund Mortimer at Ludlow, his natural response would have been to march with his army not to Pilleth but to Knighton in order to help his people. If this was his course of action he would have gone either direct from Ludlow or first by way of Wigmore, through Brampton Bryan and up the Teme. William Hatfield, author of a small book on Knighton published in 1947, expands this theory. He is believed to have used a mysterious source which the late Frank Noble tried very hard to trace, but without success. Noble quotes it in his article on the excavations at Bleddfa:

> One writer relates that in 1402, before the battle of Pilleth, the Welsh crossed the hills from Llanidloes towards Knighton, burning and slaying on all sides. Sir Edward [sic] Mortimer sent 400 men to Knighton and found all the men under arms; they had sent their women and children in wagons towards Ludlow, but as the town had a strong wall the men were determined on making a stout defence. A party advanced five miles beyond the town and found a village on fire and attacked the Welsh, who were repulsed and the party returned to Knighton ... there is scarce a house left standing between Llanidloes and Knighton.[18]

This account broadly agrees with the evidence of the three chronicles. Owain may have come via Dolgellau and Machynlleth to Llanidloes, and thence into Maelienydd. The burning village could have been Beguildy, Llangunllo or Bleddfa. But the account is rather more detailed and circumstantial than one would expect of a Norman-French official letter, which Noble believed to be its source. These important documents are more stilted and restrained in style than the story given by Hatfield. How does its author know that so many houses were destroyed between Llanidloes and Knighton? Again, if Knighton was really in such imminent danger, the families of the garrison would have been safer within its walls. It seems more likely that some writer of the romantic age embellished the chronicle accounts. It is not clear whether Mortimer was in personal command of the force which went to Knighton, but he probably was. Perhaps Mortimer repulsed the Welsh advance guard from Knighton and then, hearing that their main body had moved south to the Lugg valley, marched from Knighton to Whitton, and met them at Pilleth. Alternatively, Owain and his whole army may have been at Knighton, and retreated in case they were caught between the advancing English army and the beleaguered garrison. Whatever happened, the available evidence makes it likely that there was fighting near Knighton before the battle of Pilleth, but it is impossible to say whether this involved the main armies of Owain and Mortimer, or smaller detachments of each. If the first clash did occur at Knighton, it seems likely that Owain decided to fight at Pilleth very much at the last moment.

After considering all the evidence, the likeliest conclusion is that the English were on the northern side of the Lugg, and that they spent the night of 21 June near Whitton. One can imagine the chaotic task of arraying a semi-disciplined army into some sort of order to march against their hereditary enemies, an enterprise for which many of them may have had very little stomach. It was a midsummer morning, almost the longest day, and the chronicles say nothing about adverse weather.

Above Pilleth Church is a hillside looking like a great, green roof, in the middle of which stand four wellingtonia trees. It faces the valley, and has given the battle its other name of Bryn Glas, or Green Hill, which suggests that in the middle ages it was grassy and not wooded. There are two reasons for accepting it as the site of the battle. First, the Monk of Wigmore says 'on the hill of Brynglase'; he lived much nearer Pilleth than the other chroniclers, three of whom agree that the battle was fought on a hill, though *The Brut* chronicler says: 'this bataile was on the black hyll beside Pymaren', the Black Hill being a mile north-west of Pilleth. The Monk of Evesham and Giles's Chronicle go further, and say that Mortimer 'bravely ascended the hill'.[19] It is remarkable that we know more of the tactics employed at Pilleth than at Mortimer's Cross in 1461, another local battle, about which the chronicles tell us next to nothing.

Secondly, Bryn Glas makes strategic and tactical sense. If Owain had reached Pilleth before the English and in time to give battle there, he would have promptly placed his army in the best possible

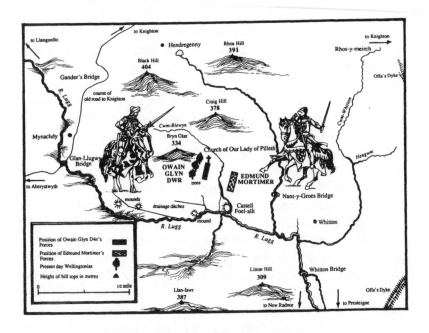

The Battle of Pilleth or Bryn Glas
Saint Alban's Day, 22nd June, 1402

position. This may well have been the point near the modern main road shown on Ordnance Survey maps as the site of the battle. Owain could have waited for the English here with part of his army, perhaps keeping his main body out of sight on top of Bryn Glas and in the shallow valley on his left. If he had then withdrawn outside the range of their arrows, as soon as Mortimer's troops began to advance they would probably have followed him up-hill, which according to the four chroniclers is exactly what they did. This seems to have been Owain's plan, with which Mortimer had to comply if he wanted to attack his enemy. The English would have no time to consider the dire consequences which might ensue, and so they were enticed onto a killing ground from which few may have been able to escape.[20]

The Rev. Jonathan Williams, whose *History of Radnor* was not published till long after his death in 1829, describes two parapets or breastworks, about 400 yards apart, and supposes that these were used by the two armies. The Ordnance Survey shows four earthworks on the flood plain: Castell Foel-allt (mentioned by Williams) and three other mounds, one near Castell Foel-allt, the others a quarter of a mile west.[21]

To make earthworks an army needs time, tools, and an obvious military purpose. If Owain had really waited for Mortimer on top of Bryn Glas, his men would have had plenty of time to dig trenches, but there is no sign of any. In fact his fast-moving army is unlikely to have burdened itself with many digging tools, or with guns, a possibility also discussed by Williams. At that time most guns were heavy siege weapons, not easily transportable. Doubts have already been expressed about the idea that either Owain or Mortimer could have foreseen exactly where a battle would be fought; an army only digs defences before a battle if it knows where the enemy will attack and has the time to dig. In 1459 the Duke of York dug a redoubt near Ludford Bridge and planted field guns on it, because the King's army were expected to attack Ludlow from the south. Finally, we are told that the battle of Pilleth was fought on a hill, not down on the marshy valley floor among the mounds.

The usual formation of an English army was lines of men-at-arms with wedges of archers a intervals, so that the lethal volleys of arrows could be shot ahead and at an angle. When the enemy losses were heavy enough the men-at-arms engaged him hand to hand, helped by the archers if possible, as for example at Agincourt thirteen years later. Archers were best suited to a defensive role, protected by a hedge or a line of sharpened stakes, not advancing uphill against a mobile enemy. Bryn Glas was to show that the usual English tactics were less suitable in hilly country, especially against a tough and well-led enemy.

At first, however, all seemed to be going well for the English, but their spirited and determined charge up-hill would have left heavily armed men winded and exhausted when the crisis came. Walsingham says: 'Clearly, being the stronger force in the field, they were not afraid of the Welsh, who were in retreat. But alas! as they hastened in their turn to the attack they were betrayed by treachery in their midst. They were unexpectedly defeated by their own archers who turned their arms against them; those who resisted were killed.' In deep disgust the Monk of Evesham descends to violent and intolerant language. 'Therefore, having come together with great impetus, the said Welshmen of Maelienydd, not of the tribe of Judah, but born to be similar traitors, traitorously turned their faces and weapons against their own lord.'

Was this action premeditated or taken on the spur of the moment? A move so sudden and well-coordinated looks like the result of some kind of plan. The Monk of Evesham says that they were Maelienydd men; perhaps they joined Mortimer's army during its march up-country, having already decided among themselves to go over to Owain at the first favourable opportunity. Perhaps one of his agents had approached them first, for the ease with which Owain marched through Wales, and the signs that he had good information about the enemy, suggest wide popular support. When Mortimer's archers deserted, they were probably far enough forward to turn and shoot at their former comrades at point-blank range, with shattering physical and moral effect. A Welsh frontal attack could have been accompanied by another on their right, if an ambush had been placed in the little valley north of Bryn Glas.

The English casualties were probably heavier than the Monk of Evesham allows. He gives the English dead as only 200, and Giles's Chronicle 400, but Walsingham seems to have much grimmer information. 'On that field more than 1,100 of our people were killed, and Edmund Mortimer was captured, together with several knights and esquires ...' This could mean half of their entire army, which is at least credible, whereas Adam of Usk's 8,000 is the wild guess of an exile in Rome without access to reliable sources. The entire English army cannot have numbered half as many. Splitting the difference between Giles and Walsingham suggests about 800 killed.

'Sir Robert Whitney and Sir Kinard de la Bere were slain and Sir Edmund Mortimer and Sir Thomas Clanvow were captured and most of the English host were slain' is Gruffydd Hiraethog's breathless summary. Whitney's brother and others of his family were also killed. 'Alas!', exclaimed Adam of Usk, 'my lord the said

Sir Edmund, whose father [Earl Roger], the lord of Usk, gave me an exhibition at the schools, was by fortune of war carried away captive.'[22]

'There was also perpetrated a crime unheard of in that age', said Walsingham, who explains that after the battle many of the bodies were obscenely mutilated by Welshwomen (probably camp followers with Owain's army rather than locals); he spares us none of the disgusting details. Two centuries later, Shakespeare echoed the horror in the scene when Mortimer's defeat is reported. Walsingham adds: 'Nor were the bodies of the dead released for burial without the payment of rewards and ransoms'. The Monk of Evesham gives further grisly details: 'the corpses were left lying under the horses' hooves, weltering in their own blood, as burial was forbidden for a long time afterwards. In the opinion of various people, that prodigy which had occurred at the birth of the said Edmund was fulfilled in this conflict.' Thomas Pennant, wishing to 'exculpate my countrywomen from this heavy charge', cited 'another ancient writer, who ascribes these barbarities to a follower of Glyn Dŵr, one Rees a Gyrch'. Indeed, the Monk of Evesham names 'a certain Welshman, named Rees Gytch, who was harsher in mind than the others; he either killed, or mutilated, or captured all who resisted him'. These are undoubtedly different spellings of Rhys Gethin, who was probably responsible both for the ghoulish ransoming of bodies, and for encouraging the women to cut them up. Pennant rather charmingly adds: 'It would have been totally unnecessary to discourage the English, by an express law [which forebade mixed marriages], from marrying such furies as the Welshwomen were reputed to be.'[23]

The chronicle evidence for siting the battle on Bryn Glas is borne out by clear evidence that exceptional numbers of corpses were buried in the churchyard. In 1847, Evan Williams of Knighton wrote that 'the funerals do not average more than two a year, this parish being one of the smallest in the Principality. In digging out graves here, great quantities of human bones are always discovered; and it is conceived there can be but little doubt of this having been the resting place of many of those who fell in the severe conflict hereafter noticed.' There is also the tradition that about this time many bones were found further up the hillside, where Sir Richard Green-Price, Bart., planted six wellingtonias in pairs to mark the site, four of which are left. Some of these bones were buried inside an unmarked stone curb in the churchyard. There do not seem to be any written records of these excavations; the trees could mark one mass grave, but the mass of bones in the churchyard alone indicates the site of the battle beyond reasonable doubt. The labour of clearing any battlefield must be immense. Men would naturally try to reduce the task by burying the bodies as near as possible to where they had fallen. If most of the slaughter was on Bryn Glas, the dead would have been carried downhill to their graves, some on the hillside, others in the churchyard. [24]

The battle of Pilleth was indeed a decisive event. From the days of William the Conqueror till the conquest of Wales by Edward I, the Mortimers had been pre-eminent among Marcher lords in aggressive energy and military might. It is a paradox that, although in the fourteenth century they gained an earldom and then a claim to the throne, the Mortimers never recovered the prominence which they had enjoyed in the thirteenth century, and up to the fall of Roger the first earl in 1330. Of his successors, only the second and fourth earls, both named Roger, showed the charisma and gifts of leadership which had made the Mortimers great. The outcome of the battle of Pilleth demonstrated that Mortimer military power was a shadow of what it had once been. The disaster severely damaged their prestige, and devalued their claim to the throne.

The history of Wales and the borders in the fifteenth century has been distorted by some very dubious traditions. Medieval history depends heavily on traditions: some may be well-founded, but others begin as clerical errors, rumours, surmise or pure fiction. Tradition can be very useful; it sometimes illuminates and adds colour to written contemporary evidence. Two centuries ago, many books on county topography and history were published; confronted by traditions, their authors often failed to discern where truth ended and fiction began. An account of the battle of Pilleth is incomplete without a study of the rich mythology which has overgrown it.

This is very apparent in several books on Herefordshire and Leominster. In 1793 a topography of Herefordshire was produced by the Rev. John Lodge (1756-1830), and in 1795 a history of Leominster by John Price (1772-1801), who taught languages. The first volume of John Duncumb's well-known history of Herefordshire emerged in 1804. Jonathan Williams (1754-1829) has already been cited. He and Price accepted a legend that after the battle of Pilleth Owain Glyn Dŵr invaded Herefordshire and took Leominster. The story was not known to Pennant, and is not supported by any contemporary chronicle or official paper, yet it has managed to hold the field ever since. Williams says that Owain 'overran the county of Hereford and carried his victorious arms to the gates of Worcester'; in 1405 Owain actually did march with a Franco-Welsh army through south Wales and Herefordshire to Worcester, and back again. Price and Williams knew much less about history than Pennant or their contemporary, Thomas Thomas, rector of Aberporth, who used chronicles for his *Memoir* of Glyn Dŵr, and observed the standard of scholarship set by Pennant, but was capable also of expressing his own point of view.[25]

A second source, which attracted Duncumb, Price and Williams, is a piece of poetic licence by Shakespeare: Hotspur, denying that Mortimer was a traitor and pleading for his release, describes a Homeric combat between him and Owain:

> When on the gentle Severn's sedgy bank,
> In single opposition, hand to hand,
> He did confound the best part of an hour
> In changing hardiment with great Glendower:
> Three times they breathed, and three times did they drink,
> Upon agreement, of swift Severn's flood.

Price and Williams decided that 'Severn' meant 'Arrow', and placed the duel on its banks near Pembridge in a fictitious battle for which no evidence exists. Williams does not substantiate his idea that Shakespeare confused Owain's supposed invasion of Herefordshire in 1402 with an imaginary one of Shropshire in 1403, when in fact Owain was invading south Wales; he was not present at the battle of Shrewsbury.[26]

Williams was a master of story-telling, far surpassing his colleagues in inventiveness. Owain defeats Mortimer near Knighton and occupies the hill-fort of Wapley, near Presteigne. Using Edward the Confessor's statute, Mortimer arrays his new army at Baron's Cross, near Leominster. Owain makes a magnificent speech to his troops, like those which Tacitus, the historian of Imperial Rome, attributes to Boudicca and Calgacus, Celtic chieftains fighting for freedom against the Romans. Mortimer is defeated and captured at Pembridge. Owain sends troops to occupy Wigmore Castle and three hill forts: Ivington, Risbury and Croft Ambrey. He takes Leominster and lives in state at the Priory, having put Mortimer in its dungeon. He punishes the monks and other enemies and rewards his followers. Prince Henry makes a treaty with him, and keeps faith with him when he becomes king. Then Owain retires to Ruthin Castle, where he passes his last years in peace. After his death Henry V renews the treaty with Maredudd ab Owain. In order to keep a watch on the Mortimers, says Williams, 'it is acknowledged by every writer who has given an account of these times that a Welsh corps was stationed at Leominster during the changeful and distracted times of Henry VI', for whom they fought at Mortimer's Cross. But George Townsend (1815-1900) disagrees: 'there is not ... sufficient evidence to confirm the local tradition.' This summary suffices to show that Williams's narrative is far more fiction than fact. His ignorance of the elementary detail that Ruthin Castle belonged to Lord Grey, Owain's mortal enemy, is amazing, and alone indicates his total unreliability as a historian.[27]

Mortimer's supposed commission of array was one piece of evidence which was misunderstood by both Price and Williams, who quotes another in support of the idea that Owain took Leominster, but to no avail:

> Richard de Lingein, empowered by the commission of our redoubted lord the Prince in the county of Hereford, and the Marches adjoining, to all those who these letters shall see or have, Greeting. Know that I have granted to one Janin de Brompton, loyal and liege

man of our lord the King, and to his servants, to bring
and sell beasts and forage in the county of Hereford,
and in the Marches adjoining, without molestation or
hindrance from anyone, as loyal and liege man to his
own use and increase, without refreshment to the
rebels of Wales; and this my letters shall be his guar-
antee. In testimony of which to the above I put my
seal.
Given at Lemestre th xi day of July, in the third year of
the reign of King Henry the fourth [1402].

This is not a commission to array troops, as Duncumb thought.
There is no mention of Owain Glyn Dŵr: nothing about Lingein
occupying Leominster after Owain's retreat, as Price thought, or of
driving Owain out by cutting off supplies, which Williams
somehow read into it. The sense is clear: trade with the Welsh was
a normal commercial activity in the border shires. Loyal subjects
must be able to trade, but not with rebels, which they persisted in
doing throughout the war. Probably similar orders against illicit
trade were often issued, with little effect. Lingein's status is not
clear, but he was probably sheriff, or an esquire to the king. He may
have issued a batch of these warrants, of which only the one in
Blount's collection survived. On 31 July 1402 the prince was
appointed to command in the king's new *chevauchée* against the
rebels, so he may already have had authority to commission officers
to issue orders in his name.[28]

We may dismiss Price's story that during his stay at Leominster
Owain arranged the marriages of his daughters to Herefordshire
gentlemen who had helped him to victory. Edward Hall (1548),
Ellis, Pennant and *Powys Fadog* repeat a copyist's error in *The
Brut*, that Lord Grey was compelled to marry one of Owain's
daughters and died in captivity. In fact Grey 'served King Henry V
in his wars in France and with his fleet, and lived to the 19th [year]
of Henry VI'. Grey is obviously confused with Mortimer, a free and
willing bridegroom. Williams overlooks Shakespeare's moving
account of the love between Mortimer and his bride:

Glendower	I am afraid my daughter will run mad,
	So much she doteth on her Mortimer.
Mortimer	This is the deadly spite that angers me,
	My wife can speak no English, I no Welsh.
Glendower	My daughter weeps; she will not part with you;
	She'll be a soldier too, she'll to the wars.

It can, however, be accepted that probably three of Owain's daughters later married into Herefordshire families.[29]

It is quite possible that Lingein's warrant was prompted by fears about Owain's future plans, and that he might follow up his victory by invading Herefordshire, but the story that he seized Leominster is not supported by the many written reports and orders which followed the disaster at Pilleth. For instance, only three days after the battle Henry IV heard 'certain news from our country of Wales, how our rebels there have recently captured our well-beloved cousin Edmund Mortimer and several knights and esquires in his company'. He would go 'to resist the malice of our aforesaid rebels', but said nothing about driving 'our rebels from our town of Leominster and our county of Hereford', which he surely would have done if there had been any substance in the fable that Owain had occupied Leominster. In fact, on 23 July the following notice was sealed:

> Licence for the good men of the town of Leomynstre, which is situated on the frontiers of the marches of Wales, to fortify the town with walls, pales and ditches, for defence against the Welsh rebels, and to compel all the men of the town to contribute to the expense according to their means.

The tax involved was called murage. Leominster was defenceless against Welsh raids. It was a monastery town with no castle or walls, unlike Ludlow or Hereford, useless for a garrison or a military base. The only permanent royal garrison was prohibitively expensive and was at Calais, home of the Wool Staple, even its lucrative trade could hardly pay the costs. On 29 July the sheriffs of Gloucester, Hereford and Shropshire were ordered, 'as the king intends shortly to go in person to Wales with divers armies', to arrange 'by 27 August at latest for the victualling of the king's lieges flowing thither and going to Wales'. This also applied to the mayors and bailiffs of Shrewsbury, Ludlow and Hereford.[30]

After Owain's victory at Pilleth, his only realistic course was surely to retire to north Wales with Mortimer as fast as possible, as he had done with Lord Grey. The idea that he risked all in a dangerous foray into country where the English could soon be expected to assemble in force seems more fanciful than ever. The sooner Owain and his followers made themselves scarce the better; they would have been anxious, like all freebooters, to seek the safety of the hills with their prisoners, sheep, cattle and other plunder. The evidence is that Owain did so; most of the subsequent damage to castles and churches was the work of raiding parties, which continued to plague the border shires for years to come. The nearest churches to Leominster named in Mascall's *Register* as 'destroyed' were Lyonshall and Byton. Both are about ten miles to the west, which implies that Leominster suffered no damage in 1402, or even in 1405 when Owain and the French may have passed through.[31]

In any case, within two months of the battle of Pilleth Owain and his men were in south-east Wales on a campaign to which the invasion of Maelienydd may originally have been a prelude until it produced a brilliant victory surpassing Owain's wildest hopes. The prisoners and the loot had first to be taken to safety before the invasion of south Wales could proceed.

A final piece of evidence that the enemy had gone away from the area three months after the disaster at Pilleth are the following orders, issued on 24 September 1402:

> Commission, during pleasure, to the King's knight, John Greyndor, with the consent of the council, of the custody of the castle and lordship of Radnor, and the villages of Presteigne, Kingsland, Norton, and Pembridge for the greater security of the same and the

adjacent country and the resistance of the malice of the
rebels of Wales, so that he answer for the issues from
time to time at the exchequer.

The castle was probably taken and the garrison massacred in the
summer of 1401, but Leland says that it was only 'partely
destroied', so the Welsh had not had the time or resources to
dismantle it. This commission confirms that it was still defensible a
year later. Greyndor was to remain in active charge of the castle
and its garrison after Prince Henry took over command at Hereford
in 1404.[32]

The hapless Edmund Mortimer joined Grey in some mountain
fastness in Snowdonia. The *carchardy* (prison) of Owain, near
Llansanffraid Glyndyfrdwy was described by Pennant as being thirteen feet square, ten and a half feet high and stoutly built; but this
was rather too near territory held by the English to be a safe place
for such valuable captives. Walsingham adds this rumour: 'there
were those who asserted that Edmund Mortimer was not captured
unwillingly, but by agreement and by premeditated treason.' There
is no confirmation of the story elsewhere, so it was probably false,
but it was the sort of innuendo which Henry IV unfortunately
preferred to believe. After a battle any men of rank in the defeated
army who had not been killed were easily captured by the victors
for ransom; they were conspicuous and too exhausted after a mêlée
in heavy armour on foot to regain their horses and escape. The fact
that Mortimer was captured after the battle of Pilleth was therefore
neither surprising nor sinister. Henry's hatred and suspicion
resulted in Mortimer becoming Owain's son-in-law and ally, but he
is never mentioned as taking an active role in military operations
until his death at the siege of Harlech in 1409.

Hardyng's verse fittingly concludes this chapter:

> Syr Edmonde then Mortimer warred sore
> Vpon Owen, and dyd hym mekyll tene,
> But at laste Owen laye hym before,
> Where in batell they faught, as well was sene,
> When Owen toke him prisoner as then ful kene,

With mekyll folke on eyther syde slayne, And set
Edmonde in prisone and great payne. [33]

CHAPTER SEVEN

The Years of Victory, 1402 to 1404

For the first two years of the war Owain Glyn Dŵr and his men experienced varying fortunes, but in 1402 they defeated and and captured two Marcher lords in as many months. Victory was to crown Owain's endeavours for another two years; the English under Henry IV's uncertain leadership failed to regain the initiative. Consequently the precarious military situation in Wales became infinitely worse. At Shrewsbury in 1403 the king defeated the Percies, but not Owain Glyn Dŵr, who was then overrunning south Wales, and whose power continued to grow. The plight of the garrisons of the Welsh castles became worse than ever. Mortimer's defection left the central Marches, formerly under Mortimer control, wide open to Welsh raids. Owain beame Prince of Wales, ruling with his own council and parliament; he made alliances with Scotland, France and the pope. His triumph at Pilleth does much to explain why the war dragged on for eight more years.

'In the following August [of 1402]', writes Gruffydd Hiraethog, 'Owen came to Glamorgan and all Glamorgan rose with him; Cardiff and Abergavenny were burnt.'[1] The possibility has been mooted that this daring stroke was conceived by Owain Glyn Dŵr and his captains as their principal operation for that summer, and that it was postponed because of the unexpected outcome of the invasion of Radnorshire. Whatever the truth may be, Owain enforced the moral impact of his stunning victory over Edmund Mortimer, and kept the momentum going with this new offensive.

The English chronicles are strangely silent, but Adam of Usk, writing in Rome, comes to our aid with a highly emotional and rather garbled report:

> Concerning such an ill-starred blow given by Owen to the English rule, when I think thereon, my heart trembles. For, backed by a following of thirty thousand men issuing from their lairs, throughout Wales and its marches he overthrew the castles, among which were Usk, Caerleon and Newport, and fired the towns. In short, like a second Assyrian, the rod of God's anger, he did deeds of unheard-of cruelty with fire and sword.

Adam's hatred of his famous contemporary helps to explain why, for the next three centuries, Owain was to be so unfavourably regarded by his own countrymen. In this war some of the Welsh themselves suffered as much from his men as from the English; Gwent does not seem to have shown any of the sympathy for Owain's cause evident in Glamorgan. Adam makes no mention of Cardiff or Abergavenny, probably because he was so distressed by the ruin brought to his homeland of Usk and Caerleon, both belonging to Mortimer. Newport was a lordship of the Earl of Stafford, and the damage done there was so great that in 1403 no revenue could be collected.[2]

On 7 August commissions were sent to eighteen sheriffs to array troops at Chester, Shrewsbury and Hereford, commanded by Prince Henry, the king and the Earls of Stafford and Warwick respectively, for a triple assault on Wales. The chancellor of the county palatine of Lancaster was ordered to send his men to Chester to join those from Derby and Shropshire. The shires of Hereford, Worcester and Gloucester sent men to the Earl of Stafford, who was lieutenant for the Marches from Wigmore to Chepstow and south Wales; his deputy was Richard, Lord Grey of Codnor. The lieutenant for the Marches from Wigmore to Holt was the Earl of Arundel. The offensive began at the end of August, and failed more dismally than its predecessors. Wales threw her very worst weather at the invader in aid of her beleaguered sons: rain, hail, even snow. King Henry himself had a narrow escape when a torrential downpour overthrew his tent when he was encamped in a meadow. A lance or perhaps the heavy central pole fell across him; he survived only because he was sleeping uncomfortably in full armour. He was lucky not to have been struck by lightning.[3]

Owain Glyn Dŵr's exultant comment on these ignominious events is well known from Shakespeare's lines:

> Three times hath Henry Bolingbroke made head
> Against my power; thrice from the banks of Wye
> And sandy-bottom'd Severn have I sent him
> Bootless home and weather-beaten back.

As usual, Hotspur is prompt with his repartee:

> Home without boots, and in foul weather too!
> How scapes he agues, in the devil's name?

No wonder the English saw Owain as a wizard who could even control and direct the forces of nature against them, and said that he was invincible. Only a commander of genius can sap the morale of his enemies like this.[4]

Henry's ignominious retreat in face of the weather and of 'the great magician, damn'd Glendower' was soon followed by some welcome news from the north. The Percies had avenged their shattering defeat by the Scots at Otterburn in 1379, when Hotspur had been captured. On 14 September they won a complete victory at Homildon Hill over a large Scottish army. The English archers had inflicted very heavy casualties. There were thirty Frenchmen among the many nobles and knights who were captured. The king demonstrated his pleasure that the Scots were so severely defeated by giving £40 a year for life to the fortunate bearer of 'the first certain news: Nicholas Merbury, esquire to the Earl of Northumberland. Yet the contrast between Hotspur's triumph and his own recent humiliation in Wales may have rankled with the king. Northumberland presented several prisoners when Parliament met in early October, but not the most important one, the Earl of Douglas.[5]

Parliament's contribution to the Welsh problem was wholly negative, and can have done nothing to conciliate the Welsh. It presented a series of petitions to the king, asking for punitive measures which Henry was very willing to grant; 'le roi le voet' gave them the force of law. Unless they were of approved fidelity, Welshmen were severely restricted in their freedom in their own country: they were forbidden to try Englishmen, to carry arms in public, to hold defensible houses or responsible offices. Arms and supplies might only be brought into towns or castles if they were English-held. Two items deserve special attention. The key role played by bards in disseminating seditious ideas is demonstrated by the ban placed on

> wasters, & rhymers, minstrels or vagabonds ... for to make commorthas or gatherings upon the common people, whom by their divinations, dreams and excitations, they draw into the Welsh insurrection and rebellion.

Another reminds us of Pennant's remarks on behalf of Welsh women:

> No Englishman married to a Welsh wife of the kindred of Owen ap Glendowrdy, Traitor to our Lord the King, or any other Welshwoman since the Rebellion of the said Owen, or who shall in time to come marry any Welshwoman, shall hold no office in Wales or in the March of Wales.

The news of Mortimer's marriage, when it was known soon afterwards, would have been seen to justify this edict.[6]

Parliament also drew the king's attention to the lamentable plight of Lord Grey of Ruthin, 'dolorously [confined] in a strong and hard prison in Wales ... for he knows that the said Lord Grey is a valiant and loyal knight'. There was no sign of any similar concern for Mortimer. It looks very much as if the text of this petition had been pre-arranged with the king, who was only too willing to help with

Grey's ransom; like any lord he had to assist a retainer taken prisoner in his service. The sum of 10,000 marks (£6,666.66) was fixed, and on 11 November 6,000 marks were handed over, with Grey's eldest son as a hostage for the payment of the balance. Grey was impoverished for the rest of his life.[7]

Thomas Clanvowe, who had also been captured at Pilleth, had been freed already, though we do not know exactly when, or how the ransom was paid. On 1 November he and his wife Perina were granted new letters patent, after he had testified on oath that the originals, granted during Richard II's reign, had been accidentally lost, perhaps when his lands had been pillaged by the Welsh. He was compensated with valuable grants, rose in the king's favour and became a king's knight. The king had presumably had a hand in his ransom; everyone wondered what would be done about Mortimer.[8]

The Earl of Northumberland seems to have adopted the role of honest broker, but he failed in his attempts to secure Edmund Mortimer's release. Henry IV believed the dubious rumour that there had been collusion between Owain and Mortimer at the battle of Pilleth. 'In the same way [the Earl's son] Henry Percy, whose wife was sister to Edmund, captive in Wales, came asking the king that he might contribute to Edmund's ransom. The king replied that he would not use the royal revenues to strengthen his enemies against him'; a speech with very similiar words is put into his mouth by Shakespeare.[9]

In fact the outcome of Pilleth was not unwelcome to King Henry: Mortimer locked up, and his military power broken. This narrow dynastic attitude was also extremely unrealistic, a fact which quickly became apparent. Henry had already committed one enormous political blunder: he had missed his best chance of ending the revolt of Owain Glyn Dŵr by refusing to hear Owain's side of his quarrel with Grey. Henry's treatment of Mortimer was even less wise: had he shown the magnanimity worthy of a king, the Percies and Edmund Mortimer might have remained loyal. Mortimer's services would have been of immense value in guarding the border counties against Welsh raids. Henry's stupidity was to cast a long shadow, but he could not have foreseen that Anne Mortimer would marry Duke Edward of York's brother Richard and produce the heir of both York and Mortimer. Henry V was just as harsh with Earl Edmund of March, on whom he imposed a vast fine for marrying without his approval. In 1415 Edmund conspired with Richard, now Earl of Cambridge, against Henry V, but survived by betraying his fellow plotters, who were all executed. The earldom of March was still paying off the fine as late as 1432, when the young Duke of York came into his inheritance.[10]

Edmund Mortimer, unjustly treated as a potential rebel, was compelled to become one. 'Being by his enemies in England stripped of all his goods and hindered from paying ransom', wrote Adam of Usk, 'in order to escape more easily the pains of captivity, he is known by common report to have wedded the daughter of the same Owen.' In November Edmund was released. He became Owain's ally, and 'with great solemnity' married Catherine, probably the eldest daughter of his former conqueror. Returning to Maelienydd, he appealed to 'Monsieur John Greyndor, Howel Vaughan, and all the gentles and commons of Radnor and Presteigne':

> Very dear and well-beloved, I greet you much, and make known to you that Oweyn Glyndor has raised a quarrel, of which the object is, if King Richard be alive, to restore him to his crown, and if not, that my honoured nephew [the Earl of March], who is the right heir to the said Crown, shall be King of England, and that the said Owen will assert his right in Wales. And I, seeing and considering that the said quarrel is good and reasonable, have consented to join in it, and ... I ardently hope, and from my heart, that you will support and enable me to bring this struggle of mine to a successful issue.'[11]

Greyndor was not only a king's knight but also an able soldier who rose to prominence as a member of Prince Henry's staff. There is no evidence that he or any of the others to whom Mortimer appealed came over to his side.

During the winter of 1403 Owain had been besieging castles which were still in English hands, like Harlech and Aberystwyth (referred to in those days as Llanbadarn, the parish in which it was situated). In March the king appointed Prince Henry, fifteen years old, royal lieutenant in Wales and the Marches, with powers to order the sheriffs of the border counties to supply troops. Despite his youth, Henry was fast acquiring the grasp of detail and flair for administration with which he was to win the Welsh war, and which were finally to place him far above any other commander of his time. Most of the great Edwardian castles of north Wales belonged to the Prince of Wales: Caernarfon, Conwy, Cricieth, and Harlech, and in the south Aberystwyth, Cardigan and Carmarthen. (Beaumaris had been granted with Anglesey to the Percies). The gross yield of the Principality had once been about £5,000 a year, but was now at rock-bottom. The earldom of Chester needed most of its net revenue of about £400 to maintain its two Welsh castles of Rhuddlan and Flint. The duchy of Cornwall, with its rich tin mines, and estates in Cornwall, Devon, nineteen other counties and also London, produced about £2,000 net. The prince's duchy and earldom could now hardly maintain his Welsh castles and pay his soldiers' wages, let alone finance a major war, so the king and council now decided to raise an army of 3,000 men at a cost of £32,000 a year.[12]

In the spring of 1403 Owain gathered fresh forces and prepared to resume operations. Prince Henry acted with speed and vigour. On 15 May he was at Shrewsbury, and wrote a letter to the Council in which he described with relish his depredations at Owain's expense:

> We took our forces and marched to a place of the said Owen, well built, called Sycharth, where we thought we should have found him ... We then marched to his other place of Glyndowrdy ... and we caused a fine lodge in his Park to be destroyed by fire, and laid waste the country all around.

One cannot help wondering what John Beaufort Earl of Somerset thought of this ravaging of estates which were now his. The prince now turned to the much more intractable problem of how to help the garrisons of Aberystwyth and Harlech. On 30 May he wrote again, as an officer on behalf of his men, upon whom all depended:

> Our soldiers want to know whether they will be paid
> for the three months of this quarter, and say that they
> will not stay here unless they are at once paid their
> wages according to their indentures ... Our castles of
> Harlech and Llanbadarn [Aberystwyth] are besieged
> and have been for a long time, and we must relieve and
> victual them within these ten days, and besides this
> guard the March [against] the rebels.[13]

Aberystwyth and Harlech guarded the northern half of Cardigan
Bay, and access by land was longer and more precarious than to
any other castles in Wales. The growing domination of the land by
the Welsh brought ever more serious problems of supply and
morale. The Edwardian castles were all sited near the sea, but
Caernarfon, Conway and Beaumaris (belonging to Hotspur) were
readily accessible from Chester. Harlech was more dependent on
the sea for supplies than the others, because it is hemmed in
between the sea and the Rhinog mountains, the wildest and rockiest
terrain in Wales; its supply routes round the Mawddach and Glaslyn
estuaries were long and tenuous. (In those days the sea washed the
very foot of the crag upon which Harlech is built, whereas today it
is about a mile away).

Two weeks after the prince's request for funds, alarming rumours
arrived from south Wales, which produced the following reaction
from the king:

> Commission of array in the county of Carmarthen to
> Thomas, Earl of Worcester [and four other men], on
> information from credible persons of the council of the
> king's son the prince in the parts of Wales that Owen
> Gleyndourdy and other rebels from those parts for
> want of victuals intend to come suddenly with no small
> posse to the marches of the county to seek victuals and
> to waste the county.

Thomas Percy, Earl of Worcester, Lord Carew and others were
commissioned to array troops to guard Carmarthen and Pembroke.

The English intelligence system had correctly predicted the movements of Owain Glyn Dŵr, but even so this commission was not executed. Worcester most likely ignored it, and the king was busy preparing for his Scottish campaign. In 1346 Edward III had taken his main army to France and overwhelmed King Philip VI at Crécy. His northern army had routed the invading Scots and captured King David I at Neville's Cross. A much less formidable and dangerous task faced Henry IV in 1403: to hold off the Scots and crush a Welsh rebellion, without even having to cross the Channel. He could have surely done it, if he had not quarrelled with the Percies, and had been able to leave them to deal with the Scots; but his relations with them must have been near breaking point already. Less than a month later Hotspur came out in rebellion.[14]

Despite this clear warning of Owain Glyn Dŵr's movements, Henry did not take it seriously, or respond with prompt and resolute action. His inertia had disastrous results, as his servants in Wales and the Marches were soon to tell him. Owain's personal losses may have fuelled the fiery energy with which he carried out his new enterprise. His aims were far more ambitious than in the summer campaigns of 1401 and 1402, when he had achieved his more limited goals. His plan was now to overrun south-west Wales. We can follow its dramatic success, thanks to the surviving letters of officials and soldiers, several of whom were Herefordshire gentry. The letters show the importance of that shire in the government of south Wales. They also give a detailed account of events during two weeks of July 1403, and they vividly illustrate the desperation and panic which were felt by men faced with overwhelming odds.

During June the people of the Builth and Brecon area rebelled. Brecon was besieged. John Bodenham, sheriff of Herefordshire and a king's esquire, had acted decisively in defence of his threatened shire, so must have been gratified to hear that he had anticipated the order of his dilatory master. On 7 July he wrote to the king: 'On the Sunday last [1 July] before we had received your honourable letter aforesaid, we were at Brecon and broke the siege; and there were killed by the men of your said county the number of 240 and upwards.' Bodenham received a well-earned reward for his expenses and resolute action: an annuity of 40 marks.

After his victory Bodenham withdrew to Hereford, apparently unaware of the menacing developments in Carmarthenshire, news of which greatly alarmed John Fairford, the Lancastrian receiver of revenues at Brecon and canon of Abergwili. It was no longer simply a matter of chastising the local riff-raff, as Bodenham had done a few days before, but facing a crisis of truly terrifying magnitude. Probably very early on Wednesday 4 July, Fairford sent off two very important dispatches. One was addressed 'in great haste' to Bodenham: Jenkin Havard, constable of Dinefwr Castle near Llandeilo and a king's esquire, had written that he was besieged by the Dwnns of Kidwelly and other rebellious gentry of Carmarthenhire. Ralph Monnington, constable of Llandovery Castle belonging to Lord Audley, was in like case, but he had even graver tidings to impart: the arrival of Owain Glyn Dŵr in person with his retinue. Fairford begged Bodenham and his colleagues to ask the king 'to supply all the Counties around you, to reinforce them and array them at once for resisting the same rebels.'

Bodenham received this on Saturday 7 July, and wrote to the king the letter which has already been quoted. He entirely agreed with Fairford. The gentry of Herefordshire had too few men to face such massive enemy forces. Reinforcements must be sent immediately, preferably led by the king in person, but Henry, who did not realise that Hotspur was now on the point of rebellion, was anxious to leave for Scotland. Bodenham sent two enclosures with his dispatch. One was almost certainly the letter he had just received from Fairford. The other was probably a copy of the letter which Fairford had received from Monnington.[15]

Fairford also wrote, enclosing Monnington's letter, to an old servant of the House of Lancaster in London, Sir Hugh Waterton. In 1377, when young Henry of Bolingbroke was knighted and made Earl of Derby, John of Gaunt retained Waterton for life as Henry's receiver and financial adviser. Later he was on Henry's council. Surely the king would listen to him and act on his advice. Waterton wrote to the king 'in haste, on Friday, before Vespers', almost certainly 6 July, when Henry IV probably set out for the north. Waterton's health was bad; he apologised for not coming to see the king about important matters earlier, but he was afraid of catching cold. Since he could not give the king the news from Wales by word of mouth, he must write. (Neither Fairford's nor Monnington's letter has survived).

'A servant of the Receiver of Brecon has now brought to me a letter of news from those parts, directed to his Master by the Lieutenant of Lord Audley at Llandovery, the which for your better information I have enclosed within these presents.' The bearer told Waterton that the rebels had burned Llandeilo and Newtown, and were advancing with fire and sword on the Lancastrian lordships of Iscennen and Kidwelly, which they failed to take because of a flood. 'Also they have driven the Chamberlain of Carmarthen towards the town, and have killed some of his men'. He ends by appealing to the king to send an army large enough for 'the preservation of your faithful lieges, and the punishment of your rebels'.

Waterton's information confirmed Fairford's recent news from Sir John Scudamore, who wrote on 5 July that the fall of Carmarthen was imminent; in fact it occurred on Friday 6 July, the same day that Fairford's servant reached London, and handed his letters to Waterton. Scudamore was constable of the rocky Lancastrian fortress of Carreg Cennen near Llandovery, which was also in danger; he was further embarrassed by the presence of his wife, her mother and their servants. (Scudamore must have had a previous wife before he married Owain Glyn Dŵr's daughter Alice; the act of Parliament already quoted disqualified any Englishman with a Welsh wife from such a post as his). He told Fairford that under a flag of truce Owain had refused a safe conduct for his family. Owain 'is about the town of Carmarthen, and there thinketh to abide till he may have the town and castle'; he aimed to take Kidwelly and invade Pembrokeshire. 'Write to Sir Hugh Waterton, and to all whom you suppose will take this matter to heart, that they excite the King hitherwards in all haste to venge him on some of his false traitors whom he hath overmuch cherished.' Scudamore's idea of writing to Waterton, a man clearly thought to have influence with the king, shows that Henry IV was well known to be irresolute, unwilling to face facts and difficult to persuade.[16]

There are very strong reasons for dating Waterton's letter to Friday 6 July, not the 13th. First, the news in Monnington's letter to

Fairford was so grave that no time could be lost in laying it before the king. Secondly, when he wrote, Waterton had apparently not heard of the fall of Carmarthen Castle, news of which would certainly have reached him by Friday13 July. Finally, it is more credible that so vital a letter reached London, 165 miles from Brecon, in three long summer days rather than ten, at an average speed of 55 miles a day. On the third day after the battle of Pilleth the king was giving his reactions to the news at Berkhamstead, 140 miles from Presteigne. There are many examples which show how fast important news could travel in those days. The battle of Bosworth was fought on the morning of 22 August 1485; the news reached York, 120 miles away, the following evening of a summer day. Duke Richard of York's death at the battle of Wakefield on 30 December 1459 was known in London, 182 miles away, on 2 January. In both examples the speed was 60 miles a day, but the more remarkable achievement of the two was surely to have delivered the news of Wakefield in only three short winter days, though the courier was admittedly helped by the moon, which was full on 1 January. One imagines that such speeds would only have been maintained in favourable weather, and with reasonably dry roads.[17]

Carmarthen Castle was surrendered to Owain Glyn Dŵr by its constable, Robert Wigmore, on 6 July 1403. This grim but expected news was sent to Fairford by Jenkin Havard at Dinefwr, probably writing early next morning; Newcastle Emlyn, guarding the middle Teifi valley in Cardiganshire, had already been given up by Jenkin ap Llywelyn. Havard, whose family was well known in Pembrokeshire, appeared to be losing his nerve under the strain; maybe the bloodthirsty threats of the rebels outside the castle walls were fully audible to the defenders. When Fairford received this letter, he had already forwarded Scudamore's to Richard Kingston, Archdeacon of Hereford, thereby shattering that gentleman's Sunday peace. Fairford then delivered another shock by sending Havard's letter as well.

Richard Kingston was not only archdeacon, but also clerk of works of the royal castle at Hereford, and also Dean of Windsor: an interesting example of clerical pluralism. Conscious that he owes his appointments to the king, he rather oddly calls himself 'votre

*Owain's possessions of Glyn Dyfrdwy c.1900 (top)
and Sycharth (below) (Richard Williams)*

Owain from his seal
(Geoffrey Wheeler)

Effigy at Montgomery Church,
purported to be Sir Edmund Mortimer
(Richard Williams)

Effigy of Henry IV at Battle Church
(Richard Williams)

The Walls of Conway Castle c.1925

The site of the Battle of Hyddgen

Ruthin Castle

Buck's 1732 engraving of Wigmore Castle from the south

*The castle mound at New Radnor,
believed site of a massacre by Owain's forces*

*Montgomery town and castle c.1925,
attacked by Owain in autumn 1401*

Castell Foel-allt above the ford across the Lugg at Pilleth

Pilleth, showing the Wellingtonias marking the mass grave on the hillside to the left, and the church in the centre
(Richard Williams)

The Church at Pilleth
(Richard Williams)

The Lancastrian castle of Carreg Cennan c.1905

Owain's parliament house at Machynlleth
(Geoffrey Wheeler)

The Martingale found at Harlech Castle with Owain's coat of arms
(National Museum of Wales)

Woodbury Hill from Abberley
(Richard Williams)

Abberley Hill from Woodbury
(Richard Williams)

The entrance to Grosmont Castle from the south-east

The hall at Grosmont Castle

*Aberystwyth Castle (top) and Harlech Castle (bottom),
both c.1900, recaptured from Owain by forces
under the command of Prince Henry*

Lawton's Hope, where Owain is believed to have died

Kentchurch Court, as sketched by James Wathen in 1795,
where Owain may have spent some of his last years

Monnington Church c.1900 at Monnington-on-Wye, long believed to be the final resting place of Owain, now more correctly thought to be at Monnington Straddle

petite creature' in his letter dated 8 July, but is emboldened to overcome his nervousness at speaking so bluntly to his master by the
dire news from Carmarthen:

> May it please you to prepare to set out with all the
> power you can muster, and march day and night for the
> salvation of these parts. And may it please you to
> reflect that it will be a great disgrace as well as loss,
> to lose or suffer to be lost, in the beginning of your reign,
> a country which your predecessors have won, and for
> so long a time peacefully possessed. For people are
> talking very maliciously.

The same day came the news that Carmarthen and Newcastle
Emlyn had fallen; at this new bombshell he redoubled all his exhor-
tations in a postscript.[18]

Although the king was preoccupied with his expedition against
the Scots, which still had priority over Wales, on 10 July he belat-
edly ordered £1,000 to be paid to his son. This desperately needed
grant was very likely the fruit of a letter which the prince had
recently written to Thomas Fitzalan, Archbishop of Canterbury and
Chancellor, whose counsel and moral support he greatly valued.
Known as Archbishop Arundel, Thomas was brother of the earl
who had been Owain's patron and Richard II's enemy, also of Joan
de Bohun, dowager Countess of Hereford and grandmother of the
prince, whose affection for the archbishop appears from his
frequent use of the phrase 'very dear and heartily beloved uncle'.
(After 1407 the prince's relations with the archbishop became less
cordial, because he was at odds with his father and Arundel over
the government of the realm). The prince was weighed down by
official cares, especially as his right-hand man, the Duke of York,
had gone to join the king at Leicester, no doubt for the abortive
Scottish campaign. Although he was responsible for the safety of
Herefordshire, he was short of money to pay his troops who, like
those at Aberystwyth, would desert if they did not get their wages.
The archbishop's opinion would have carried great weight with the
king.[19]

Meanwhile Jenkin Havard wrote to Fairford again on Wednesday 11 July: on Monday Lord Carew had advanced from Pembrokeshire 'with a great retinue' towards St. Clears, ten miles west of Carmarthen, where he and Owain spent Tuesday in fruitless negotiations. That night Owain was at the port of Laugharne, returning to Carmarthen in the morning to divide the spoil; the Welsh were undecided whether to burn the town and castle. 'They have goods and victuals plenty, for every house about us is full of their poultry, and yet wine and honey enough in the country, and wheat and bran and all manner victuals.' Owain's strength was given as 8,240 spearmen.

The sequel is told by the mayor and burgesses of Caerleon in a letter to their brothers at Monmouth. Owain had based himself at Carmarthen. A strange tale ensues, which shows both Owain's cautious nature, and his love of Celtic lore and divination: the side of this extraordinary man which so infuriated Hotspur, but which was such a vital element in his character. Owain invited Hopkin ap Thomas of Gower, a famous litterateur and patron of bards and prose writers, 'to come and speak with him upon truce ... that in as much as he held him master of Brut, that he should do him to understand how and what manner it should befall of him'. The very word 'Brut' suggests ancient origins; it was the kind of esoteric learning, lore and prophecy associated by Geoffrey of Monmouth with Merlin. Hopkin warned Owain that he would very soon be taken prisoner 'between Carmarthen and Gower ... under a black banner.' The Welsh were not alone in succumbing to the lure of magic and divination; Henry IV's widowed Queen Joanna and Duchess Eleanor of Gloucester were to fall from grace in this way. By his advice Hopkin succeeded in keeping Owain away from his home country of Gower; perhaps Owain also read into this a warning to be very careful of an ambush by Lord Carew. If he did, the affair must have considerably enhanced his reputation for bearing a charmed life.

The captain of Kidwelly reported that Lord Carew was expecting to meet Owain in battle on 12 July, but that Owain had sent 700 of his own men into the hill country north of Carmarthen 'to search the ways', as he wanted to be sure of his line of retreat, but they met Carew and his men, and most of them were killed. The letter from Caerleon ended exultantly: 'Be glad and merry, and dread ye nought for we hope to God that ye have no need. And we do you to understand that all these tidings be sooth without doubt.'[20]

The euphoria of the Caerleon burgesses, prompted by the defeat of Owain's men, was destined to prove premature in the long run. Though this disaster may have helped to reduce the impetus of Owain's campaign in south Wales, his attention may also have been distracted by the rebellion of the Percies against Henry IV. Hotspur had been particularly angered by Henry's refusal to help Mortimer regain his freedom; the last straw was probably his demand that Hotspur hand over the Scottish prisoners he had recently captured at Homildon Hill, notably the Earl of Douglas. The king had a right to ransom but the refusal of the Percies to obey illustrated only too clearly a political problem confronting any usurper: it was hard for Henry IV to command the respect and obedience of a powerful family whose support had helped him to the throne and who thought that they had been ungenerously treated. They had held the Scottish March and contained the Welsh revolt at very great cost, for which he had failed to repay them fully. Thomas Percy thought that he was inadequately endowed with land to maintain his rank as Earl of Worcester. There is a story that Henry angrily refused to recoup Northumberland's expenses whereupon Hotspur said:

> 'Shall a man spende his good, and put himself in perille for you and your realm, and ye wil not helpe him in his need?' The king was wroth and saide to him, 'Thou art a traitour! wilt thou that I sholde socoure myn enemies, and enemies of the realm?' Sir Henri Percy saide, 'Traitor am I none, but a trew man, and as a trew man I speak.' The king drow to him 'Not here, but in the field.'[21]

The outcome was the best known event of the reign: Henry's hard-won victory at Shrewsbury. He was at Nottingham on 12 July while on his way to help Northumberland against the Scots, when he heard that Hotspur had declared his rebellion at Chester two days earlier. Hotspur's army was made up not of the northern Percy affinity, but of men from Cheshire and north Wales, loyal to the memory of Richard II, who had raised his retinue there. Hotspur and his uncle Thomas, Earl of Worcester, advanced on Shrewsbury. If they hoped to find Owain Glyn Dŵr there, they must have been badly out of touch with recent events in south Wales, where Owain and his army were too deeply committed to come to their aid. Faced by this dire threat to his throne, Henry for once acted vigorously and decisively. After a forced march he reached Shrewsbury before Hotspur, and defeated and killed him on 21 July 1403. The casualties on both sides were heavy. Worcester and other leaders of the rebellion were executed after the battle. Henry spared his enemies no indignity, even the dead Hotspur. London, Bristol, Newcastle upon Tyne and Chester were singled out for the dubious privilege of displaying the quarters of this great man's body 'as long as they will last'. The living rebels were drawn on hurdles to the place of execution where they were beheaded. None of this can have helped Henry IV's reputation, though the conduct of Worcester, a royal retainer, was generally condemned. Giles's Chronicle accused him of ensuring that the parley before the battle failed, so that many men were killed, a charge repeated by Shakespeare. Giles also says that Worcester wanted the king dead, as he would do better under his kinsman, a reference to the story that Hotspur aimed at the crown; Walsingham reported that his troops had shouted 'Henry Percy King!'[22]

During the battle Prince Henry sustained a nasty wound in the face from an arrow, which needed surgery. Two days later the Earl of Arundel, Lord Berkeley, Edward Charlton, Hugh Burnell an Lord Audley were appointed 'to govern the marches of England towards Wales and resist the invasions of Owin de Gleyndourdy and other rebels there, as the king's son the prince of Wales cannot attend to this'. It seems doubtful whether the effects of this wound fully explain the fact that Prince Henry's lieutenancy in Wales was to be virtually in abeyance until the following year.[23]

Through his own courage and resolution, and thanks to the loyalty and massive strength of the Lancastrian retinue, Henry IV had survived the most serious crisis of his reign, but he had been very fortunate. Hotspur had acted so precipitately that he had given Owain insufficient time to come to his aid; but would Owain have taken the risk of joining battle so far from the cover of the Welsh hills? When he did so two years later, he was in the company of a French expeditionary force. It can be argued that it was his best chance of final victory but, on the other hand, even if Henry IV had been defeated at Shrewsbury, it is difficult to believe that the English would have permanently tolerated an independent principality of Wales.

Henry's victory at Shrewsbury did nothing to ease the situation in Wales, which became even worse. Only two days after the battle, another message of gloom was penned by the elderly uncle of the Earl of Warwick: William Beauchamp, Lord Abergavenny. The king had entrusted to his care Pembroke, Tenby and several other castles in south Wales: a crippling burden in addition to his own castles of Abergavenny and Ewyas Harold.

> My most sovereign liege lord, I would most humbly beseech you, and in very great bitterness of heart, that it would please you of your great grace and compassion to remember my poor and suffering person, who am in very great disease and distress at present and to extend to me with all speed your succour and gracious aid in this case, which is very perilous and pitiful; or otherwise I judge myself destroyed at this moment ...

The Welsh were by then east of the Black Mountains; they had captured one of his soldiers between Hereford and Abergavenny.[24]

Archdeacon Kingston wrote on 3 September that 'there were come into our county more than four hundred of the rebels of Owen ... and many other rebels besides from the Marches of Wales, and they have captured and robbed within your county of Hereford many men, and beasts in grea numbers, our truce notwithstanding'. He commended to the king Miles Walter, the valiant esquire who brought the news. His very unrealistic request vividly displays his alarm, but he ends with his bluntest warning yet:

> to send me this night, or early tomorrow morning at the latest, my most honoured Master Beaufort, or some

other valiant person ... with one hundred lances and six
hundred archers, until your most gracious arrival to the
salvation of us all ... For, my most dread Lord, you will
find for certain that, if you do not come in your own
person to await your rebels in Wales, you will not find
a single gentleman that will stop in your said county.

The archdeacon was referring to Thomas Beaufort, later Earl of
Dorset and Duke of Exeter, who greatly distinguished himself in
the French wars. The warning with which he ends his letter gives,
however, yet another example of what Henry's servants thought of
his reluctance to act decisively. [25]

Adam of Usk, hearing of the latest mayhem in Wales, gives a
hostile and confused account of how, after the battle of Shrewsbury,

Owain and his manikins ... marched through Wales
with a great power as far as the sea of the Severn, and
brought into subjection with fire and sword all who
made resistance and also those beyond the same sea,
sparing not even churches ... And then with a vast spoil
he retired for safety to the northern parts of Wales,
whence are spread all the ills of Wales ... amid smoth-
ered curses on his open adulteries.

A raid across the Severn estuary could have provoked the
seaborne reprisal led by two esquires from Bristol mentioned by
Adam. They pillaged Llandaff Cathedral, and were driven off with
heavy loss by the country people. [26]

The defence of Wales and its Marches depended on the Marcher
lords, whose appeals had to be taken seriously, and in August the
king reluctantly agreed to come to Worcester. From Pontefract he
sent a special commission to the sheriffs of thirty-five shires, a
verbal net of fine mesh through which no servant of the Crown,
Principality of Wales or Duchy of Lancaster could hope to slip:

All knights, esquires and yeomen of those counties
who, by grant of King Edward III, the late king,

Edward late prince of Wales, or the king's father, confirmed by the king, or of the king himself yearly take any fees, wages or annuities of the king or are of his livery and retinue, shall under pain of forfeiting such fees etc. and all else which they may, cease every excuse and hasten to draw towards the town of Worcester, every man well furnished and arrayed as his estate demands ...

One can readily imagine how Owain must have felt on receiving a similar writ three years earlier, which Grey had deliberately handed to him with only three days to spare.[27]

At Worcester on 8 September the king issued orders to the surveyor of castles, the Bishop of St. David's, and sixteen other persons for the re-equipping, repairing and restocking of twenty-two castles in the southern Marches. Three Herefordshire castles, Lyonshall, Stapleton and Huntington, were presumably still defensible against the Welsh.[28] More tangible evidence to illustrate the devastation caused by Welsh raids can be found in the Chancery records, in the grants made by the king to those lucky enough to have access to him. In February 1403 the castle of Clifford and the lordship of Glasbury were granted to Robert Whitney, because his father, uncle and several relations had been killed at Pilleth, and his castle and most of his estate destroyed by the Welsh. In March 1403 Thomas Coke, an Englishman resident at or near Radnor, was given a total of about £30 from the forfeited lands of local rebels to compensate him for damage to his property. In February 1405 John Bedell of Hay, another Englishman, who had been loyal to the king and had suffered losses, was granted lands in the king's lordships of Hay and Bronllys, forfeited by eight named rebels.[29]

From Worcester King Henry IV took the usual route through Hereford and Brecon, up the Usk valley and into that of the Tywi to Carmarthen, where he arrived on 24 September. This was his third invasion of Wales, which was as fruitless as its predecessors, although at least this time the weather seems to have been tolerable. He met with little resistance, and left the Earl of Somerset in charge, later to be replaced by the Duke of York. No sooner had the king withdrawn, than the rebels resumed their domination of the countryside, though at least Carmarthen had been recovered.[30]

Henry IV could not reconquer Wales, or defend his coasts, or his lands in France, unless he had enough ships, and the men to work and fight them, all of which added to his financial burdens. The transport of supplies and troops was perhaps even more important than fighting. In the late summer of 1403 provisions were ordered for Carmarthen from the Pembroke ports, and a massive order went to Bristol to supply Aberystwyth, Cardigan, Cardiff and Newport. Hereford was responsible for the inland castles: Builth, Clifford, Hay, Brecon, Dinas and Carreg Cennen. Wheat, oats, fish, ale and wine were the staple items, but 'the king's brother' Somerset, who was in command at Carmarthen, also had honey and salt to enliven the diet of the medieval soldier.[31]

Warfare at sea was very haphazard in the middle ages, when the chances of two fleets actually meeting and fighting were slim. It consisted more of piratical raids by the French, Bretons, Flemings and Spaniards as much as by the English, who were at a disadvantage in the days when square-rigged ships could not tack against the south-westerlies. French and Breton raiders frequently had the weather gage, so could attack without warning wherever they chose. They were already helping the Welsh, who had few ships of their own. If Owain was to win and hold the great coastal castles like Kidwelly, Aberystwyth, Harlech and Caernarfon, he could only do so with the aid of French reinforcements brought by sea. He was also helped by Henry IV's perennial shortage of money; supplying the castles by sea was very expensive. Aberystwyth and Harlech were especially vulnerable, as their lines of communication were so long and hazardous.

On the Feast of St. Michael and All Angels (29 September) a letter was written to the king by his constable of Kidwelly:

> Harry Doun and all the rebels of South Wales, with the men of France and Brittany, are coming towards the Castle and Town of Kidwelly with all their ordnance, and have destroyed all the grain belonging to your poor lieges of every side of your said castle and town;

and many of your poor commons have fled into
England with their wives and children, and the others
are in your said castle in doubt of their lives.

The attack failed, but support for the revolt from across the
Channel, especially when its leader in south Wales was a man as
formidable as Henry Dwnn, was a worrying development.[32]

In November the French fleet under Jean d'Espagne sailed to
Gwynedd, and tried to take Caernarfon Castle. The garrison seems
to have shrunk to about forty men from the hundred who had been
there at the beginning of the war, far too few, one would have
thought, to hold so vast a fortress, yet the assault failed. On 12
January it was reported by Reynald of Bayldon, one of the keepers
of Conwy Castle, that the rebels were moving people and livestock
from Anglesey to the safety of Snowdonia, 'lest Englishemen
shulde be refreshitte therwith'. The French and Owain were
preparing for a fresh assault on Caernarfon. On 15 January this
news was forwarded to the king by William Venables, Constable of
Chester, who sent even worse tidings next day: the second succes-
sive assault on Caernarfon was about to begin. Owain and the
French were better equipped this time, with engines, sows and very
long ladders; perhaps the first time the scaling ladders had been too
short. A sow was a wheeled vehicle made of timber and protected
against fire by raw hides, the crew of which could undermine walls
like rootling pigs. Venables wrote:

In the town and castle there are not more than twenty-
eight fighting men, which is too small a force; for
eleven of the men who were there at the last siege of
the place are dead; some of the wounds they received
at the time of the assault, and others of the plague.

Harlech's predicament was equally grim. The garrison had
numbered ten men-at-arms and thirty archers in 1404, but by 15
January 1404 it had been reduced by pestilence and desertion to five
Englishmen and about sixteen Welshmen, according to Venables.
Bayldon explained how one Welsh keeper had been taken prisoner

by his compatriots; his successor, also a Welshman, suffered the same misfortune having aroused the suspicion of his own men and been relieved of the castle keys. Probably both were deserters.

Accustomed as they were to wine as part of their diet, the French did not take kindly to campaigning in barbarous countries like Scotland and Wales where such delights were rare luxuries. This may explain a report of 26 February, by Henry of Scarisbrec, Lieutenant of Conwy Castle, that six French ships were about to land their cargoes of wines and spices in the Llyn peninsula; Scarisbrec thought that 'if they were taken hastily it were great profit, in a great abashing to our enemies'. In another letter that day he told the Constable of Chester that Owain had been to Harlech. Most of the garrison had agreed with him 'to have deliverance of the Castle at a certain day for a certain sum of gold, & the day is in right hasty time bot he wot not when'.

As late as 23 April a Council meeting ordered John Stevens of Bristol and Lord Carew to array five ships with men-at-arms and archers and relieve the castles of Cardigan, Aberystwyth, Harlech and Caernarfon; 'and to drive away Jean d'Espagne, knight of France, who with certain warships has laid siege to the said castles of Caernarfon and Harlech, for the safeguard and defence of the realm'. At that date Aberystwyth and Harlech had still not surrendered to Owain; it is not known when he won this resounding double victory, but it cannot have been long afterwards.[33]

The castles had been captured as they were too remote for the English to reach by land routes dominated by the Welsh, and too dangerous to relieve by sea in the face of the French naval squadron. Owain was now master of most of Wales with a good claim to be its ruling prince, and able to seek the formal recognition and support of France. Abbot Walter Bower summed up Owain's achievement:

> It is a fact that, by the providence of God himself, within three years the Welsh had expelled all their enemies, and had further extended their marches to the final boundaries of the same kingdom established by Brutus, who had first divided Britain with his brothers.[34]

CHAPTER EIGHT

Owain Glyn Dŵr, Prince of Wales

When Parliament met in January 1404, the king was severely criti-
cised for financial incompetence, though too little allowance was
made for his grave problems. Perhaps in self-defence, he handed
'the custody of our country of Wales to our very dearly beloved son
the Prince as our lieutenant in those parts'. This may seem a very
heavy burden to place upon so young a man, but the signs are that
Henry was eager for responsibility; in the last four years he had
already gained much experience. As Prince of Wales and Earl of
Chester he was by far the greatest magnate in Wales. His abundant
energy was combined with maturity and military skill beyond his
years. In May the appointment was formally notified to the council;
Thomas, Earl of Arundel, and Edward, Duke of York, were to safeguard the borders of north and south Wales repectively. Despite
York's reputation under both Richard II and Henry IV as a time-
server and trouble-maker, he was an able man at both politics and
war, which may explain why he was so successful at getting out of
trouble. Although one suspects that Henry IV never really trusted
him, York was one of those people who have a talent for being
indispensable.[1]

A very important letter to King Henry IV, written at Shrewsbury
on 21 April, bears stark witness to the terrifying growth of Owain
Glyn Dŵr's power. Although the manuscript is badly damaged and
the wording often uncertain, there is no doubt as to the grim
meaning:

> Most excellent and mighty sovereign lord, we
> [humbly] beseech your highness that you may hear
> how your loyal lieges of your county of Salop are in
> great doubt and despair from day to day at the malice
> [and mischief] which your Welsh rebels and their
> adherents are purposing to do and sooner or later will
> do with all their might in your said county, [threat-
> ening] your said lieges with the destruction of their
> goods and chattels ... [Most excellent lord, may it
> please you to show grace and favour to your said
> lieges, and to send them some of the men-at-arms and
> archers who have come into these parts with our most
> redoubted lord the Prince. Your said rebels and the
> French, knowing that this county is less well guarded
> than your other counties adjoining your marches of
> Wales, were intent on a *chevauchée* into your said
> county before the coming of our lord the Prince] ...
> Most mighty lord, a third of your said county has been
> destroyed and devastated by your said rebels, and your
> lieges formerly living there have left to gain their meat
> and sustenance elsewhere in your realm.

News of Prince Henry's return to the area earlier that month had
presumably reached Shropshire; the appeal for his help may well
indicate his rising prestige. A French naval squadron was known to
have contributed to recent Welsh victories, but there is no evidence
that the French had assisted in recent Welsh *chevauchées*; they sent
no army to Wales till 1405. The lieges of Shropshire may have
exaggeretaed in saying that a third of their county, the largest in
England with no sea coast, had been looted; but the damage immediately 'adjoining your marches of Wales' was endorsed by the
Bishop of Hereford in 1406. The terror aroused by Welsh war-
parties could well have driven the inhabitants of a larger area to
seek refuge further afield.[2]

There is an example which suggests that some raiders may have
penetrated more deeply eastwards. This is the Cistercian abbey of
Buildwas, north of the Severn and some twelve miles east of

Shrewsbury, 'whose possessions have been in great part burned and destroyed by the Welsh rebels so that divine services and other charges and works of piety cannot be maintained there according to the ordinances of the foundation.' If the Welsh could cause havoc so deep into Shropshire, few of the inhabitants can have felt safe, though the damaged property may have been further to the west.[3]

The situation in Herefordshire was indeed serious. 'The Welsh rebels in great numbers have entered Archenfield, which is part of the county of Hereford, where they have burned houses, killed people, taken prisoners and ravaged the land with great dishonour to the king', the sheriff and his colleagues reported to the council on 10 June. 'We have no other forces at present to help us but those of our lord Richard of York [brother of the duke] and his soldiers, who are too few.' Perhaps the lieges of Shropshire were right to complain that neighbouring shires were better protected; we are not told that there was any similar garrison at Shrewsbury. The council was asked to prevail upon the king to send reinforcements, and its attention was respectfully drawn to what Archdeacon Kingston had already said on the subject.[4]

King Henry reacted to this grave news by ordering Prince Henry to direct operations from Worcester, where on 26 June he described the situation in sombre terms. Rebels from south Wales, victualled for fifteen days, were burning and destroying in Herefordshire. The prince had ordered enough men from the four border counties to help Richard of York. He warmly commended the Earl of Warwick to the royal favour for the fine body of troops which he had provided at his own expense. Perhaps it was now that the nunnery of Aconbury, about six miles south of Hereford, suffered grievous damage from the Welsh; the king himself may have ordered compensation when he was in Hereford in September 1405. Another payment, of five marks, was ordered to assist Llanthony Priory which had also suffered badly.[5]

Further disasters followed. The fall of Aberystwyth and Harlech gave the signal for the overrunning of south Wales, not just a great raid like that of August 1402. The principal event was the capture of Cardiff, which is mentioned only in the *Eulogium*. Strangely enough Gruffydd Hiraethog, who had recorded its burning in 1402, tells us nothing about it. It sounds as if the damage was probably very much worse this time:

> Owain took the town and burned it, except for the street in which the Friars Minor lived, which for his love of the friars, together with their convent, he allowed to stand. In addition he took the castle and destroyed it, and took away many valuables which had been deposited there. When the Friars Minor asked him for their books and silver which they had deposited in the castle he replied: 'Why did you put your goods in the castle? If you had left them at home, they would have been safe.'

One can only hope that Owain was still in a position to restore their goods to the friars, and that he did, unless his men had already purloined them. The incident gives a rare glimpse of Owain's character and humour.[6]

By midsummer 1404 Owain's writ ran throughout most of Wales. The English still held eight castles round the edge of north Wales: Welshpool, Oswestry, Flint, Rhuddlan, Denbigh, Conwy, Beaumaris and Caernarfon, but the country outside them was controlled by Owain's troops. Owain's power was at its zenith. In August there was an air of despondency in a review of the situation by the council. The Cheshire revenues of the Prince of Wales were not enough to maintain the Mortimer castle of Denbigh, as well as the prince's own castles in north Wales, and the king was asked for a grant of £1,000. He would have been even less pleased at having to approve a truce between the people of Shropshire and 'the land of Wales', because the lord of Powys was in a similar position. Nothing could illustrate the ascendancy of Owain Glyn Dŵr at this time more conclusively than this humiliation of the King of England and his council: they were unable to rule Wales, and were forced in effect to recognise her independence.[7]

The latest handout of £1,000, like the previous one, may have resulted from Prince Henry again confiding in Archbishop Arundel. He was not under indenture and received no money for defending

114

the Marches. His council had entered into bonds for such large sums of money that he had had to pawn a valuable piece of silver, which he explained when writing to the council from Worcester on 26 June. He informed the archbishop that Convocation had sequestered the fruits of the priory of Little Malvern because the prior was absent from its meeting. This was patently unjust as he had received no summons. Moreover, 'the said Prior has covenanted to sustain great charges to guard the English March toward Wales against the malice of the rebels', and could not meet his obligations. The prince hoped that the archbishop would countermand the sequestration, and ask the Bishop of Worcester 'if he could aid the guard of the said march with his men and goods, for the salvation of the peace and of his possessions'. In other words, everyone must contribute to the common cause, since Prince Henry would need as much money as he could get. In July he took over from Richard of York, basing hinself and his household at Hereford and Leominster, where they were to remain at his cost into the following year, guarding the river valleys against the Welsh, and closely supervising military operations.[8]

The signs are that Prince Henry was now determined to take the offensive and wrest the initiative from Owain Glyn Dŵr. This could explain a serious Welsh defeat which occurred at about this time, and of which the only evidence which we have is provided by Gruffydd Hiraethog:

> In the same year was the slaughter of the Welsh on Campstone Hill [Camstwn], and another of the English at Craig y Dorth, between Penclawdd and Monmouth town. Here the more part of the English were slain and they were chased up to the town gate.

Campston Hill is near the Lancastrian castle of Grosmont, and Craig y Dorth in the Trothy valley near Monmouth. There is every reason to think that the English were led by Richard Beauchamp, Earl of Warwick, who had impressed the Prince of Wales so much with his well-armed men, and was in the area at about that time. It is possible that he almost captured Owain himself, and seized his banner from its bearer, Ellis ap Richard. A picture which may represent this feat is in an illustrated biography of Earl Richard, who was to become one of the most distinguished Englishmen of his time. This book is well known for its fine scenes of warfare in the fifteenth century. The Welsh then avenged this bloody defeat by the English with a pursuit and a massacre of their foes, but it was a Pyrrhic victory; none would have seen more clearly than Owain that the English were more numerous and could stand such heavy losses more readily. Next year the Welsh would suffer crushing disasters in Gwent, turning the tide at last against Owain Glyn Dŵr.[9]

Owain was already well on the way towards establishing an independent Principality of Wales. He began negotiations for a French alliance in the spring of 1404. The King of France, Charles VI, was born in 1368, nearly a year after his late brother-in-law, Richard II of England. In 1392 he had gone mad and never fully recovered, but during his lucid periods tended to favour the Duke of Orléans, who advised continuing the war with England, but was bitterly opposed by the Duke of Burgundy. The early reign of Charles VI had been marked by grave civil disorders, and by a disaster comparable with Crécy or Agincourt: in 1396 a crusading army, mostly of picked French knights, had been massacred by the Turks on the Danube at Nicopolis. The political state of France was thus exceedingly precarious, and the French were not as dangerous to England as they had been under the able Charles V. Nevertheless, the Orléanist party wanted to give all possible aid to the Scots and Welsh against 'Henry of Lancaster', as they called the king who had deposed the pro-French Richard II. Henry had sent Richard's French Queen Isabelle home to her father without her dowry, thus surrendering 'a valuable bargaining counter'. He was diplomatically isolated, but hoped that he could restore the Anglo-Breton alliance of Edward III's time by marrying Joan, widow of Duke John IV of Brittany, and secure a much-needed naval ally. But hostilities continued between English and Breton seamen, who gave their active support to Owain Glyn Dŵr at a crucial stage in the war.[10]

Another aspect of foreign affairs which concerned Owain was the Great Schism. From 1309 until 1378 all popes had resided at

Avignon, where they were controlled by the French kings, and tried to mediate between France and England. In 1378 a rival pope was elected at Rome; he and the Avignon pope excommunicated each other. Both then sought allies, and encouraged wars between Christian princes which were cynically called crusades. The kings of France and Scotland supported the Avignon pope, and the English were loyal to the one at Rome. So at the moment was Owain Glyn Dŵr, as this important example shows. Lewis ab Ieuan was formerly rector of Byford, by which name he is usually known, a church on the Wye above Hereford. After many years at Rome, in April 1404 the pope had made him Bishop of Bangor. Owain found him a valuable councillor, but in 1406 it finally became necessary, in order to maintain the French alliance, for Owain to transfer his allegiance to the Avignon pope. In 1404 another able Welsh churchman joined Owain: John Trefor, an adviser to Henry IV, who had been consecrated Bishop of St. Asaph at Rome in 1395. He had been in good standing with the king, and in 1399 had advised parliament to conciliate the rebels.[11]

After the recent humiliation of Henry IV, and the Welsh successes that winter, the time was ripe for Owain to approach the King of France. The *Religieux* (Monk) of Saint-Denys explains in his history that Owain thought the French the bravest of all the nations and natural allies for the Welsh. Owain was also encouraged by the fact that he was related to Owain Lawgoch, who had died in the service of Charles V. On 10 May 1404, at Dolgellau, 'Owain, by the grace of God Prince of Wales' wrote to Charles VI, commending 'Master Griffin Young, doctor of decretals, our chancellor, and John Hanmer, our very dear cousin'. Gruffydd Young had been in favour with Henry IV, but had gone over to Owain in 1404; later he was appointed Bishop of Bangor by the Avignon pope, replacing Lewis Byford. The envoys were royally entertained, and their requests were promptly granted: for arms to be bought in Paris, embarked on the Seine and transported safely to Wales. They were also promised that, at an opportune moment, a corps of troops under Jacques de Bourbon, Count of La Marche, would be sent to help Owain. Negotiations with the Count and the Bishop of Chartres followed, leading to a formal league on 14 July.

Owain's letter and the treaty are in the French National Archives. The alliance was directed against 'Henry of Lancaster, adversary and enemy of both parties, and against his adherents'. The count of La Marche was advised as to the best ports in Wales, the best routes, and the most fertile and best provisioned areas.

> The king, who was then in good health, and who had loaded the envoy with presents, talked familiarly with him about the state, way of life and customs of the Welsh, and asked him what his brother [Owain] loved best in the world. On the envoy replying that it was arms, the king, in order to please the Prince of Wales, gave to the ambassador at the moment of his departure a royal, gilded helmet, a cuirass and a sword, and charged him to offer them to his brother.[12]

It is a pity that we have to rely on Adam of Usk, that most ungracious of witnesses, for one of the most important events in Owain's career:

> Owen and his hillmen, even in their misery, at Machynlleth, usurping the right of conquest and other marks of royalty, albeit to his own confusion, held, or counterfeited or made pretence of holding parliaments.

Owain may have used as a model for a Welsh parliament an assembly called by Hywel Dda at Hendy-gwyn-ar-daf (Whitland) in Carmarthenshire in the tenth century. Machynlleth was well placed in the centre of Wales and in the area which Owain controlled; it was also near one of his newly-won castles, Aberystwyth, and within reach of the other, Harlech, which he had made his capital. With his experience, Owain based his state on the English pattern, with his own chancery and seals. During excavations at Harlech in 1923 one of Owain's personal possessions was found: a bronze boss from the martingale of his horse, with four lions rampant, his device as Prince of Wales, and probably lost when he had held court at Harlech, for there is no evidence that he was in the castle during the siege. (This poigant token of a great man has a parallel in English history in the Alfred Jewel from the marshes of Athelney).[13]

It is always said that another parliament was called at Harlech, but the date is as obscure as that of the Machynlleth assembly. In a letter to the king dated 30 July, probably in 1405, Sir John Stanley said that he had been told by two gentlemen from Flint, David Whitmore and Jevan ap Meredith that Owain had called the most important men who were obedient to him from every commote in Wales. The purpose of this assembly was to offer to make a treaty with the king, but nothing more was heard of this proposal, or of the parliament itself.[14]

The main object of any English king in calling Parliament was usually to raise money, though it was also an occasion for majesty and nobility to be on display. No doubt Owain had both of these aims in mind. It is impossible to say whether he was able to raise any taxes, though it does not seem very likely when the normal administration of the country had broken down. Also he had the immensely expensive problem of financing a war. In 1407-1408 Prince Henry's 2,400 soldiers cost £6,825 for only six months; hardly any magnate received that amount per annum. War was expected to pay for itself; the *chevauchée* was intended both to plunder the enemy and to break his resistance by destroying his resources. The English example was followed by the Welsh with their raids into those parts of Wales, like Pembroke, which were hostile to the cause, and into the English border shires. These areas were also made to pay a sort of Danegeld. There were even accusations that Owain received large sums in cash or kind from well-wishers in England. Such a resounding coup as the capture and ransoming of Lord Grey of Ruthin was a fortunate bonus, but lesser prisoners were also seized. Looted livestock must have been an important means of financing the war and feeding the troops for both sides, but with so many enthusiastic raiders in the field it is a moot question as to how much reached Owain's coffers. There was also a limit to the endurance of a poor country like Wales. Before the war Wales could produce £60,000 a year, but by 1405 two Gwent lordships, Newport and Abergavenny, were yielding nothing, which was probably the general pattern.[15]

Owain's assumption of his high title and resounding powers did not win universal acceptance in Wales; some of the southern *uchelwyr* were bitterly resentful. One of his enemies was a Brecon gentleman, a small, red-haired man named Dafydd ap Llywelyn, generally known as Dafydd Gam, meaning 'One eyed'. His family had for a long time been tenants and servants of the former earls of Hereford. It is hardly surprising that Welshmen with such long traditions of profitable service were hostile to Owain Glyn Dŵr. While making this point Professor Davies also quotes David Powel, the sixteenth century historian, who says of Dafydd Gam that 'he was a great stickler for the House of Lancaster'. Thomas Ellis tells the following story:

> David Gam, a gentleman of Brecknockshire, came hither upon his summons, but with a bad intention to murder Owen for his master King Henry's sake and service: but David's plot being discovered, he was seized upon and committed to prison, and he would surely have been put to death, had not the greatest upholders of Owen's cause interceded for his life ... David, being pardoned and set at liberty, went home to his country, but, contrary to his promise of fidelity, vexed exceedingly the friends of Owen. Owen, hearing this, entered the marches, destroying all before him. He burned David Gam's house, but David kept himself out of his reach.

There is, however, a serious difficulty about this story: Walter Bower, who was well informed about the severe defeat which the Welsh were to suffer at Pwll Melyn in May 1405, says that Dafydd Gam was one of the captains in the English service on that occasion. As a member of the Prince's retinue, involved in military operations in the southern Marches, Dafydd Gam was unlikely to have attended the Machynlleth parliament. The fate of Owain Lawgoch, however, shows that the English were quite capable of arranging the murder of a dangerous enemy. A Welshman in the royal service like Dafydd Gam could have pretended to go over to

Owain's cause and try to kill him, well aware that he was unlikely to survive the attempt. Whatever truth there may be in this story, it is certain that in 1412 Dafydd Gam did fall into Owain's hands, and was ransomed by the king's order. If he really did plot to kill Owain his fate would surely have been that of Hywel Sele, a cousin of Owain, who tried to shoot Owain while they were out hunting near Dolgellau. He was killed without delay and his body was hidden, it is said, in a hollow tree.[16]

The year 1404, which ended in gloom for the English, fell far short of Owain's hopes. The English were then fighting the French and Bretons in the Channel; they were aware of Owain's overtures to the French, and alarmed at the implications. Their fears were realised when in May a French ship was taken into Dartmouth, having aboard three French knights and two esquires, also a Welsh esquire who was perhaps Owain's liaison officer, though we know neither his name nor anything else about him. The king ordered the sheriff of Devon to send them all to him for questioning. At midsummer the English raided the south coast of Brittany whose Admiral, Guillaume Sieur de Chastel, had driven them off and defeated their fleet with heavy loss, capturing many ships and prisoners. He then landed at Dartmouth with 1,200 troops but was defeated in his turn and driven off by the English.[17]

The omens seemed right for Jacques de Bourbon, who commanded his fleet to assemble at Harfleur, and also at Brest, where he was joined by twenty Spanish ships. Richard Young, Bishop of Bangor, warned King Henry on 2 August, saying that they numbered 500 'bassinettis' and 200 crossbowmen; bassinets were the pointed helmets worn by men of rank. The most reliable chronicler, the Monk of Saint-Denys, says that there were sixty-two ships, 800 men-at-arms 'with a great number of crossbowmen'; Enguerrand de Monstrelet gives the numbers as 1,200 'knights and esquires'. The Monk says that they sailed from Brest and Harfleur about mid-August. According to Monstrelet, they first sacked Plymouth and, sailing to Saltash, returned to St. Malo, fearing an English attack; they lost twelve ships with all hands. Another chronicler, Pierre Cochon, remarks acidly that 'they burned one poor village, a fine feat by a great number of knights, and then went home having done nothing more. Thus they spent 100,000 francs ... money belonging to the poor people of France.' The Monk, like other Frenchmen, felt thoroughly ashamed of what is called, in a chapter title, the 'Malheureuse issue de l'expedition du comte de la Marche'. Wind, weather and sea had all been favourable.

Perhaps the count was negligent and too fond of the pleasures of Paris, but there was a lot of naval activity at the time in the Channel. The Spaniards as well as the Bretons were eager to attack the English, and La Marche's men may have seen more prospects of rich pickings in piratical raids on the English coast. The French repulse in Plymouth Sound was followed by an equally unlucky Breton attempt on Falmouth. La Marche's expedition never passed Land's End, but frittered away the sailing season in this ignoble cruising. The basic reason for this dismal performance was probably the lack of any effective leadership in France.[18]

The sense of stalemate persists into 1405, and the continuing dominance of the Welsh can be seen in a letter of 7 February to the council from Thomas Fitzalan, Earl of Arundel. Commenting on an ordinance passed by Parliament in October 1404 to guard the Marches of Wales, Arundel wrote: 'I have been ordered by the King our sovereign Lord to remain at Oswestry on the march of North Wales for 8 weeks continually with 30 men-at-arms and 100 archers.' Only one week was left of the time stipulated in his indentures, and no further ordinance had been made for the marches, 'to the great joy and comfort of the rebels of our lord the King.' When the time was up he must withdraw, having too few troops; 'the said rebels are as high and haughty as they are at present because the said ordinance is deferred and delayed.'[19]

In February came a rather melodramatic affair which could have had serious consequences for Henry IV. Lady Despenser arranged the escape of the young Earl of March and his brother Roger from their imprisonment at Windsor Castle, probably intending that they should go to Owain Glyn Dŵr. The plot involved her brother Duke Edward of York, who was owed £13,000 by the king for his services in Wales and Gascony, but had little chance of repayment. The party got as far as Cheltenham before they were caught. Lady Despenser accused York of plotting to assassinate the king, and called for a champion to take him on in a duel, offering herself to be burnt if York won. William Maidstone, her esquire, threw down his gage before the king, and York threw down his; but the king ordered Duke Thomas of Lancaster to arrest York, who was taken to the Tower. Thomas Mowbray, Earl Marshal and son of Henry IV's enemy, was accused of being privy to what the Latin text quaintly calls 'the subtraction of the March boys'; he admitted that he knew of it, but gave it little encouragement, and the king forgave him. Allegations were also made against Archbishop Arundel, who refuted them without difficulty. York got away with a spell of imprisonment at the Lancastrian castle of Pevensey and was released in October. 'Perhaps', suggests Mr. T.B. Pugh, 'he managed to buy his pardon from the insolvent king.' York's military and political talents were so useful to the king that he was restored to the council at a salary of £200 a year. The affair must have shaken Henry; he was merciful to Lady Despenser and the boys, but he vented his rage on the unfortunate locksmith who had made the keys to the boys' quarters.[20]

It is probably no coincidence that this affair took place at about the same time as the sealing of the Tripartite Indenture in the archdeacon's house at Bangor, a famous event in Owain's career. Shakespeare's scene contains the memorable exchange of wit, argument and repartee between Owain and Hotspur, but he places it *before* the battle of Shrewsbury. The Tripartite Indenture and the attempt to take the Mortimer boys to Wales seem to have been components in the latest plot against Henry IV, which is borne out by the fact that one of the plotters was the recently pardoned Thomas Mowbray. The master-mind was, as usual, the Earl of Northumberland, pardoned for his part in the 1403 rising. Another conspirator was Lord Bardolf, formerly a royal councillor. It is uncertain who were the English representatives at Bangor, though we know that Mortimer was not one of them and that Hotspur was dead. Bishops Trefor and Byford signed for Owain. The treaty gave Wales and the border shires to Owain, the region north of Trent to Northumberland, and southern England to Mortimer. There is an element of fantasy about it, unlike the pragmatic and forward-looking policies which Owain was proposing for Wales. We are again in the wonder-world of Brutus, who divided the kingdom with his brothers:

> Owain and his heirs are to have the whole of Cambria or Wales, divided from Leogrea, which is commonly called England, by the bounds set out below, namely: following the River Severn from its estuary as far as the north gate of the city of Worcester, and from that gate directly to the ash trees, commonly called in the Cambrian or Welsh tongue *Onennau Meigiawn*, which grow on the road leading from Bridgnorth to Kinver; thence directly by the high road, which is commonly called the old or ancient way, as far as the head or source of the River Trent; thence directly to the head or source of the River Mersey, thence following that river to the sea within the bounds described above.[21]

There is a hamlet called Six Ashes where an ancient group of these trees once stood, nearly half way between Kinver and Bridgnorth on the A458 road, parallel to which, and about four miles north, was a Roman road roughly following the B4176. This looks like the 'ancient way' referred to; it passed a village significantly called Chesterton (from *castra*, a Roman fort), near the road from Bridgnorth to Wolverhampton, and joined Watling Street near the foot of the Wrekin. Leogrea was an old Welsh name for England. There was a sound reason for the Welsh to claim the area west of the Severn, as it would be a good buffer zone against English aggression, while the river itself formed a clearer border than Offa's Dyke. On the other hand, that region had been part of the Anglian kingdom of Mercia, and its English inhabitants could hardly be expected to take kindly to this act of annexation by Wales.[22]

Owain's hopes and plans were to prove illusory; his fortunes were soon to receive blows from which they never really recovered. In March 1405 the Prince of Wales wrote exultantly to his father from Hereford, announcing at last a major victory:

On 11 March your rebels from the districts of Glamorgan, Morgannwg, Usk, lower and upper Gwent assembled to the number of 8,000 men, by their own account. They advanced the said Wednesday morning and burned part of your town of Grosmont in your lordship of Monmouth. I at once sent my well-beloved cousin Lord Talbot and a small detachment of my household. They were joined by your faithful and valiant knights William Newport and John Greyndor, who together were but a small force ... And there, by the aid of the blessed Trinity, your people won the field and vanquished all the said rebels.

It should be noted that this victory was won by mobile companies acting in concert, under orders from the prince's headquarters at Hereford. Talbot was in charge of the household troops; Greyndor and Newport were leading a separate company who probably included the Radnor garrison. The dead were reckoned at 800 to 1,000, in both the battle and the pursuit, the prisoners having been questioned 'on pain of death'. Grosmont was the birthplace of Henry, the first Duke of Lancaster, whose daughter Blanche had married John of Gaunt.[23]

Worse was soon to follow for Owain's cause. Gruffydd Hiraethog writes:

A slaughter of the Welsh on Pwll Melin Mountain, near Usk, where Gruffydd ab Owen was taken prisoner. It was now that the tide began to turn against Owen and his men. At this time Glamorgan made its submission to the English, except a few who went to Gwynedd to their master.

Walsingham gives the date as 5 May, which is usually accepted. The site of Pwll Melyn, which means Yellow Pool, has not been identified. We rely largely on Adam of Usk for the details:

Griffith, son of Owen, with a great following made
assault ... on the castle of Usk, which had been put into
some condition for defence, and wherein at that time
were the lord Grey of Codnor, Sir John Greyndor, and
many other soldiers of the king. For these same lords,
sallying forth, took him captive, and pursued his men
even to the hill-country of Higher Gwent, through the
river Usk, there slew with fire and the edge of the
sword many of them, and above all the abbot of
[Llantarnam]. And they crushed them without ceasing,
driving them through the monk's wood where the said
Griffith was taken. And their captives, to the number
of three hundred, they beheaded in front of the same
castle near Ponfald; and certain prisoners of noble birth
they brought, along with the said Griffith, to the king.
The which Griffith, being held in captivity for six
years, at last in the Tower of London was cut off by a
pestilence.

If Adam was correctly informed, the battle ended in a cold-
blooded massacre worse than any atrocity in the Rising we know
of, including the killings at Radnor.

Abbot Walter Bower's account of Pwll Melyn is of great interest;
he first confirms what Gruffydd Hiraethog says about the submission of Glamorgan, and then the successful direction of strategy by
the prince:

When Henry prince of England, who still held the title
of Wales, aimed to attack with a large army and totally
destroy Wales, he sent Lords Cobham and Grey of
Codnor, and David Gam, to exterminate them.

Bower seems not to have realised that Henry was responding to
another Welsh assault on Gwent, but he agrees with Adam about
Grey, who with Greyndor would have been commanding the
Brecon and Radnor troops. Bower may well be right about Cobham
the future title of Sir John Oldcastle, one of the prince's most

trusted knights; perhaps he and Dafydd Gam were in charge of some household troops sent by Henry from Hereford to join Grey and Greyndor, as on the previous occasion before the battle of Grosmont. Bower goes on to say that many were killed, and that the prisoners included Gruffydd ab Owain, whom he wrongly calls Prince of Wales, 'that not insignificant warrior, Hopkyn ap Thomas', and many others.[24]

Bower's most notable contribution to the tragic story of Pwll Melyn is the obituary of a Welsh warrior monk, John ap Hywel, Abbot of Llantarnam. This was a Cistercian abbey near Caerleon, whose mother house was Strata Florida. John deplored the oppressive government under which the Welsh suffered, but denounced the Welsh themselves for their vicious and evil ways. He called them to live in the same way as the last of the Britons in their struggle with the Saxons, and to fight faithfully for country, lands, possessions, children and wives: to suffer for the liberty of their fatherland even to death. He heard confessions, gave absolutions, and inspired the men by every means to prepare for battle. The perfect military chaplain, he met a soldier's death with seventy other Welshmen, earning, it was hoped, the reward of eternal life. His heroic conduct was contrasted with that of an unnamed friar, who had promised the soldiers before the battle that they would sup with Christ before their innocent blood, shed by the enemy, had cooled. When they saw him seeking safety in flight they exclaimed: 'O holy friar, do you hope to return to the battle, so that in accordance with your promise, you will by this fate deserve to sup with Christ?' His answer was: 'I assure you that it is for your good that I am fasting today, and therefore it is not convenient for me to sup with the Lord tonight.' It is a relief to be able to end the grim story of the battle of Pwll Melyn on a lighter note.[25]

At first it seemed to the English that their greatest enemy had also fallen. According to Ellis,

> among the dead bodies was found one much like unto Owen, whom they supposed, and gave out, to be Owen that was slain; but upon further enquiry, it was found that it was not Owen, but his brother Tudor, who very

127

much resembled him, and was often taken for him being hardly distinguished asunder, only Owen had a little wart above one of his eyebrows, which Tudor had not. The report of Owen's overthrow and death disheartened the Welsh exceedingly; insomuch that the people of Glamorgan submitted unto the king, save some few, who went unto Owen, when they understood he was alive.

Even without this false rumour Pwll Melyn was an appalling calamity, and armed intervention by the French was more vital now than ever before.[26]

In June came a third disaster. The deputy lieutenant in Ireland, Stephen Scrope, attacked Anglesey; our knowledge of what happened depends on an eighteenth century historian of Beaumaris named William Owen. Scrope beat the Welsh at Rhos-y-meirch and recovered Beaumaris. It is uncertain when or how the Welsh had taken this concentric castle, the most formidable of all the Edwardian fortresses, but it had fallen since August 1404, when it had still been in English hands. The Welsh fled across the Menai Straits into Snowdonia, and the English ravaged the island, taking away valuable loot to adorn the churches of Dublin. The loss of Anglesey, the granary of north Wales, was catastrophic and foreshadowed final defeat.[27]

CHAPTER NINE

The French in Wales, 1405

King Henry IV now felt encouraged to invade south Wales again, but no sooner had he reached Hereford in mid-May than he heard bad news from the north. The Earl of Northumberland, the indispensable warden of the East March toward Scotland, was pardoned after the battle of Shrewsbury, but was now again in rebellion, with Mowbray, Lord Bardolf, the Archbishop of York, and Bishops Byford and Trefor as Owain's envoys. Henry acted as resolutely as when he had heard of Hotspur's revolt before Shrewsbury; he was at Derby on 28 May, and in ten days had captured and executed the archbishop and Mowbray. Northumberland himself, Bardolf, and the Welsh bishops escaped to Scotland. Archbishop Richard Scrope was an aristocrat and a member of a rich Yorkshire family, widely respected for his austerity and piety. Richard II had raised him to the see of York; he had supported the king's deposition, but was by nature a reformer rather than a rebel. He had joined Northumberland only to protest against the heavy taxes born by clergy and laity. His execution made him a martyr, and Henry was accused of the crime of sacrilege. It laid yet another burden on the conscience of a king who had always tried to be a devout churchman. There seems little doubt that as a result Henry's health became even worse; he already suffered from a weak heart and epilepsy.[1]

The northern rebellion distracted the king's attention from Wales, and offered the Duke of Orléans a golden opportunity of sending an effective force to help Owain Glyn Dŵr. French military assistance was all the more urgently needed to restore Welsh morale, severely shaken by the disasters at Grosmont and Pwll Melyn. The Monk of St. Denys says that 'the dukes of France' wished to fulfil the promise of aid to Owain Glyn Dŵr and to remove the shame of Bourbon's failure by some notable feat of arms. They resolved to send 'auxiliary troops commanded by illustrious knights, the marshal de Rieux, the sieur de Hugueville, grand-master of the crossbows of France, and the sieur le Borgue de la Heuse'. Though the Monk does not give the full names of 'these three captains', he seems otherwise to be correct. The master of crossbows was Jean de Hangest, sieur de Hugueville. Robert de la Heuse, seigneur des Ventes, was known as Le Borgue (One-eyed). Cochon names Hangest and Heuse but omits the marshal. Monstrelet says that the leaders were a marshal of France whom he later calls de Tries, and the master of crossbows. The Monk says that the army was levied in Brittany and Normandy; it consisted of 800 *hommes d'élite* (men of rank), 600 crossbowmen and 1,200 light troops. The *hommes d'élite* were the heavy cavalry: knights, esquires and other superior men-at-arms.

According to the Monk, they had to wait a month for a favourable wind, but towards the end of July they sailed from Brest in two large vessels of war and thirty small ships. Monstrelet speaks of their being delayed for fifteen days by a contrary wind. If this means that they were becalmed at sea, it might help to explain the disaster mentioned by Walsingham: during the voyage nearly all the horses died of thirst owing to a shortage of water. This may have been due to inexperience in a difficult transport operation, or to incompetence. As horses cannot vomit, seasickness could have been the cause. Whatever the reason, it was just the sort of mishap which the French would have preferred to forget. The loss of their trained war horses, or destriers, would have very seriously reduced the fighting power of the heavy cavalry. Early in August the French sailed into Milford Haven, where the Monk says that Owain was waiting for them with 10,000 men; Monstrelet, however, places this meeting at Tenby.[2]

Of all Welsh harbours Milford Haven is nearest to France, a fact which was to have profound consequences in the fifteenth century.

Two French expeditions used it during the Wars of the Roses. French, Breton and Irish troops are thought to have landed there in 1461 to join Jasper Tudor's army which was defeated at Mortimer's Cross by Edward of York. In 1485 a stronger French force than either of the previous two landed there, led by Henry Tudor with his English exiles. His challenge to an unpopular usurper won him increasing support in Wales and England, which was why the French at last succeeded in causing a political revolution in England.

Henry IV heard the news of the landing on 7 August, when he was at his castle of Pontefract. He at once issued a commission of array, ordering the sheriffs of Hereford and seventeen other shires to bring to Hereford 'all knights, esquires, yeomen and other fencible men ... the lord of Hugueville and many other of our French enemies' had arrived at Milford Haven in order to help 'our Welsh rebels' in their evil intentions towards 'our faithful lieges'. The news had probably reached Hereford on its way north. The usual pompous orders for general mobilisation, over the name of a king who inspired little confidence, may have been read with a sense of weariness and resignation, but the prospect of fighting the French as well as the Welsh could have had its appeal.[3]

Meanwhile the Welsh and French were treating Pembrokeshire, 'Little England beyond Wales', as enemy territory. The Monk of St. Denys tells the story so lucidly that it seems best to follow him for the main details, and fit in other evidence as it arises. The allies advanced with fire and sword on Haverfordwest. Monstrelet tells us that its captain was Thomas Earl of Arundel, but this is thought unlikely. From its strong castle 300 men in full armour and many archers made a determined sortie. The French and Welsh had the better of the fierce battle which followed; they killed forty men, captured sixteen and drove the rest off. But the castle and town were too strong to be taken, despite the French siege artillery. The defenders lost seventy killed; the Welsh casualties are not mentioned. It is said that the French lost very few men, but among the dead was 'a famous knight, called Patrouillart de Trie, who was deeply mourned by all his companions.' Pennant says that his brother was Renaud de Trie, Admiral of France, one of the commanders of the French force, the others being Marshal de Rieux and Jean de Hangest. Monstrelet does not mention Marshal de Rieux; perhaps by Marshal de Tries he means the admiral, whom neither the Monk nor Cochon includes among the French leaders.

After several assaults the French abandoned the siege of Haverfordwest. Meanwhile an independent company of their troops won a consolation prize by takiing Picton Castle, four miles east of Haverfordwest, and on the way to the next objective:

> The same day a detachment guarding the foragers pushed forward as far as the castle of Picot, and forced it to surrender after the first assault. The French went away laden with booty from wasting the country, and marched with fire and sword, arriving at a fortified port, called Tenby. Having resolved with one accord to besiege and take this town, they posted their cross-bowmen all around it, and set up their siege engines. They were actively making their preparations, and were on the point of delivering the first assault, when they saw in the distance a fleet of thirty ships, well provisioned and full of men of war, who were coming to the aid of the inhabitants.

Their own ships were beached, they could not float them and, incredible as it may seem to us, they lost their nerve and retreated, hoping to avert the enemy's attention. The panic quickly increased; though they were not being pursued, and had with them 2,000 Welsh 'knights', they fled in disorder, abandoning their siege engines, artillery and baggage. The Monk may not have been fully aware of the recent disasters in Gwent, or of their probable effects on Welsh morale. The understandable anxiety of the French for their ships, their lifeline with home, can also be detected here and on other occasions.

A note of disapproval can now be heard through the measured tones of the Monk. 'After this shameful flight, having burned, as was their custom, the villages which they reached en route, they arrived before the strong castle of St. Clears and prepared to besiege it.' The garrison were ready to give in if Carmarthen did so, but the Monk does not tell us the result of this curious offer, or of the siege of St. Clears. On the other hand, he recognised that Carmarthen with its strong walls was very important to the king of England. 'The archers and men-at-arms, who formed the garrison [of Carmarthen], made frequent sorties and upset the Welsh very much. Also the Prince of Wales [as the Monk calls Owain] swore an oath that he would not leave until he was master of the place.' The Welsh and French took up their stations on each side. French sappers armed with pickaxes cut trenches and breached the wall.

The defenders, fearing that the French were about to scale the walls, decided to parley. They offered to give up their arms and goods as long as they were spared and could stay in the town. Owain seems to have been more generous than they expected; according to Walsingham, he gave them letters patent, whereby they could go free to any of the King's towns in Wales, or in England if they preferred. It was a useful opportunity of displaying his princely power. The Welsh, who had not yet reached the wall and had perhaps been bystanders, praised the French for their valour, accepted this offer, and sacked and burned the town, destroying most of the walls. 'From there the two armies marched on a strong castle named Cardigan whose inhabitants, frightened by the fate of their neighbours, were eager to capitulate.'[4]

After taking Carmarthen (and presumably Cardigan) the allies started their advance on England. It is a pity that the Monk refers to the journey to Worcester only as a march of sixty leagues; we now have to rely on the less sure guidance of Monstrelet, but must be grateful for his account which is the only one we have of this remarkable affair. The army traversed Glamorgan; 'le pais de Linorguie', Monstrelet's phrase, was probably the nearest the French could get to the Welsh name, as Dr. Nash, the historian of Worcestershire, suggests. It was certainly the easiest route into England if they wanted to challenge Henry of Lancaster. Another clue to the route taken is that the French were much interested in the original Round Table of Arthur, which was the usual name for the Roman amphitheatre at Caerleon, also 'the noble abbey of Arthur', probably Llantarnam. They were no doubt equally intrigued to hear that Carmarthen meant 'the city of Merlin', so strong was the appeal of any story from 'the Matter of Britain' among the chivalry of those days.[5]

We can only guess which route they took from Caerleon; the shortest would have been via Monmouth and Ross to Worcester. The disadvantage of going via Hereford was that it was not only a less direct way into England, but also that Hereford was a very strong city with a large royal castle, well manned and the main base for operations against south Wales; it would be a tougher problem than Carmarthen and much better avoided. When the allies reached Worcester they sacked the suburbs, probably the area west of the Severn, which would have been hard to cross; Monstrelet does not support the local tradition that they broke into the city itself.

About the end of the sixteenth century the antiquary William Camden was exploring the country west of Worcester, and wrote: 'About seven miles below Temebury, the river [Teme] passeth under Woodberry-hill, remarkable for an old intrenchment on the top, vulgarly called Owen Glendowr's camp; which notwithstanding is probably of greater antiquity.' Woodbury Hill is a large Iron Age hill-fort south of Great Witley, and eight miles north-west of Worcester. It was visited by Thomas Pennant in the company of Dr. Nash; the accounts of the two historians are very similar. Today Woodbury Hill is accepted as the position where, about the middle of August, the Franco-Welsh army fortified themselves.[6]

After hearing of the French landing and sending out his orders, King Henry took no decisive action until 19 August when he was at Leicester. The news of the Franco-Welsh advance into England spurred him on to demonstrate again how fast he could march, as when he had heard of the rebellions of Hotspur and Scrope. In three days he reached Worcester, and soon arrived at Great Witley. Nash suggests that he may have taken up his station about a mile north of Woodbury on Abberley Hill, which is very steep and too sharp-topped to carry a hill fort, though his army could have camped on the level ground to the west, near the Clock Tower. This agrees with Monstrelet's account of what followed:

> Each party drew up in order of battle on two eminences, having a valley between them, and each

waiting for the attack of its opponent. This contest,
who should commence the battle, lasted for eight days;
and they were regularly every morning drawn up in
battle array, and remained in this state until evening,
during which time there were many skirmishes
between the two parties, when upwards of 200 of
either side were slain, and more wounded. On the side
of France three knights were slain, namely Sir
Patrouillart de Trie, brother to the marshal of France,
the Sieur de Martelonne, and the Sieur de la Valle.

Patrouillart had probably been killed already at Haverfordwest.
The flat area immediately south of Great Witley, between that
village and the foot of Woodbury Hill, was probably where the
jousting took place. After the disastrous losses of their horses at sea
the French would have been at a grave disadvantage in these chivalrous activities.

The French and Welsh were also much oppressed by
famine and other inconveniences, for only with great
difficulty could they obtain any provision, as the
English had strongly guarded all the passes. At length,
on the eighth day that the two armies had been looking
at each other, the King of England, seeing the enemy
were not afraid of him, retreated to Worcester, but was
pursued by some French and Welsh, who seized on 18
carts laden with provisions and other baggage, upon
which the French and Welsh marched back to Wales.[7]

The position was similar to that at Crécy or Poitiers, as no doubt
both armies realised. On each occasion the King of France had had
a weary and hungry English army at his mercy. He had been
advised to let starvation do its work, but the hotheads had
demanded the chivalric solution, with the most appalling consequences. The same thing was to happen again ten years later at
Agincourt. A medieval general preferred to avoid a pitched battle
unless he had a good chance of victory. Henry IV had nearly lost a

battle two years before; he was, understandably, in no mood to take unnecessary risks. Time was on his side, and he used it in a most admirable and shrewd manner. Ardent young knights and esquires could practise their martial valour and skill in combat with the traditional enemy, winning renown and valuable prisoners for ransom, while they rejoiced at their good fortune in having such chivalrous adventures.

It is not surprising that this deep penetration by a French army into England during the Hundred Years' War seems to have survived in folklore. A recent book on this fascinating but elusive subject offers two examples. In one, Sir John Washbourne of Wichenford, half way between Great Witley and Worcester, took a Frenchman of rank prisoner. Sir John was then absent in the king's army. Lady Washbourne tried to seduce the interesting guest, but he resisted her, and she stabbed him to death. The remorseful lady, ghost story and indelible bloodstains inevitably follow, but the basic details are quite credible, especially as Wichenford is near enough to Woodbury for memories to linger. The other was a tradition in a farming family at Martley, five miles south of Great Witley, that an ancestress had been shot by a Frenchman as she rode pillion behind her husband. Whatever one makes of these stories, they at least match the written records, which those of the Leominster school of history do not. It is of course possible that such stories were made up long after by somemone who had read Nash or Pennant, and felt moved to spin a yarn to enliven a long winter evening.[8]

Despite its ultimate futility, this French invasion of England was the first since Louis, son of Philip II of France, had come with an army to the aid of King John's rebels in 1216. The lack of information about the affair in English chronicles may well be due to acute national embarrassment, but it ought to be better known. The views expressed in a private letter which we are fortunate enough to have were probably pretty generally held. Far from harm's way and probably at her home at Bytham, Lincolnshire, Joan de Bohun, dowager Countess of Hereford and the king's mother-in-law, was writing on 28 October to an old friend, Sir Hugh Waterton. By then the French had probably returned to their base in Pembrokeshire.

The old lady was in a very disgruntled frame of mind, because of accusations against her brother Archbishop Arundel and herself, after the northern rebellion. She expresses herself very oddly, but the gist of her remarks about the enemy invading England and getting as far as Worcester is that she had heard no worse news since the French fleet burned Plymouth [in August 1404]. She had heard nothing about the enemy since but words, maybe a criticism of the conduct of the war by King Henry; the proverb that 'hard word break no bones' may express her feelings. She also seems to think of the sea as the source of ill tidings, in which she is probably referring to the activities of the foreign freebooters at this time, and the fact that they all too often snatched the initiative from the English. It recalls the description of the sea as a wall or a moat in the famous speech by the dying Gaunt in *King Richard II*.[9]

The confrontation at Woodbury Hill had results as decisive as might have ensued from a pitched battle. Henry IV had won an almost bloodless victory over enemies who had penetrated deep into his kingdom. Owain and the French now knew that there was no support for them or their cause in England. They must have been profoundly ignorant of the political situation in England to suppose that anyone seriously believed in Richard II's survival. Even when they had landed in force, the French had not been able to give Owain the help which he needed if Wales was to be free. Owain must have realised, with bitter disappointment, that his last chance had gone and that final defeat was only a matter of time.

We know nothing about the retreat to Pembrokeshire. The direct route from Great Witley is up the Teme valley to Tenbury, and through Leominster and Brecon to Llandovery and Carmarthen. The legend of Owain's capture of Leominster, and occupation of Ivington Camp and other hill-forts after the battle of Pilleth may reflect a tradition that he took that way home with his French allies in 1405; but there is no place name in the Leominster district like 'Owen Glendowr's Camp' to suggest that he was about for any length of time. The hungry retreating army would have done a good deal of damage during its homeward journey unless a truce had been made with the sheriff and other local gentry, who may have agreed to supply them as long as they kept moving on and refrained from looting, the accepted policy in the border counties when buying off Welsh raiders. This would have suited the French; their passage through Herefordshire has left certainly no tradition of pillage.[10]

If the French were hearing the latest news, it would have given them every reason to get back to their ships as fast as possible. Henry IV was ordering a large army to gather at Hereford, and the invaders were in grave danger of having their retreat cut off. Jean de Hangest and Jean de Trie would also have been very concerned by the growing threat to their ships. Walsingham tells us that Lord Berkeley and Henry Pay had burnt fifteen French ships in Milford Haven, but does not say when. Fourteen other ships were intercepted 'sailing towards Wales in support of the said Owen. In these ships the Seneschal of France and seven other named captains were taken prisoners.' This may explain Monstrelet's statement that 'the French fleet was at sea, having on board some men-at-arms to defend it, and made for a port which had been pointed out to them, where they were found by their countrymen on their retreat from England'. We do not know which port this was, but the French may have decided that it was too dangerous to remain in Milford Haven, where it would be harder to escape if the English caught them at anchor. Perhaps there had also been so much plundering that provisions were very scarce, which is what the Monk seems to imply when he says that, after their march, the French were afraid 'of having to suffer from hunger because of the barrenness'; he is very likely referring to the effects of their ravages during their earlier passage. They had reason to beg Owain to let them camp somewhere else till they could have a fleet to carry them home, so 'he gave them three separate quarters where they stayed till the Feast of All Saints'.

All Saints' Day is 1 November, which helps us to date the letter of the Countess of Hereford. After finding their ships, says Monstrelet,

> The Marshal de Tries and the master of the crossbows having embarked with their men on the fleet, put to sea and made sail for the coast of France, and arrived at St. Pol de Leon without any accident. But when they had disembarked, and had visited their men, they found they had lost upwards of sixty men, of whom the three

knights before mentioned were the principal. They then departed, each man to his home, except the commanders who went to wait on the king and the princes of the blood at Paris, by whom they were received with much joy.

The Monk gives more detail; he thought the conduct of the commanders of the expedition outrageous:

> Then, knights and esquires embarked on six little vessels, leaving in Wales 1,200 light troops and 500 crossbowmen under the orders of a Picard esquire, named le Begue de Belay, until they were sent more ships for their return. One must emphatically blame those who returned to France for having abandoned the people who had fought for their glory, who had always been the first in the assaults and had saved them from more than one danger. Meanwhile the nobles, under whose orders the men-at-arms had been placed, stayed loyally with them; they provided generously for their needs, assembled ships from all parts and brought them home towards Lent.

In this outburst the Monk plainly distinguishes the *hommes d'elite* from the ordinary soldiers; they made sure of their berths, apart from a few who, like le Begue de Belay, honourably elected to remain with their men. Thus the losses reported by Monstrelet were only of noblemen. Probably all the surviving crossbowmen and light troops remained behind; there is no record of the casualties among them. The Monk made clear his feelings that their leaders had showed much greater devotion to duty than the senior captains, whose conduct on this occasion may help to explain the poor discipline in French armies so apparent in the battles of the Hundred Years' War. One would have thought that after all the fighting and marching the losses would have been quite severe, though the number given for light troops who were left behind was the same as when they sailed from France, which is unbelievable.

The reports used by the chroniclers indicated heavy fighting; siege operations and assaults are usually very bloody in any age. The losses from sickness, hunger, desertion and exhaustion during a long march could be as heavy as in a battle.[11]

The presence of the French troops for most of the winter enabled the rebels to force their hereditary enemies in Pembrokeshire to pay £200 for a truce lasting from November until 1 May, which had the blessing of Francis Court, now appointed lord of Pembroke by the king. The council expressed their strong disapproval of such an ignominious bargain with the king's rebels, but they were forced to accept the fact that his writ, and that of the Marcher lords, no longer ran in most of Wales. The men of Pembrokeshire were left with no alternative but to pay up, exactly as Shropshire had had to do the previous summer.[12]

After withdrawing their remaining troops during the Lent of 1406, the French made a final attempt later that year to help their allies. They sent twenty-eight troopships which the English intercepted; eight were captured, but the rest escaped and reached Wales. Nothing more is known of this expedition, which cannot have posed a serious threat. Jean de Hangest and his colleagues can have derived no great satisfaction from their recent adventures; he himself had been put to such great expense that he received royal permission to sell his estate of Ayencourt, near Montdidier, for about two hundred *livres*. The Duke of Orléans probably thought that it would be hard to persuade any other nobles to undertake a similar venture, as it was now clear that Owain's military effectiveness was confined to Wales. But Orléans was still in control of royal policy and wished to preserve the Welsh alliance; it is therefore likely that he was behind a royal proclamation of October 1406, which seems to refer to the recent expedition. The reason given for not sending more help to the Welsh was the lack of support from friends of King Richard II. The 'Auld Alliance' of France and Scotland against England had long been used to curb English aggression; a similar alliance with an independent Prince of Wales might have been equally useful, but the outcome of the 1405 expedition had been very disappointing to the French, and disillusionment had resulted.[13]

CHAPTER TEN

Owain Glyn Dŵr at Bay, 1406 to 1412

The French expedition of 1405 had failed partly because it found no support from friends of Richard II, who was presumed by most people to be dead, or from anyone else in southern England. Henry IV had defeated his northern rebels, and was at last firmly in control of his kingdom. There was now no threat from any magnate, especially the Mortimers, who were in no position to assert their claim to the English crown. Considering that Owain's hold over Wales was beginning to crumble as early as 1406, it is remarkable that he was able to go on fighting for another six years.

King Henry IV had already sent out orders on 19 August for a muster at Hereford; on the 29th a further writ went to the sheriff of Lancaster for more soldiers. The royal army then marched to relieve Coety Castle in Glamorgan. Wales again rose to the occasion with the most ghastly storms and floods. The Welsh captured forty royal baggage wagons, with provisions, treasure and jewellery, which must have been a welcome addition to Owain's warchest. The king and his sodden troops withdrew to Hereford, and Owain was safe from further effective action for the rest of the year.[1]

During the autumn a mysterious state of affairs was revealed which, if true, gave some disturbing indications as to the sources of Owain Glyn Dŵr's funds. Professor Ralph Griffiths has given us an enthralling glimpse into the underworld of fifteenth-century England. First of all, John Oke of Newent, Gloucestershire, was a livestock thief with an extensive practice stretching as far as Essex and Berkshire. In August 1405 he was in prison at Huntingdon where he made a startling confession to the sheriff and coroner, with an accusation of treason against one of the king's trusted officers, Sir John Scudamore. The same month another thief, John Veyse from Holbeach in Lincolnshire, who had been arrested in February, was examined in the same gaol and told a very similar story. Under the shadow of the gallows, they had nothing to lose by 'appealing' others of treason; but we have already seen from the Oxford affair how grave were the risks run by an 'approver' if he tried the patience of judges and juries too far. Oke and Veyse exceeded this limit, and in December they were convicted and hanged.

Since the start of the revolt Oke claimed to have collected £6,870 from twenty-seven of Owain's English friends. Eleven of them were members of religious orders and gave £4,100, of which £1,400 came from St. Edmund's Abbey in Suffolk. Oke had paid it over to Sir John Scudamore, Owain's receiver, in twenty-six separate installments. He met Scudamore at various places, but mostly in areas where Scudamore's military duties could have taken him, for instance Carmarthen, Cardiff, Newport, Abergavenny, Brecon, Huntington, Madley (near Hereford) and Radnor; also Montgomery and Beaumaris, which are less likely. We know less about Veyse, because his confession is lost. His agent was John Swineshead, probably from the place of that name in Lincolnshire.

It is significant that the monasteries were in eastern England, an area known to both men: Ramsey, Thorney and Crowland (Benedictine), Woburn and Warden (Cistercian), Huntingdon and Thetford (Augustinian). This last order was well represented on Oke's list; Launde Abbey, the prior of which was hanged for treason in 1402, was also Augustinian. Of all the orders, the Franciscans were the most opposed to Henry IV. Professor Griffiths points out that accusations of treason against religious orders were in tune with the anticlerical sentiments of those nobles and knights who were attracted by Lollardy, like Sir John Clanvowe and his friends. Archbishop Arundel complained to the king that some household knights were irreverent at Mass. He had also heard them attacking the clergy for their wealth. Walsingham said that the Earl of Salisbury had refused the last rites of the Church before he was beheaded at Cirencester in 1399.

Walsingham could easily have come from St. Albans to Huntingdon for the trial of Oke and Veyse. His description of part of it could be first-hand evidence. 'A thief, a sawyer by trade', who was under sentence of death at Huntingdon, accused fifty-nine abbots and priors of collecting money for Owain Glyn Dŵr; Walsingham does not name the man. John Cokayn, one of the three justices, asked him to say which of two monks was the Abbot of Ramsey, whom he claimed to know. He failed the test and was hanged at once.

Sir John Scudamore was the king's constable of Kidwelly, Monmouth and the Three Castles in Gwent, and acted in the same capacity for the prince at Carmarthen; but he had a relative, Philip or Philpot Scudamore, who was a rebel. He had certainly met Owain in 1403 at the siege of Carreg Cennen. Henry IV refused to believe the charges against Scudamore, whose career was not affected. His subsequent marriage to Owain's daughter Alice assumes importance at the end of Owain's life.

How much truth if any there was in all these allegations can never be known. Many people were unsure of their allegiance to a usurping king. As Professor Griffiths suggests, the charges could have been cooked up by the two men as they lay in prison awaiting trial. On the other hand, they were clever rogues who could have met important people in the course of their nefarious lives; they may well have heard tittle tattle which added much needed verisimilitude to their otherwise bald and unconvincing narratives. But they may also have gleaned some really compromising information. As the poet John Dryden wrote of Titus Oates's accusations, which gave rise to the story of the Popish Plot of 1678: 'Some truth there was, but dash'd and brew'd with lies.' Oates was a notorious character in English history who resembled Oke and Veyse in having a thoroughly shady past.[2]

On 8 March 1406 Owain received a letter in the name of Charles VI which persuaded him that the French alliance might still bear fruit, if only he transferred his allegiance from Rome to Avignon.

He called a council of magnates and clergy at Pennal, between Machynlleth and Aberdovey, where a lengthy answer to the French proposal was drawn up, setting out Owain's conditions for his recognition of Benedict XIII of Avignon. Benedict was to confirm all grants, appointments and dispensations made by Roman popes since the Schism. There was to be a Welsh church fully independent of the Archbishop of Canterbury. The Bishop of St. David's was to be archbishop, and his province would include Lichfield, Worcester, Hereford, Bath and Exeter, recalling the grandiose ideas behind the Tripartite Indenture. All grants of Welsh benefices which had been made to English monasteries were to be revoked. Wales was to have two universities. Like other papally-sponsored wars of the age of schism, the war with the English was to be a crusade, against the usurpation and other crimes of Henry of Lancaster. The diplomatic effect of all this would be to make Wales fully independent from England. The Pennal policy and its execution seem to have been Gruffydd Young's work, for Lewis Byford may still have been loyal to Rome, and in 1407 Pope Benedict replaced him as Bishop of Bangor with Gruffydd.[3]

Pennal was the final demonstration of an independent Welsh foreign policy. The year 1406 brought Owain further disappointments on top of the unsuccessful French expedition. Gruffydd Hiraethog wrote: 'Gower and Ystrad Tywi and Ceredigion yielded and took the English side', meaning the loss of all of south-west Wales. Ystrad Tywi was the valley of the River Towy, the greater part of Carmarthenshire. On St. George's Day, 23 April, Walsingham records the severe defeat of a Welsh army, in which a son of Owain was slain, though we are not told which son, where this happened, or who the English commander was. In June Northumberland and Bardolf were defeated by Edward Charlton with troops raised in Shropshire and Cheshire, and driven from Wales. They went to Paris, where Orleans refused to help them, and were seen by Adam of Usk: 'because I, too, often held converse with them, I thereby drew down on myself the greater wrath of king Henry, when he knew thereof.'[4] Such remarks make one wonder whether Adam had an inflated sense of his own importance; he cannot have been one of the king's major worries.

Events beyond Owain's control turned the diplomatic climate irrevocably against him; he could succeed only as long as the situation was favourable, but Welsh fortunes were soon to be in irreversible decline. In March 1406 James, heir to the Scottish throne, was sent by his father Robert III to France. The dying king feared that the young prince would be in danger from Robert Stewart, the ambitious Duke of Albany, who would be regent. It was perhaps as a result of a tip-off by Albany that an English ship captured James on his way to France. The news killed the old king, and Albany ruled Scotland as a client of the English, who kept James I as a hostage till 1424. Owain could expect no further help from the Scots.[5]

Despite the ignominy of the rebels exacting protection money from the king's lieges in Pembroke, Owain's cause was failing and the time had come to seduce the Welsh from their allegiance. In April 1406 the king formally notified Lord Grey of Codnor, responsible for the defences of the southern border, that the Prince of Wales, his lieutenant in Wales and the Marches, was now given full discretion to grant the royal grace and pardon to all rebels who submitted. John Bodenham, who had won the king's favour for his services as sheriff of Herefordshire in 1403, was appointed receiver of all fines, fees and payments for the redemption of confiscated lands. In June Parliament demanded that the prince should hasten to Wales to do his duty. It may be tempting to think that this demand reflects the myth of Prince Hal wasting his time with low companions in the taverns of Cheapside, but in fact Parliament was probably being rather unfair. Although Prince Henry was still lieutenant in Wales, Welsh affairs were less demanding as Owain's power declined, and he could devote more of his time to the council, whose business was probably making it difficult for him to leave London. In 1407 he attended two-thirds of the meetings which are known to have been held.[6]

War weariness and the sense of impending defeat soon made the new policy effective. This was demonstrated in what can best be called a public ceremony at Beaumaris in November 1406. From six commotes in Anglesey, a total of 2,112 men assembled before Prince Henry's commissioners to submit. The clergy too turned out to see fair play. The fines came to £537 7s 0d; a lot of money, but Anglesey was richer than most of Wales; maybe it had also suffered less than other parts. The unconditional surrender of Anglesey, the bread-basket of North Wales, indicated that defeat was now inevitable. In growing numbers, the Welsh were coming to realise that Owain's cause was doomed, and it was time to make terms with the enemy. Wales was devastated, and the people could endure no more.[7]

As long as Owain Glyn Dŵr held the castles of Aberystwyth and Harlech, the English could not claim to have won the war. The siege of Aberystwyth in 1407 has great dramatic interest, because for the first time there was a direct contest of wills between the rival Princes of Wales, although during the summer the Welsh commander at Aberystwyth was Rhys Ddu (Rhys the Black) of Anhuniog, formerly sheriff of Cardigan. In May Prince Henry undertook to serve for six months with 200 men-at-arms and 600 archers. He had with him a galaxy of military talent, including several familiar names: the Duke of York, the Earl of Warwick, Lord Carew, Lord Audley, John Talbot, Francis de Court, John Oldcastle and John Greyndor. The siege did not go well, owing to indiscipline in the English army. It was difficult for Henry at his age to exert his authority over so many experienced colleagues; it might have been better if there had been fewer stars in the firmament around him.[8]

By September Rhys Ddu and his colleagues decided that they must treat with the enemy. Richard Courtenay, Chancellor of Oxford University, came to draw up the Indenture which gives the names of the dramatis personae, and much else about this remarkable affair. An indenture meant a legal contract between two parties; the word reflects the ancient practice of cutting the deed in half along a zigzag, when each party was bound by it and kept half. This one was made 'before the castle of Arburustwich, situated near the new town of Lampadere', between Henry, 'Prince of Wales, Duke of Aquitaine, Lancaster, Cornwall and Earl of Chester' the King's Lieutenant 'of the one part, and Rees ap Gruffith ap Lluellin ap Jenkin' and eleven others 'of the other part'. There was to be a truce of six weeks due to end on 24 October 1407, during which the Welsh could come and go freely as long as they did not attack any ships or molest anybody. Four of Rhys's 'Complices' would be hostages: Richard ap Gruffydd (Abbot of Strata Florida), Jenkin ap Rhys, Maredudd ab Owain, and

Gruffydd Thomas ap Roderich, the last three of whom were esquires of Cardiganshire. Owain Glyn Dŵr then had until All Saints' Day (1 November) to evacuate the castle and to remove all guns, bows, arrows, crossbows and other equipment.[9]

The sequel is told by Gruffydd Hiraethog:

> Before the day [ending the truce] Rhys the Black went to Gwynedd to ask Owen's leave to surrender the castle to the English. Owen kept Rhys with him until he had gathered his power around him and then went back with Rhys to Aberystwyth, where he threatened to cut off Rhys's head ... whereupon the castle was given to Owen.[10]

Parliament warmly thanked the prince for his efforts; on his knees before the king he gave what can only be called a glowing testimonial to the Duke of York, against whose 'honourable estate and name' there had been slanderous allegations. 'Had it not been for his good advice and counsel my said Lord the Prince & the others in his company would have been in very great peril and desolations.' The duke had worked very hard to give comfort and courage to the whole company, and was 'a loyal and valiant knight'. There can be no doubt that the prince's praise of York was heartfelt and sincere; on a previous occasion he had told Archbishop Arundel how much he relied on York. At Agincourt he gave York command of the van, the post of honour, where York lost his life, as Shakespeare relates. Indiscipline and slackness are also apparent in a request by Parliament to the king to order 'the Lords of the Marches of Wales to guard their Castles, Fortresses and Country ... without charge to the Realm of England'.[11]

Bitter complaints were laid before the same Parliament by members for Shropshire and Herefordshire about the devastatation caused by the Welsh raiders in recent years: sheep, cattle, and moveable goods stolen, people kidnapped and held to ransom. The war had given this age-old practice an extra incentive, because the Welsh were now also embittered by defeat and by a natural desire for vengeance, both of which encouraged them to go on raiding the hereditary enemy. Matters may have been worse in Shropshire. There were complaints about the behaviour of Richard II's men who passed through Shrewsbury on their way to or from Ireland in 1398, and the effects of the battle of Shrewsbury were felt locally. Shropshire had to pay the heavy cost of defence against the Welsh, but no doubt the same was true of Herefordshire. It was said that the Welsh burned Shrewsbury, but there seems to be no definite evidence to support this. Shrewsbury itself would have been been hard to attack, as it is a walled town with the Severn on three sides, but the suburbs on the opposite bank were exposed to Welsh plunderers.[12]

Owain had held Aberystwyth without French help, which was a remarkable achievement when the Welsh had so few ships, and at the end of 1407 he was still firmly in control of this vital castle. However, that November his ally, the Duke of Orléans, was murdered by order of the Duke of Burgundy, who was now in power and willing to make peace with the English. Lord Burnell, the Bishop of Durham, Sir Thomas Erpingham and Hugh Mortimer were the English envoys; enough survives of a badly damaged copy of their orders to make it clear that Owain was to be excluded from the terms of the truce. France was much weakened by the civil war which followed the murder of Orléans. The English also made a truce with Brittany, which together with Scotland and France would give Wales no more support against England. One after another the allies of Owain Glyn Dŵr had ceased to be effective, and his foreign policy had now collapsed irrevocably.[13]

To add to the woes of the suffering people, the year 1408 opened with 'a most harsh winter, with abundance of snow, lasting through the months of December, January, February and March; it caused almost all the blackbirds and thrushes to die of hunger and cold'. In February, Owain's last English allies, the Earl of Northumberland and Lord Bardolf, were defeated and killed at Bramham Moor by the sheriff of Yorkshire. When I heard these things, I ... gave thanks to Him who foreseeth what is to come, for that I had stayed behind', was Adam of Usk's pious comment. Ralph Neville, Earl of Westmorland, a Lancastrian retainer, was now in control in the north. Lewis Byford, who had been with Northumberland, was captured, but he had already been superseded as Bishop of Bangor by Gruffydd Young. The English soon persuaded the Roman pope to replace him with Benedict Nicholls, canon of Salisbury. Byford had not borne arms and escaped with his life, but his goods and valuables were seized, and he was imprisoned. Owain had lost his influence with both popes, and his diplomatic isolation was now total.[14]

It has always been agreed that the capture of Aberystwyth and Harlech in 1404 had set the seal on Owain's claim to the title of Prince of Wales. A year after Bramham Moor he had lost both castles. After the long entry in his chronicle on the first siege of Aberystwyth, Gruffydd Hiraethog says:

> Now began the second siege of the above castle and, without stirring from the spot, it was won; thence the host went to Harlech, where many gentlemen of Wales met their death; at last the castle was perforce given up to the English.

Having had too many cooks to spoil the broth at the first siege of Aberystwyth, this time Prince Henry seems to have managed on his own, while the Talbot brothers, Gilbert of Goodrich and John (Lord Furnival), began the siege of Harlech. Aberystwyth surrendered in the late summer. It is not definitely known when, but probably by 23 September 1408, when Prince Henry appointed his valet, William Malbon, rhaglaw [bailiff] for life in the commotes of Genau'r-glyn and Anhuniog 'in our county of Cardigan'. This looks very like the rewarding of a servant for his devotion to duty at the end of an arduous operation. The office itself and Anhuniog had been forfeited by Rhys the Black for his rebellion.[15]

The prince then joined the Talbots at Harlech, the siege of which was probably more difficult and more expensive than that of any other castle in Wales. Its remoteness compelled the besiegers to rely on ships to deliver cannon, powder, arms, victuals and other supplies, but time was on their side. The Welsh now had no allies or ships to help them to break the siege. Bombardment by cannon and archers sweeping the walls with arrows must both have had a shattering effect on the morale of the defenders; 1,500 quarrels or crossbow bolts were used at Aberystwyth and Harlech, as well as longbow arrows. A letter to the king shows that guns could be as dangerous to their crews as to those at the receiving end. A brass gun called the 'Messenger' burst at Aberystwyth, as did also the 'King's Daughter' at Harlech and another being tested by Anthony the Gunner at Worcester. But perhaps in the end hunger and disease were decisive in reducing these castles.[16]

Edmund Mortimer was present at Harlech, if not actually in command, and was among the casualties referred to by Gruffydd Hiraethog. Since the death of the first Earl of March most of the Mortimers had died untimely deaths, and he shared the fate of so many of his unlucky family, for he was killed or died of the plague. Adam of Usk tells of the prisoners taken at Harlech. They included Owain's wife, Margaret, and two daughters, one being Edmund's wife Catherine, and their children: their son, Lionel, and three daughters. All were taken to London. A note on 27 June 1413 by an Exchequer clerk, after the accession of Henry V, is of interest:

> To John Weele, esquire. In money paid to his own hands, for the expenses of the wife of Owen Glendourdi, the wife of Edmund Mortimer, and others, their sons and daughters, in his custody in the city of London at the King's charge, by his command ... £30.

If this sum had been properly spent they should have been well looked after, but a later entry, on 1 December, makes this doubtful:

> To William del Chambre, valet of the said Earl [Arundel]. In money paid to his own hands, for expenses and other charges incurred for the burial and exequies of the wife of Edward [sic] Mortimer and her daughters, buried within Saint Swithin's Church, London ... £1.

Owain experienced family tragedies which would have crushed any ordinary man, but eventually it was with members of his family that he finally found a place of refuge.[17]

Several years earlier, Marcher lords and sheriffs of the border shires had fallen into the habit of making truces with the Welsh, whose raids they were unable to check. Perhaps it was a sign of war-weariness that as late as 1409, when it was plain that Owain's cause was failing, they were still doing this, and the king found it necessary to order them to do their duty. On 3 November 1409 he told the Earl of Arundel, Edward Charleton, Lord Grey of Ruthin and Sir Richard Lestrange that he had heard how their officers 'on their own authority, and without our warrant or knowledge, were making truces with Owin de Glendourdy and our other rebels in those parts' which did not bind the Welsh 'to abstain from war'. The king ordered his lieges to return to their posts of duty without delay, and to make war on the rebels with all their might. Equally stern orders went to the sheriff of Hereford. The lamentable results of rebel activity often appear in the records. The bailiffs and burgesses of Shrewsbury had been let off £47 of tax in February 1408, 'in consideration of the great losses which they have sustained by the malice and invasion of the Welsh rebels'. In September the same year the king's esquire, Robert Middelton, was excused an annual rent of six marks on his land which had been plundered by rebels in the lordship of Montgomery.[18]

Adam of Usk almost assumes centre stage here. He had left Rome on 11 June 1406, and wandered in the Netherlands and northern France. In 1404 the king had rejected the pope's request that Adam succeed John Trevenant as Bishop of Hereford, or so Adam says. In 1407 Benedict XIII had named him as Bishop of Llandaff, but at Bruges a herald, entitled Lancaster king of arms, had warned him of the continuing wrath of Henry IV. Adam declared to the herald that he would enter Wales pretending to be Owain's man, but seek the protection of his old patron, Edward Charlton. His first attempt failed; 'This declaration saved me my life ... eight ships of Devon chased me for two livelong days', but he luckily found refuge at St. Pol de Leon. At last he reached Barmouth safe and sound, but a dangerous area which was still loyal to Glyn Dŵr. 'When I had gotten from [my lord] letters of leave to come unto him and to rest safe with him, I gat me by night and in secret unto him at his castle of Pool'. The reader will be relieved to hear that Adam finally received a royal pardon in 1411, and was able to practise his profession in peace till he died at Usk in 1430.[19]

The last adventure of Owain Glyn Dŵr, the last explosion of his old aggressive spirit, was a raid into Shropshire in 1409; but the royal rebuke administered to the Marcher lords seems to have put them on their mettle. It is fortunate that at this juncture Adam of Usk was at Welshpool, where he was able to observe and record the tragic outcome:

> While I there abode, among the other gentlemen of Owain's party, three men of fame, to wit Philip Scudamore of Troy [near Monmouth], Rhys ap Gruffydd of Cardigan, and Rhys ap Tudur of Anglesey, being taken by the captain of the same castle, were drawn to the gallows and hanged; the first at Shrewsbury, whose head is still there set up beyond bridge, the second at London and the third at Chester.

Adam does not say how these men came to be captured, but this question is answered by Gruffydd Hiraethog, who is our only other source for this affair. He omits Rhys ap Tudur, but otherwise he tells us more, giving the year 1409 and saying what happened and where:

> The men of Owen made an attack on the borders of Shropshire and there Rhys the Black and Philip Scudamore were captured. The one was sent to Shrewsbury and the other to London to be drawn and quartered. Thenceforth Owen made no great attack until he disappeared.[20]

CHAPTER ELEVEN

The Disappearance of Owain Glyn Dŵr

Henry of Lancaster had triumphed over all human enemies. His English rebels were all dead. He held the King of Scots. France was divided by the feud of Orléans (the Armagnacs) and Burgundy. The Bretons were no threat. Owain Glyn Dŵr was beaten even if he was still free. These achievements had been won at a heavy cost, for Henry IV was now a broken man. During 1410 and most of 1411 the Prince of Wales and his advisers ruled England as a sort of unofficial regency. This may have taken the pressure off Owain, because already Prince Henry, eager to be king, was actively thinking of his claim to the French throne, and had become Captain of Calais. His Beaufort uncles, Thomas and Bishop Henry of Winchester, were trying to persuade Henry IV to abdicate on account of his ill-health, which made him even less willing to act decisively; he disliked the policy advocated by Prince Henry and the Beauforts of an alliance with the Duke of Burgundy, who was the most powerful of the French princes. In this metaphorical sense Shakespeare was right to follow the tradition, which began with Monstrelet, that the prince tried on the crown as his father slept. Prince Henry had his critics at court, perhaps supporters of his brother Thomas Duke of Clarence, with whom his relations were tense. For example, in October 1411 six of his knights were arrested over some dispute with Clarence's retainers. Prince Henry had also to refute allegations that he had embezzled funds at Calais and even plotted to seize the throne. This was unlikely as, considering how ill his father was, he would not have to wait long for it. The story that Chief Justice Gascoigne imprisoned him for contempt has never been proved, though Gascoigne was dismissed when Henry became king. In 1412 Henry IV recovered his health sufficiently to resume control of his government, and there was even a threat of civil war, but the prince and his father were reconciled by the time of the king's death. The fact that the Lancastrian dynasty could be riven by such a serious dispute and survive it intact proves that it was now strongly established.[1]

By now Owain Glyn Dŵr was no longer a serious threat. His movements become increasingly obscure, though he and his men waged a guerilla war for two more years. Their only recorded exploit was that in 1412 they captured Dafydd Gam, who was said to have tried to murder Owain at Machynlleth in 1405. Maybe while being taken prisoner he tried to escape and nearly killed Owain, who would have been the loser had he returned the compliment. Henry IV ordered John Tiptoft, constable of Brecon, and William Butler, receiver, to pay Dafydd's ransom, which was 'allegedly seven hundred marks':

> Our chosen esquire Luellin ap Howel, father of our chosen esquire David Gamme and tenant in our domain of Brecon, has told us that the said David was violently seized by our rebel and traitor Owen de Glendourdy, and kept in strict imprisonment ...

Prince Henry had spent much of the war in the border shires, latterly in Herefordshire. In this time Dr. Griffiths notes that he collected 'a large number of annuitants and retainers who would go on to serve him as king.' A notable member of Henry V's retinue in France was Dafydd Gam. The story is that, the evening before the battle of Agincourt, he was sent by the king to report on the numbers of the enemy: 'An't please you, my liege, they are enough to be killed, enough to be taken prisoner, and enough to run away.' It is also said that Dafydd, his son-in-law Roger Vaughan, and

Walter ap Lhwyd all fell fighting in defence of the king, who knighted them as they lay dying. Roger Vaughan's alabaster effigy, with a Lancastrian SS collar, is in Bredwardine Church. He had married Dafydd's daughter Gwladys, whose second husband, William ap Thomas, was another notable Welsh soldier who became councillor to Richard, Duke of York. The grandsons of Dafydd Gam by both marriages were staunch Yorkist partisans in the Wars of the Roses. Owain Glyn Dŵr was unfortunate in failing to win the loyalty of so valiant a man as Dafydd Gam.[2]

The end of Owain's story was mysterious, like so much of his life, and English official sources say next to nothing about it. Henry IV's order for Dafydd Gam's ransom was followed by a general pardon including all rebels except murderers, rapists, Owain Glyn Dŵr and Thomas of Trumpington, that curious character whose name keeps cropping up; he was a spurious Richard II in whose survival no one can have believed any more. In 1413 occurs the following entry in the Issue Rolls:

> To a certain Welshman, coming to London, and there continuing for a certain time to give information respecting the conduct and designs of 'Ewain Glendourdy'. In money paid to his own hands for his expenses, and as an especial reward for the cause aforesaid ... £1.

This seems fortunately to have been a complete waste of a large sum of money. Wales was saved the spectacle of one of her sons becoming a traitor as infamous as John of Menteith, who surrendered William Wallace to the English in 1304, or Neil Macleod of Assynt, who in 1650 sold Montrose, a helpless fugitive, to his enemies. John Buchan comments: 'It is remembered as the solitary case of a Gael who betrayed a suppliant for gold'.[3]

After the capture of Dafydd Gam in 1412 the official view, probably for the rest of Henry IV's reign, was that Owain was somewhere in north Wales, because there were military posts at Bala, Strata Florida and Cymer Abbey near Dolgellau, though not actually in Snowdonia. This is confirmed by Adam of Usk; though

Adam is obscure and not always reliable, he is one of our earliest sources for the last days of Owain Glyn Dŵr, of whom he writes as maliciously as usual:

> Owen, with his only surviving son Meredith, miserably lay in hiding in the open country, and in caves, and in the thickets of the mountains. To make all safe, and to curb fresh rebellions by means of the king's soldiers and at his costs, the glades and passes of Snowdon and of other mountains and forests of North Wales were held guarded.

A tradition now began, with Owain and a band of devoted friends living an elusive and miserable life. Adam was probably right to include Maredudd in this band, in view of Henry V's subsequent offers to pardon him as well as his father. Writers hostile to Owain took up this idea in the following century.[4]

There are three inseparable problems about Owain's last years: how were they spent? When and where did he die? The belief that Owain was holding out in north Wales until 1413 may have given rise to an idea that he died in those parts, for which there is little if any evidence. Ellis says that Humphrey Humphreys, who was formerly Bishop of Bangor and a noted scholar, declared that Owain, Prince of Gwynedd, who died in 1138, was in fact the occupant of a tomb in Bangor Cathedral, wrongly supposed to be the burial place of Owain Glyn Dŵr. An even more unlikely assertion was that Owain died at Wolfscastle in Pembrokeshire, for which no evidence exists.[5]

Certainly Owain was compelled to keep out of sight if he was to escape his enemies. This became easier after Henry IV's death in March 1413, and Owain was now in much less danger. Henry V, the chivalrous rival Prince of Wales, felt no animosity towards a vanquished foe who had fought so bravely; Owain could do no more harm, now that his rebellion had burned itself out. Also, once Henry V was on the throne his French expedition was uppermost in his mind; he wanted to conciliate the Welsh and recruit Welsh soldiers, of whom many joined his army. On 5 July 1415 he ordered Gilbert

Talbot 'to communicate with and treat with Owin Glendourdy of Wales' and to offer him and the other rebels his royal grace and pardon if they desired it. There is, in Dr. Phillips's opinion, little doubt that Owain was still alive at that date. Henry Dwnn was one of those who accepted the amnesty, but Owain never did.[6]

The first question to be answered is whether there is enough evidence to give a date for the death of Owain Glyn Dŵr. He was apparently alive as late as 5 July 1415. A long entry for 1415 by Adam of Usk is mostly about the Agincourt campaign, but it ends with a note on Owain's death:

> Died Owen Glendower, after that during four years he had hidden from the face of the king and the realm; and in the night season he was buried by his followers. But his burial having been discovered by his adversaries, he was laid in the grave a second time; and where his body was bestowed no man may know.

Since his pardon in 1411 Adam had received ample preferment from Archbishop Arundel. He could go where he liked, and hear all the latest gossip. Usk is only about twenty miles from the very part of Herefordshire where Owain is believed finally to have found refuge. This may be why Adam seems to know more than he is prepared to admit. He gives no date or place for Owain's death, maybe because he respects the need for secrecy.[7]

Other Welsh fifteenth-century sources are unanimous that Owain died on 20 or 21 September 1415, the Eve and Feast of St. Matthew. The chronicle used by Gruffydd Hiraethog says that after his defeat in 1409:

> Owen made no great attack until he disappeared.
> 1412 Rhys ap Tudur of Anglesey and Ednyfed his brother were captured. They were executed in Chester.
> 1415 Owen went into hiding on St. Matthew's Day in Harvest, and thereafter his hiding place was unknown. Very many say that he died; the seers maintain that he did not.

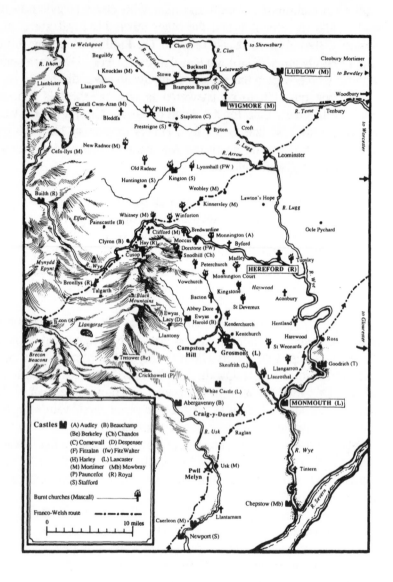

The south-eastern Marches

As Dr. Phillips suggests, all this probably referred to Owain's death. The seers were comparing his disappearance to that of Arthur, who vanished into the mists of Avalon. Like Arthur, Owain was asleep but would awake at his people's call. Gruffydd Hiraethog was the main source used by Robert Vaughan and Thomas Ellis:

> After the year 1411, Owen was so weakened, his men deserting him, and returning to the king's obedience, that he was forced often to change his quarters and keep less in sight.
> A.D. 1415, death put an end to Owen's life and misery upon the Eve of St. Matthew.

The only difference with Gruffydd Hiraethog is that St. Matthew's Day 1415 is given for Owain's death, the day on which Owain and his men had first taken to the woods in 1400. It is worth noticing that the chronicle used by Gruffydd Hiraethog agrees with Adam of Usk about the year when Owain Glyn Dŵr ceased to make war.[8]

Two other fifteenth-century Welsh sources confirm the Eve and Feast of St. Matthew as the time of Owain's death. One of these, which is known to have been among Vaughan's papers, gives St. Matthew's Day, 21 September. There is also a Welsh paraphrase of *The Brut* written by a fifteenth-century poet, which gives 20 September for the raid on Ruthin in 1400 and also for Owain's death. Sir John Lloyd thought that Gruffydd Hiraethog was repeating the date of Owain's flight in 1400, and that Owain had died later. Phillips believes that this is pure coincidence; since three independent fifteenth century sources give 20 or 21 September 1415, one or the other is probably the date of the death of Owain Glyn Dŵr. He adds that Adam of Usk and two further early sources confirm this belief. Lloyd thought that the new offer of a pardon on 24 February 1416 meant that Owain was still alive; it was made to Maredudd ab Owain who might be 'more tractable than the broken, yet unconquered old warrior.' But the order to Gilbert Talbot differs from the previous one: Talbot is 'to communicate with and treat with Meredith ap Owyn, son of Owyn de Glendourdy', with no hint that Owain was still alive. Maredudd was granted his pardon in 1417, but there was no word from Owain. The unanimity of the primary sources is not absolute proof of the date of Owain's death, but there seems to be no good reason to doubt it.[9]

The very strong tradition that Owain's life ended somewhere in western Herefordshire now requires detailed discussion. It springs from some very early sources which were tapped by Vaughan, Ellis and their predecessors:

> Some say he died at his daughter Scudamour's, others at his daughter Monington's house. They had both harboured him in his forlorn condition. They say that he was fain to go up and down, disguised in a shepherd's habit, to his daughter and other friends' houses.

A Herefordshire antiquary named John Webb, writing in 1833, accepts the date of Owain's death and the tradition that he died at Monnington-on-Wye:

> It is said that [Owain] retired to his most esteemed daughter Mary [sic] Monington in Herefordshire ... Browne Willis Esq in his history of the Bishop of Bangor says, Owen Glendŵr died, and was buried at Monington, the 20th of Sept. 1415 ...[10]

Those writers, Welsh as well as English, who are hostile to Owain, take up the theme of misery harped on by Adam of Usk and continued by Ellis; they prefer to think that he died of hunger and privation. English writers of the sixteenth century agree, but they are uncertain where he died. About 1436 Humphrey Duke of Gloucester, Henry V's brother, invited to England an Italian scholar, Tito Livio, with a commission to write a life of the king. Tito accepted the general opinion that such a rebel deserved a wretched end and died in misery. An English translation of 1513 says:

> This Owen, for feare and in dispaire to obtain the
> King's pardon, fledd into desart places without
> companie; where in caves he continued and finished
> his misserable life.

There are several manuscripts of this translation, one of which gives some very interesting additional information, that Owain died

> vppon the toppe of Lawtons Hope Hill in Hereford-
> shire, as is their stated and affirmed.

Lawton's Hope is between Leominster and Hereford, near Canon Pyon and west of Dinmore Manor. This link in an early tradition between Owain's name and a minor hilltop in north Herefordshire is perhaps rather too curious to be summarily dismissed. The passage is copied by Edward Hall, who adds that Owain starved to death. Similar gloating and moralising can be found in *The Mirror for Magistrates*, where Owain's fate is summed up as follows:

> How Owen Glendour seduced by false prophesies took
> upon him to be prince of Wales, and was by Henry
> then prince thereof, chased to the mountaynes, where
> he miserably dyed for lacke of foode.[11]

Pennant, Price and Williams agree that he died in Herefordshire, though Pennant was of course better informed. He knew about Talbot and the pardon. He followed Ellis in the date and place of Owain's death, at the daughter's house at Monnington-on-Wye where he was buried in the churchyard. Price agreed about Monnington, but added that he may have died of hunger in *Harewood* Forest (eight miles from Hereford on the Ross road). Williams said that the malice of the clergy gave rise to the story that Owain wandered in exile, and died of hunger in *Haywood* forest (three miles south of Hereford) though he preferred his own theory about Owain's retirement at Ruthin.[12]

Owain's presence in Herefordshire was due to his married daughters. His family had consisted, says Ellis, of 'Griffith and five sons more, who came all to be men and perished, in their father's war, without issue'. In fact Gruffydd died in prison; Maredudd survived the war, and was pardoned. There were several illegitimate children. There were five daughters: Catherine, Alice, Janet, Margaret and Isabel. Ellis names Isabel first, and says that she married Adam ab Iorwerth, without explaining who he was. Assuming that Owain and Margaret Hanmer married in 1383, which is by no means certain, it would have been possible for her to have produced eleven children by 1400, when their eldest child, perhaps a boy, would have been only sixteen: not too young for a girl to have married— Mary Bohun was about eleven when she married Henry of Bolingbroke. After the Rising had begun Owain had other things on his mind than his daughters' marriages, yet they are inseparably linked to the problem of his last years. The first datable marriage was in 1402, of Catherine to Edmund Mortimer, a brilliant match, and a much more important husband in rank than Sir John Scudamore, who married Alice. Under the statute of 1401, Scudamore could not have been in command at Carreg Cennen in 1403 with a Welsh wife. Therefore he must have married Alice later. If Catherine was the first daughter to marry, and her husband was a member of so great a family as Mortimer, she must surely have been the eldest. She died first, so Alice presumably succeeded her as Owain's heir. This does not agree with the usual genealogy, which omits Catherine's name and makes Alice the eldest, but it is borne out by the evidence.[13]

The marriage of Alice and John Scudamore was well known after Owain's death, because in 1430 Scudamore tried to have his father-in-law's outlawry reversed, and to recover Glyn Dyfrdwy and Cynllaith in his wife's right from John Beaufort Earl of Somerset who, a prisoner of the French since their victory at Baugé in 1421, appealed to Parliament. Scudamore incurred the anger of John's brother Edmund, and was dismissed from his posts under the statute of 1401 forbidding an Englishman to marry a Welshwoman.

There is no early evidence for Janet's marriage to Sir John Croft, but it was accepted in the next century, is in the Croft pedigree and has never been doubted. Sir John was governor of Mark Castle in the pale of Calais during the war, and 'was frequently employed in negotiations in Flanders between 1402 and 1404'. When either marriage took place is unknown, but possibly as late as 1412, when Owain 'disappeared'. Since the marriages were unlawful, they may well have been as secret as the whereabouts of the elusive father-in-law. The marriage of Margaret (Mary) to Roger or Richard Monnington is less definite, but it is still based on an early tradition. The Monningtons held Monnington-on-Wye as tenants of Lord Audley, a Cheshire magnate and lord of Llandovery (where in 1403 Ralph Monnington was his constable), also of Cemaes in Pembrokeshire.[14]

Sir John Scudamore's principal residence was Kentchurch, a manor house in the hidden upper valley of the Monnow near Pontrilas. He also held the manor of Monnington in Straddel, from the Welsh *Ystrad* which means a broad valley; it is in the Golden Valley. Ellis and later writers who had perhaps never heard of it, may have confused it with the home of the Monningtons at Monnington-on-Wye, which being in English territory seems a less likely place both for Owain's refuge and for his grave. There can be little doubt that, of the daughters' houses in southern Herefordshire, only Kentchurch could be called a secure hiding place, though a descendant, Owen Croft, argues in favour of his family home in the north of the county:

> There is a tradition that a Welshman could always get a night's lodging with a palliasse of straw in the attic floor - a large one at Croft Castle, and it may well be that this comes down from the time of Glendower ... [Kentchurch] was too apparent a bolt hole for him to have been there over long; and the very fact that Croft Castle has never been mentioned gives an idea that it may have been frequently used by Glendower during his last years. A further likely place is another manor of the Scudamores (now belonging to Guy's Hospital) overlooking the Golden Valley, and known as Monnington Straddle [sic]. It is probable that all three were used by the proud old warrior, all off the beaten track, and all easy to get away from.[15]

Owen Croft seems to have thought that Glyn Dŵr might still want to slip across the border into Wales; he seems not to have considered the perils of the journey to Croft, through country whose inhabitants had many scores to settle with the Welsh. In fact the Scudamore manors, which were in Welsh-speaking country, were Owain's only safe haven. Croft would not have been 'easy to get away from', and escaping from Margaret's home first involved crossing the Wye.

Owain may still have longed to see Janet before he died, and to have risked the journey to Croft, 'disguised in a shepherd's habit'. The direct way from Kentchurch would have been past Haywood and Lawton's Hope, both of which are associated with his death; Harewood is decidedly off the route. Perhaps on the journey home from Croft he was either taken ill or died at Lawton's Hope. His friends thought it safer to avoid Hereford and to carry him along the Roman road from Canon Pyon to Kenchester and Monnington-on-Wye, where they buried him by night. This is a plausible explanation which links three places associated with Owain, and to which Adam of Usk's brief story may serve as a sequel. This seems to imply that Owain's enemies were foiled before they could act by the prompt removal and reburial of the body, perhaps at Monnington in Straddel or Kentchurch; only a faithful few knew the site of the grave, which was forgotten. If Owain had died at Haywood, his followers would probably have carried the body straight back to Kentchurch, about fifteen miles.

These attempts to reconcile the various traditions about where Owain died or was buried cannot be verified, but the result suggests that it may be better not to ignore these odd details entirely; when put together they do make a certain amount of sense. Whatever the truth about the death of Owain Glyn Dŵr, the confusion between the two Monningtons has undoubtedly complicated the issue. It is probably best to finish with Sir John Lloyd's verdict:[16]

> Legend was bound to gather around the latter years of so striking and weird a figure as that of Glyn Dŵr, and my own feeling is that there is very little one can maintain on this head with any confidence. The Monning-

ton Straddle *[sic]* suggestion is the farthest point to
which I am prepared to go and even that I put forward
with some hesitation.

Perhaps Owain preferred peace and security for the little time left
to him. Kentchurch and Monnington in Straddel offered the surest
refuge, but both are close enough to English territory for the
English to have learnt of Owain's whereabouts, had he been in that
area for any length of time. Perhaps Henry V, whom very few dared
to disobey, had given stern orders that Owain was to be left in
peace; when he sent Gilbert Talbot to offer Owain a pardon, he may
have known very well where he was to be found. While Owain
lived no attempt seems to have been made to disturb him, even if
some malignant locals may have tried to desecrate his grave.

Returning to the legend of the 'disappearance' of Glyn Dŵr, Dr.
Phillips mentions a tradition in Welsh medieval literature that a
man named Owain would return one day to save his country, like
King Arthur. The well-known story by Elis Gruffydd, a soldier in
the Calais garrison during the reigns of Henry VIII and Edward VI,
can be used to support this messianic idea. Early one morning
Owain Glyn Dŵr and his friend and neighbour, the abbot of Valle
Crucis, met on the Berwyn moors above the Dee valley: 'You are
early, Father Abbot!' said Owain. 'No,' replied the abbot, 'it is you
who are early, a hundred years before your time.' Another story
tells how, faced by inevitable defeat, Owain saw that he could not
fulfill this prophecy and would be seen as an impostor. He therefore
went into hiding, covering his tracks by ordering a fake burial at
Llanrhaeadr-ym-Mochnant, a church to the south of the Berwyn.
Other reasons to account for his disappearance were that he had no
more money to pay his troops, or that he went to France for help
and never came back, or that he and his men were sleeping in a
cave, while they awaited their call to return and save Wales.[17]

At Kentchurch there is a panel with a painted portrait of an
ascetic, clean-shaven, elderly man. It may be the work of a Flemish
artist of the early fifteenth century, in which case the man must
have been someone important, as the painter would have earned a
large fee for such a picture. Though some have argued that it is

Owain Glyn Dŵr, the majority favour Sion Cent, a poet who was Owain's contemporary, and who may even have been his chaplain.[18]

Sion Cent has his place in Welsh history. Sir John Clanvowe and other Lollards condemned earthly glory, wealth, and covetousness. The horrors of the recent war prompted the rise of a school of Welsh poets who had similar ideas without being Lollards; there is no sign that Lollardy persisted in Wales after Sir John Oldcastle's death. Sion Cent was the most prominent of these bards. His message was austere and ascetic. Life and its joys were transitory. Riches and pleasures were vain. He condemned the wealthy who disobeyed the Church's teachings, indulged in the pleasures of the flesh and failed to carry out the works of mercy enjoined by Christ. He attacked his fellow poets for their servile flattery of the powerful, whom they praised for their fake generosity when in fact they oppressed and exploited the poor and needy.[19]

Owain could have shaved and dressed like the man in the portrait for additional safety, but the picture reflects what is known of Sion Cent's character. He was probably one of those men whom ordinary people found alarming; he became a wizard in Herefordshire mythology, known as John o'Kent, in league with the Devil, and a bogy man whose name mothers used to frighten their children if they misbehaved. 'Look out or Jackie Kent will have you!' was a warning which Owen Croft said could still be heard in his lifetime, like the name of Boney in Napoleonic times. It is anyone's guess as to whether Owain used Sion Cent's name as an alias, which with his famous reputation as a magician survived for centuries in Herefordshire folklore. [20]

CHAPTER TWELVE

Owain Glyn Dŵr's Place in History

Having usurped the throne, Henry IV began his reign in a weak position and with insufficient authority, which was further diminished by his political ineptitude. He failed dismally to reconcile Owain and Grey, to put down the ensuing revolt, or to make any real effort to end it by negotiation, which greatly prolonged the war in Wales. Henry's quarrels with the Percies and Edmund Mortimer were probably avoidable, and cost him dearly. Seizing the throne also meant diplomatic isolation. The French, Scots, Bretons and Spaniards gave as much help as possible to Owain Glyn Dŵr. The Lancastrian dynasty was not fully in control of the realm until 1408.

King Henry IV's physical courage did not compensate for his military incompetence; his knowledge of the art of war was as rudimentary as his understanding of politics. In particular he entirely failed to appreciate the peculiar problems of defeating an enemy who was a genius at guerilla warfare. He was unable to realise that the *chevauchée* was worse than useless in a country like Wales; it was only a clumsy, brutal and wasteful reaction to an elusive foe, who was then able to seize and hold the initiative, forcing the English to use the network of castles solely for defence. These supine tactics brought the English to the nadir which their fortunes reached in 1404. The castles had been built as bases from which mobile forces could seek out and defeat the enemy. Once these tactics were revived under the skilful leadership of Prince Henry, the English were able to contain the Welsh within the ring of fortresses which guarded the English border and the sea coasts. In effect it was a vast siege of the whole of Wales, which became possible once the English were in full control of all the supply routes by land and sea. They also used the castles inside Wales in the same aggressive manner, supplying them by the lines of communication which ran from Chester, Shrewsbury, Worcester and Hereford up the river valleys. By the end of 1407 the English had regained complete control of the sea from the Welsh and their French allies.

Prince Henry was involved in the recovery of his principality from 1400 on. The stresses of war weeded out incompetent officers; the youthful prince had many able captains to advise him and to lead his troops in the field as his responsibilities grew. He learned steadily that it was a war of logistics. There were far more sieges than pitched battles. Castles had to be supplied and their garrisons paid. The prince learned how to command men, but also how to raise money, and order and pay for stores of all kinds. He and his council responded to the financial crises of 1403 and 1404 by creating what Dr. Griffiths calls a secret war treasury, which was the key to his methods of waging war. His Welsh experience was later put to excellent use in France. 'But the lessons learnt were more than purely military, for it was in Wales that Henry came to appreciate the fundamental truth that money is vital to the successful pursuit of war.'[1]

It must be stressed that the Rebellion of Owain Glyn Dŵr was not only a war of independence, but also a civil war, in which Welshmen fought against Welshmen as well as against the English. It undoubtedly caused appalling destruction and suffering in Wales and the border counties of England, with a legacy of even greater lawlessness than ever before. Medieval warfare always involved destruction and rapine, in which Owain was typical of his times. English methods in France, Scotland and Wales, and those of the Welsh rebels were all equally barbaric. For the next two centuries Welsh writers, as well as John Leland and other English travellers, deplored the dreadful destruction of towns, manors, monasteries, castles, and the humbler tenements of the poor. Bare gables and ruined battlements stood as mute witnesses. It is not surprising that

Owain's countrymen put the blame on him, but the first well-known compliment was paid to Owain by William Shakespeare, at a time when rebellion was unfashionable. Once the urge to destroy was unleashed, destruction was deliberate and thorough, whenever and wherever the Welsh had time to vent their hatred on their oppressors, especially in Marcher lordships and the adjacent border areas. Castles, manor houses, monasteries and big farm buildings were set on fire, after all moveables of any value had been taken. Mills were seen as symbols of unpopular lordship and were usually wrecked. Livestock was driven off. Towns were specially hated because the Welsh were excluded from their trade, and with few exceptions they suffered severely. Many small towns like Nefyn, Overton-on-Dee and New Radnor were so badly damaged that they reverted to the status of village, in fact if not in theory.

The war was considered by Richard Davies, who was Bishop of St. David's during the reign of Elizabeth I, to have permanently damaged the cultural life of Wales, with the irreparable loss of books and writings. Church property was not exempt; Owain destroyed Abbey Cwm Hir, and Henry IV sacked Llanfaes and Strata Florida. As the medieval church was heavily involved in politics it had to pay the price in wartime, since it was also rich and an easy target. In the middle ages plunder was an important means of financing war, which the Welsh attacks on Herefordshire and Shropshire demonstrate.[2]

When the Rising began, the aim of Owain and his adherents was probably to make an honourable settlement with the king as soon as possible; but war gains its own momentum, and those who start it tend to lose control of events if they cannot attain their objectives quickly. Those who have held Owain solely responsible for this appalling war and the resulting ruin have overlooked certain facts. The economy of Europe had been declining since the beginning of the fourteenth century; cooler, damper weather had caused poor harvests and famine during its second decade. The plague too disrupted trade and the rural economy. In Wales and the Marches, the severe burden of the Hundred Years' War had combined with the heavy exactions of the English lords to make Wales ripe for some eruption, even if Owain had never arisen. In the early years, the momentum behind the war was largely provided by the Welsh people, who saw it as a war of liberation and were ready to make the sacrifices which are unavoidable if freedom cannot be won or defended.

Finally, national recovery from even the most awful war can be amazingly rapid. Anglo-Welsh relations had always had a more peaceful side to them. The traditional Welsh trade with the English border shires and towns was so vital to the Welsh war effort that, although illegal, it had if anything increased during the war, and promoted recovery afterwards. The English tended to turn a blind eye to the penal laws of Henry IV, because the need for Welsh assistance in ruling the country was as great as ever. The truces made by Marcher lords and by the border counties with the Welsh, which Henry IV condemned, may also have helped towards reconciliation with the *uchelwyr* and a return to normal life. The seaports of the north and south coasts of Wales could only recover their prosperity in partnership with the English ports, Chester and Bristol respectively. Chester had prospered from trade with north Wales, but 'certainly in 1445 the impoverishment of the city was still attributed in part to the loss of Welsh trade as a result of the rising.' Also, perhaps, the River Dee was already silting up.[3]

Though the immediate results of the Rising were so dire, Owain's career cannot be dismissed as totally negative and destructive. In the story told by Elis Gruffydd, the comment of the abbot of Valle Crucis that Owain was a hundred years before his time could have another interpretation to the one suggested by Dr. Phillips. It may reflect a feeling among the Welsh that by his victory and accession to the throne Henry Tudor had taken up their cause where Owain had laid it down, becoming not only Prince of Wales but also King of England.[4]

The position of Owain Glyn Dŵr in world history is worth considering, both as a man of war and as a statesman. Owain had extraordinary gifts as strategist, tactician, administrator and diplomat, but above all in his power to inspire people in his own day and down to the present time. He has won a place in that select band of national leaders of genius and charisma who could bring victory out of apparently hopeless situations: Alfred the Great and

Elizabeth I in England, Wallace and Bruce in Scotland. John Hus in Bohemia and Joan of Arc in France both died as martyrs; they lost in the short run, but won enduring fame. Owain's war of independence also failed, but by fighting against great odds he saved the soul of Wales.

Intelligent Englishmen at the time may have realised that Owain Glyn Dŵr's Rising was the justified protest of a proud people, whose valiant struggle for freedom had earned them the right to be treated with greater respect in future. The night before the battle of Agincourt the disguised Henry V overheard Fluellen reprimanding his friend Gower for shouting his name, saying that it was no excuse if the enemy were being much noisier. This was when Henry approved Fluellen's 'care and valour', his sense of discipline. The king probably remembered actual incidents during the Rising, when English troops had given their position away by the noise they made, to which Dr. Griffiths refers. No doubt English soldiers admired the important contribution made by their Welsh comrades to the new armies in France, in which some rose to high command. Welsh participation in English affairs had already been growing during the fourteenth century; David Hanmer, Degory Sais, Adam of Usk and Owain himself were all examples of this. After the war this tendency continued unabated. Since England was too strong to be overcome by force of arms, able Welshmen promptly seized any opportunity for advancement offered, either in Wales or in England.[5]

The most ambitious Welshmen found their way in politics: a rough game, which easily turned into war if the politicians lacked the necessary skill. Herefordshire and adjacent areas were hotbeds of violence and brigandage, a situation which contributed to the political troubles of Henry VI's reign. Out of it grew a feud between the families who were descended from Owain: the Scudamores, who remained loyal to Lancaster, and the House of Dafydd Gam, the Herberts and Vaughans, who were adherents of the House of York. The proximity of Croft Castle to Ludlow and Wigmore led the Crofts, also descended from Owain, to seek the good lordship of York. From the local point of view this quarrel was finally settled in 1461 at Mortimer's Cross, better known for the victory which enabled Edward, Earl of March and Duke of York, to seize the throne and become King Edward IV.[6]

The extraordinary outcome of the Wars of the Roses was that the throne was won by a branch of the royal family who sprang from the secret marriage of Henry V's widowed queen with Owen Tudor, a Welshman whose family were related to Glyn Dŵr and had been his allies. Jasper Tudor had escaped from Mortimer's Cross, which cost Owen his life, and after the extinction of the House of Lancaster at Tewkesbury worked for the succession of his nephew Henry, which came about at Bosworth Field in 1485. This remarkable event might well not have happened but for Owain Glyn Dŵr's Rising.

As a strategist, Owain must rank very high. His ability to mystify, mislead and surprise the English led friend and foe to think that he was a magician. During the Second World War British soldiers said the same about a famous German general, whose adversary, General Auchinleck, wrote to his commanders: 'Our friend Rommel is becoming a kind of magician ... to our troops ... Even if he were a superman, it would still be highly undesirable that our men should credit him with supernatural powers.' It was reliably reported that Rommel had a sixth sense, or intuition, about the enemy's intentions; from his knowledge of the English, Owain probably had similar hunches about what they would do next. Owain and Rommel were similar as tacticians; both would seize and hold the initiative, always attacking the enemy, and keeping him off balance. Some of Owain's English opponents were incompetent, but others were very able indeed, especially the rival Prince of Wales, who learned the arts of war fighting the Welsh under Owain Glyn Dŵr. In this sense it would be fair to call Owain Henry's principal tutor in warfare. Some might rate Owain as only a guerilla leader of genius, but this would in fact be high praise; to wage war successfully for so many years against armies which were much stronger both in numbers and equipment demanded very high military talents.[7]

In order to estimate Owain Glyn Dŵr accurately, he has also to be seen as a statesman who was able to see beyond the war. He gave signals that he was ready to treat with the enemy, to seek a just peace and reconciliation. Since Henry IV was unwilling to make any positive response, Owain had to seek allies: Northumberland and Mortimer in England, and then the Scots and the French. Owain seems to have had reconciliation in mind when he made his reported overture to Henry IV from the Harlech parliament; he had every reason to want peace first so that he could carry out his far-sighted plans for Wales. Reconciliation, however, is only possible if the victor wins over the vanquished by a genuine display of generosity, respect and moderation. The reason why the Welsh rebelled in 1400 was that the English had signally failed to exhibit these qualities, but it was still not too late for peace-making if only Henry IV had been a greater man, and had listened to the advice of the Percies.[8]

Scipio Africanus was not only one of the greatest Roman commanders, but also a great statesman who could see that beyond defeating Hannibal in battle lay the even greater task of making an honourable peace with him. Neither Scipio nor the Duke of Wellington, whose views on peace with France were similar, was a prince intending to establish a dynasty. Owain Glyn Dŵr had this ambition and cannot be wholly acquitted of the faults which go with it. Ellis writes: 'The history printed by Caxton, 1520, says that Owen's war endured twelve years largely. His policy cannot be commended, in that he did not come in person to Hotspur and join his whole power. His cruelty made the people to hate him, and his covetousness made his soldiers by degrees to forsake him. His valour and conduct were excellent.'[9]

This quotation gives the verdict on Owain usual before the revision of the seventeenth century, but its stacatto style may imply that the writer was copying it without necessarily agreeing that it was entirely fair. Owain was unable to come to Hotspur's aid. There is no reason to think that he was more cruel, ruthless or covetous than most of his English opponents. Support dwindled mainly because the Rising had failed. No doubt Owain loved wealth, but he needed it both to finance war and to establish his power. Covetousness is a charge often levelled against powerful and ambitious people. Wealth is only seen as a vice when it is accompanied by stinginess; when it is combined with generosity it is forgiven. Everyone praised Owain for his princely hospitality to all at Sycharth.

During his short reign as Prince of Wales Owain Glyn Dŵr showed that his aim was to give Wales an equal place among European states with her own foreign and ecclesiastical policy, and above all her own pride. He did not have the chance to realise his ambition of winning independence for Wales; maybe it was an impracticable dream, but at least Henry V showed by his attempts to include Owain in a general amnesty that he wished to show magnanimity to a brave but defeated foe. Maybe he also admired the heroic response of the Welsh nation to the genius and the inspired leadership of Owain Glyn Dŵr. His chief and immediate concern, however, was to placate the Welsh; he wanted to recruit them for his war in France, and to prevent any possible revival of the Franco-Welsh alliance.

Owain Glyn Dŵr was a man of extraordinary greatness, who showed the foresight and wisdom of a true statesman. His plans for Welsh universities and a Welsh church with its own archbishop were in line with what the Scots had recently achieved; the fact that they are a reality today might be held to illuminate the prophetic wisdom of the abbot of Valle Crucis. A Welsh Parliament is now possible.

> His political programme of 1404-6 was broad and imaginative, and it seems not only to have convinced his own countrymen but the French and Scots as well. That it should ultimately have failed is no discredit to him or his men. What is surprising is not his downfall but that he was successful for so long.[10]

In the tragic aftermath of the rebellion a new self-confidence and self-respect developed among Welshmen. For about the last century Owain Glyn Dŵr has become recognised as the father of modern Welsh nationalism, a verdict with which all would surely agree.

APPENDIX ONE

Castles in south Wales & the Marches

In November 1401, the defence of the following castles guarding the southern and south-eastern Marches was reorganized. The men were to serve for three monhs at the same wages as for Cardigan:

Cardigan (Prince of Wales)—50 men-at-arms at 12 pence a day each, and 120 archers at 6 pence a day each, paid by the king to Thomas Percy, Earl of Worcester, as captain by the king; already the prince's resources were overstretched.

Aberystwyth or *Llanbadarn* (Prince of Wales)—30 men-at-arms and 40 archers

Builth (the king)—Sir John Oldcastle (captain), 20 men-at-arms and 40 archers

Carmarthen (Prince of Wales)—20 men-at-arms and 40 archers

Brecon (the king)—20 men-at-arms and 40 archers

Llandovery (Lord Audley)—10 men-at-arms and 20 archers

(A man-at-arms, also called a lance, includes his armed servants).[1]

In September 1403, King Henry IV sent a writ to Guy de Mone, Bishop of St. David's and surveyor of castles in south Wales and the Marches, with a 'strict order' in view of the threat by Owain Glyn Dŵr and other rebels to the king, realm and lieges of Wales under pain of losing his castle and all its lordships, manors and lands, to furnish the castle 'with fencible men, victuals, armour, artillery and all things needful for the purpose, that no damage or peril shall arise by his default or negligence or by careless guard thereof'. The persons named were to receive 'like writs' for their castles, situated between Pembrokeshire and north-west Herefordshire.

Llawhaden (Pembrokeshire)—the Bishop of St. David's

Llandovery—John Touchet, Lord Audley

Laugharne—Henry Scrope

Crickhowell—John Pauncefot

Tretower—James Berkeley (successor to the Picards of Ystrad Yw in right of his wife)

Abergavenny and *Ewyas Harold*—William Beauchamp (brother of Richard, Earl of Warwick)

Goodrich—Thomas Neville of Furnival, whose wife, Angharad, was the widow of Richard Talbot; their son Gilbert became Lord Furnival

Eardisley—Nicholas Montgomery (of Derbyshire); the castle belonged to Anne, widow of the Earl of Stafford, who had recently been killed at the battle of Shrewsbury, in right of her mother Eleanor Bohun

Caerleon and *Usk*—Edward Charlton; who had acquired them through his marriage to Eleanor Holland, widow of Roger, 4th Earl of March

Caerphilly and *Ewyas Lacy*—Constance, widow of Thomas Despenser, Lord of Glamorgan (d. 1400)

Manorbier—John Cornewall, husband of Elizabeth of Lancaster

Painscastle and *Clyro*—Richard Beauchamp, Earl of Warwick, lord of Elfael. *Roylle*, the name in the order, is probably *Clyro*, where there was a 'Royal Meadow'

Huntington—Anne Stafford (see Eardisley)

Lyonshall (*Linhales*) and *Dorstone*—Walter Fitz Walter

Stapleton—Richard Cornewall, Lord Burford

Brampton Bryan—Brian Harley

Snodhill or *Snowdoun* (Golden Valley)—John Chandos

Similar orders were also issued in September for *Cardiff* (the king), *Newport* (Earl of Stafford), *Kylkenny* (*Carreg Cennen*) (the king), and *New Radnor* and *Kenflyc* (*Cefnllys*) (Earl of March).[2]

176

3. A Council minute, dated April 1405, gives the details of castle garrisons and other companies of troops in south Wales:[3]

(a) *Castle Garrisons*

		Lances	Archers	Total
Brecon	Lord de Grey	40	200	240
Radnor	Lord de Grey	30	150	180
Abergavenny	Lord Bergavenny	80	400	480
Hay	Earl of Arundel	16	80	96
Carmarthen	Sir Thomas Beaufort	120	600	720
Newcastle Emlyn	Sir Thomas Beaufort	10	50	60
Cardigan	Sir Thomas Beaufort	60	300	360
Aberystwyth	Prince of Wales	40	200	240
	Totals:	396	1,980	2,376

(b) *Other Companies*

	Lances	Archers	Total
The King's personal retinue	*144	720	864
(* '144 men-at-arms', not 'lances')			
Indentured from 26 April to 22 June	400	120	520
Lords appointed to go with the King			
Duke of York ('for *Newport*')	50	260	310
Earl of Warwick	20	100	120
Earl Marshal (Mowbray)	20	120	140
Earl of Dunbar	14	28	42
Lord Lovell	30	60	90
Totals	678	1,408	2,086

When in the late summer of 1404 the Prince of Wales took over at Hereford, he abandoned defensive tactics and began to direct operations in a far more effective manner. Castle garrisons formed flying columns at short notice, like the Brecon and Radnor troops under Lord Grey of Codnor at Grosmont in March 1405, and at Pwll Melyn in May. Henry IV's *chevauchée* into Wales was abandoned at the news of Scrope's rising in May, but he moved rapidly both against these rebels, and later to confront the French.

All the evidence is of more mobile English forces, suggesting that most of the soldiers including the archers were mounted, which had become normal practice during the later stages of the French war. 'Lance' meant both the mounted soldier and his armed servants. Probably there were more than 3,000 combatant troops altogether. The term 'men-at-arms' is used only for the king's retinue, whereas the troops indentured for two months are lances.

The eight castles were seen more as bases for mobile mounted companies than as static defensive posts, except probably for Aberystwyth, which fell at about this time to the Welsh. Later that year they also took Carmarthen and Cardigan with French help. The commission of September 1402 to Sir John Greyndor had indicated New Radnor as the most important castle of that area, and his garrison was now designated as one of the flying columns. In 1405 he recorded that since 1402 the revenue raised in the lordship was £462.0s.19d, and that the wages of the garrison had cost £877.4s.6d.[4]

APPENDIX TWO

Robert Whitney & Thomas Clanvowe

Whitney and Clanvowe were gentlemen from south-west Herefordshire, both of whom suffered from the destruction of their property and ensuing loss of income. Clanvowe's manor of Ocle Pychard, between Hereford and Bromyard, was probably safe, but his other was Cusop, near Hay, right in the disaster area, like Whitney's castle and estate. Many of Whitney's male relatives had been killed at the battle of Pilleth; Clanvowe had been captured there, and, from the state of his affairs, had probably needed help to pay his ransom. Since both men had suffered in different ways on the king's behalf, he had a clear obligation to compensate them.

> Whereas the father of Robert Whiteney, esquire, and his uncle and a great part of his relations were killed on the king's service at the taking of Edmund Mortimer and the substance of his living is burnt and destroyed by the Welsh rebels so that he has no castle or fortress where he can stay for the resistance and castigation of the rebels, the king grants to him the castle of Clufford and the lordships of Clufford [Clifford] and Glasbury with all lands, rents, services, fees, advowsons, royalties, liberties, franchises, jurisdictions, escheats, fines, ransoms and other commodities and full punishment and execution of all rebels of and in the said lordships with all forfeitures and escheats, which castle and lordships before they were

burnt, wasted and destroyed were of the value of 100 marks yearly, to hold from 15 October last during the minority of Edmund son and heir of the earl of March, and so from heir to heir, so that he cause the castle to be repaired and stay in it for defence during the war and answer for any surplus yearly at the Exchequer.[1]

Clanvowe was captured at Pilleth. We know nothing of his ransom, though he was free before 1 November 1402, as we learn from his reporting the loss of letters patent issued in 1395 and 1397 by Richard II, and confirmed in 1400 by Henry IV. He had twice benefited from grants made to him from the estates of the Countess of Oxford, which had reverted to the king after her death.[2] Finally, we learn what the letters patent had conferred:

> Grant for life to the king's knight Thomas Clanvowe of 40 marks [£26.66] and to him and Perin his wife of £20 yearly at the Exchequer from the morrow of Easter last, in lieu of grants by letters patent of Richard II, confirmed by letters patent dated 31 October, 1 Henry IV, from the fee-farm rendered for the castle and cantred of Builth; as the castle and cantred have been so destroyed by the rebels in Wales that no payment has been made for five years past, and his own lands and lordships adjoining the marches of Wales have been likewise destroyed, and the king's letters of confirmation have been surrendered as concerns the annuities, and he has taken oath in Chancery that the letters of Richard II have been lost and will be surrendered if found. If the sums be in arrear for one quarter and the country pacified they shall have the annuities from the said fee-farm.[3]

Henry IV had been ready to ransom Clanvowe and to restore his livelihood and that of Whitney by generous grants and annuities. His refusal to help Edmund Mortimer, commander of that unlucky expedition, is therefore all the harder to excuse, though it can be readily explained. The other point arising from these extracts is the evidence of the devastation in two Marcher lordships.

Destruction of Churches in the Diocese of Hereford, 1406

The extent of the territory exposed to Welsh raids up to 1406 is shown by a Return submitted to the Exchequer by Robert Mascall, Bishop of Hereford (1404-15), naming those benefices in the archdeaconries of Hereford and Shropshire which had suffered so severely as to be exempt from paying the king's aid. The area affected was within the western boundary of the diocese, from the River Severn to the River Monnow. Thirty churches were destroyed in the Archdeaconry of Hereford, and twenty-two in that of Shropshire—a total of fifty-two churches spread through five deaneries. This band of country was less than ten miles wide; but the moral effect of the raids extended far beyond. It caused such a feeling of insecurity that the people of Shropshire and Herefordshire felt compelled to make treaties with the Welsh, and in effect to ward off their attentions, by paying a sort of Danegeld.

1. Damage suffered by the Bishop of Hereford
His 'temporalities' had been destroyed at Bishop's Castle, Lydbury North and 'Bysshopeswer'. His manor of 'Berton' had been devastated to the value of 'vili' [misprint for 8 marks?], and his manor of Tupsley to the value of 10 marks.

2. Archdeaconry of Hereford

Deanery of Hereford: Kingstone 'with glebe lands', Madley 'with the vicar's glebe land'.

Deanery of Archenfield: Dukestone, Hentland, Kenderchurch (St. Cynidr, Kenedric), Llangarron, Llanrothal, Monmouth, St. Dubricius (St. Devereux), St. Weonards and one whose name is illegible.

Deanery of Weobley: Bacton, Bredwardine, Clifford, Cusop, Dorstone 'with the glebe land', Eardisley, Kington 'with the glebe land', Lyonshall 'with the glebe land', Moccas 'with the glebe land', Peterchurch, chapel of Snodhill Castle, Vowchurch, Whitney and Winforton.

Deanery of Leominster: Byton, New Radnor, Old Radnor, Titley and Prestmede (Presteigne) 'with the vicar's glebe land'.

3. Archdeaconry of Shropshire

Deanery of Clun: Ashton, Bishop's Castle 'with the vicar's glebe land', 'Bromptone', Clun 'with the vicar's glebe land', Bucknell, 'Leodone' (Lydham?), Lydbury North 'with the vicar's glebe land', Moore, Stowe, 'Wantenovere' and Wentnor.

Deanery of Pontesbury: Alburbury 'with the vicar's glebe land' and with the wordly possessions ('temporalia'), goods and moveables ('mobilia') of its prior, Chirbury 'with the glebe land of the precentor of Wenlock', Hawood, Meole Brace 'with the vicar's glebe land', Montgomery, Newton with the 'temporalia' of the abbot of Wigmore, Pontesbury 'with the glebe land', Pulverbatch, Shrawardine, Westbury and Worthen.

APPENDIX FOUR

Bastard Feudalism

The Latin word *foedus* means an agreement, treaty, compact, oath or law. It gives us words like federal, confederate and feudal. The feudal system was based upon the tenure of land, which was held in exchange for military or labour services; a tenant-in-chief held directly from the king. Any tenant, whether a baron, a knight or an unfree peasant, did homage and swore fealty to his or her lord.

Feudalism was a military system which prevailed throughout Europe for a thousand years, but it did not produce reliable armies. The Angevin kings (1154-1217: Henry II, Richard I and John), who ruled half of France as well as England and the Marches of Wales, preferred to recruit mercenaries. A magnate who served all three, William Marshal, Earl of Pembroke, built up a household of knights who were not his feudal tenants, but took his fees in payment for their services. Under Edward I (1272-1307) this practice was formalised by legal agreements called indentures. The earliest surviving example was drawn up at Wigmore Castle in 1287 between Edmund Mortimer and Peter Maulay, a Yorkshire knight.[1]

During the wars of the three Edwards with Scotland and France, armies raised by written contracts began to replace the old feudal host; soldiers took indentures for an agreed period, seldom more than six months. Magnates had their retainers who usually served them for life, attending them when summoned to do so. The composition of a lord's retinue depended on whether he was on a peaceful journey, or a military campaign. It might include not only soldiers, but also councillors, stewards, clerks, pages, chaplains, and other servants. A retainer was not necessarily his lord's tenant; some other magnate might pay him a fee or annuity in cash. The wider grouping of people dependent on a lord, and from whom he drew his retinue, was called his affinity, and was primarily but not exclusively based on his estates.

Affinities were the great power centres of the later middle ages. By far the largest was that of the dukes of Lancaster: Henry of Grosmont, and his son-in-law John of Gaunt, even mightier subjects than Marshal, but just as loyal to the king. Henry the third duke was less scrupulous, however, and usurped the throne. The greatest affinities were drawn from many different shires, like those of Lancaster and of Duke Richard of York, whose affinity was strongest in the Welsh Marches where he held the Mortimer inheritance. The affinity might include elderly, retired servants (male and female), to whom the lord paid fees, annuities, or pensions.

About a century ago the rather unfortunate title 'bastard feudalism' was applied to this perfectly logical development. The economy of late medieval Europe became more complex, and the use of coin increased. Landlords became willing to accept cash rents from peasants who could afford them, instead of labour services. In England this trend began early in the thirteenth century. The Black Death caused such a shortage of labour that landowners had no alternative but to pay wages for it at the going rate.

Throughout the middle ages the gentry served magnates in their retinues, and on their estates. A knight or esquire relied on the 'good lordship' of the magnate of whose affinity he was a member, especially in his quarrels with his neighbours, which were usually about land. These quarrels often led to violence, which was common in those days, especially when justice could not be obtained, as was often the case. Lord Grey's seizure of Owain Glyn Dŵr's land is one example. Consequently respect for royal authority would decline; feuds would break out between groups of gentry who were probably the retainers of rival magnates. This was the root cause of the mayhem and private wars which flourished in the latter part of Henry VI's reign, leading to the Wars of the Roses and the fall of both Lancaster and York. Edward IV had difficulty in controlling his brothers Clarence and Gloucester, sons-in-law of the late Warwick the Kingmaker, and overmighty subjects with great affinities of their own. The Crowland Chronicler, an important but anonymous observer who had served both Edward IV and Richard III, thought that if the three 'had been able to avoid dissention, that triple cord could have been broken only with the utmost difficulty.'[2]

Like any state, the medieval kingdom worked best if there was harmony. A wise king cultivated the support of his nobles, who in their turn looked to him for patronage. To do justice, he had to be impartial. This was not the case under Edward II, Richard II and Henry VI, all of whom allowed factions to develop at court. It was also difficult for usurpers like Henry IV or Edward IV to rise above faction and to win the respect of magnates who had helped them to seize the throne. Henry VII's position was unusually strong; he held all the lands of Lancaster and York, and no subject was mighty enough to challenge him.

It is easy to put all the blame on kings. The arbitrary rule of Richard II was the main reason for the accession of the House of Lancaster, just as the weakness of Henry VI contributed to its fall. But greedy and ambitious subjects were also greatly to blame, also those magnates who failed to give the king proper counsel and support. The upheavals which occurred, from the fall of Edward II in 1327 to the flight of James II in 1688, were not only due to royal incompetence.

Livery and maintenance were the particular abuses which have done most to give bastard feudalism a bad name. A livery was the medieval equivalent of a uniform, harmless unless it became the badge of a faction. In remote areas leading magnates might be regarded more highly than the king: Percy in the north, Mortimer in the Welsh Marches, Courtney in the west country. Their liveries could then be symbols of disorder, like the scarves and colours of football supporters, causing similar alarm when at times of trouble rival magnates invaded London with large and well-armed retinues.[3] Maintenance was the widespread practice whereby magnates and country gentry 'maintained' the causes of their retainers in the courts, which involved the control and corruption of sheriffs and juries.

The Tudors did not get rid of either overmighty subjects, or bastard feudalism, or the abuses associated with them. The minority reign of Edward VI was followed by the attempt of John Dudley, Duke of Northumberland, to exclude Mary and install Jane Grey as a puppet queen. The court of the ageing Elizabeth I was rotten with factions. The queen's spoilt favourite was Robert Devereux, Earl of Essex; another subject too big for his boots, he led his gang in a disastrous coup against his rival Robert Cecil, which failed ignominiously in 1601.

During the seventeenth century overmighty subjects appeared in both France and England, where Charles I was publicly beheaded. Charles II's reign produced a Kingmaker: the Earl of Shaftesbury most skilfully used the rent-a-mob methods employed against Charles I before the Civil War. In 1678 the 'Popish Plot' enabled him to whip up anti-Catholic hysteria, but he failed to exclude James, Duke of York, from the throne in favour of the king's bastard son James, Duke of Monmouth. Despite his religion, James II lost his throne because he abandoned the sensible policies of his brother Charles II, isolating himself by arbitrary methods which Richard II might have envied. A comparison between the seventeenth and fifteenth centuries demonstrates that in any age it is unwise rulers and weak governments who get into trouble. It is no use blaming the system for bad policies.

APPENDIX FIVE

Sir John Clanvowe and Lollard doctrine

The life of Sir John Clanvowe throws an interesting light on the society in which the young Owain Glyn Dŵr grew up. Owain could well have met Sir John, pre-eminent among the gentry of Herefordshire, a notable soldier, diplomat and knight of the chamber to Edward III and Richard II. He was one of the leading knightly intellectuals of his day and a friend of Geoffrey Chaucer. It is now thought that he, not Sir Thomas Clanvowe, was the author of the poem 'The Cuckoo and the Nightingale', on the theme of courtly love; it has even been attributed to Chaucer himself.

The teaching of John Wyclif attracted Clanvowe and several other knights who had developed a more serious outlook, illustrated by Clanvowe's other work 'The Two Ways'. This rather turgid religious tract on the narrow way to Heaven, as opposed to the broad way to Hell, shows a sound knowledge of scripture, but studiously ignores the Church and its teachings. Clanvowe wrote it when he was a successful middle-aged man, disillusioned with the vanity of court life and with war; Lollardy included in its teachings a reaction against militarism. Clanvowe nailed his colours to the mast when he wrote: 'Such folk the world scorneth and holdeth them lollers and losels [good-for-nothings] ... but surely God holdeth them most wise and most worshipful'. He was one of seven knights who were known Lollards; another was John Montague, later Earl of Salisbury. Clanvowe and his close friend William Neville died near Constantinople in 1391, probably on pilgrimage.

Clanvowe and his friends flourished in a more tolerant age, before the upheavals of Richard II's reign and the rebellion of Owain Glyn Dŵr, who avoided any taint of Lollardy, and walked the strait path of orthodoxy; he could not otherwise have won the support of the Pope or the King of France. There was to be little sympathy for the Lollards who rebelled against Henry V, led by Sir John Oldcastle, Lord Cobham. Owain's Czech contemporary John Hus professed Wyclif's doctrines and was burned in 1415, the posthumous hero of a national revolt.[1]

The following is an extract from 'The Two Ways', in modern spelling:

> This treasure here upon earth is false, and passing, and unsavoury. And, therefore, as Saint Paul saith, and also it is said here before, 'Take we savour in those things that been above in heaven.' And with the savour of them we should despise these false, unsavoury things that been here on earth, the which would lightly, if we took savour in them, bring us in to the broad way of hell, for thither hath the savour of earthly things led many on. And that witnesseth Saint Paul there as he saith thus: 'Those that will be made rich are fallen in to temptation and in to the devil's panter [trap] and in to many unprofitable and envious desires the which draw men to manslaughter and also bring men to loss of body and of soul.' And, therefore, by this, and by many other authorities, and also by kindly skill, we may well see that these that men here call riches been none very [true] riches but thing of nought that letteth [preventeth] men to gather them the fair riches of heaven, the which been very riches. And, therefore, take we savour in the riches above and despise we all that is here beneath upon earth that would let us to go in the strait [narrow] way that leadeth to the bliss of heaven. And also the worships [praises] of this wretched world that men desire so greatly, if that we

188

been well advised, they been none worships, nor they oughten not with truth to been called worships. And we may be right siker [sure] that before God, that is very truth, they been neither riches nor worships, for before God all virtue is worship and all sin is shame. And in this world it is even the reverse, for the world hold them worshipful that been great warriors and fighters that destroyen and winnen many lands, and wasten and thieven much good to them that have enough, and that dispenden [spend] outrageously in meat, in drink, in clothing, in building, and in living in ease, sloth, and many other sins.

APPENDIX SIX

Owain Glyn Dŵr: A Summary

1357-59? Born, probably at Sycharth.

1380? Studied at Inns of Court.

1383? Married Margaret Hanmer.

1384-5 In retinue of Sir Degory Sais, on Richard II's Scottish campaign.

1386 Gave evidence at Chester in suit of Grosvenor v. Scrope.

1387-8 In the retinue of Richard Fitzalan, Earl of Arundel, fighting in the naval battle of Cadzand.

1397 Arundel executed; Owain in retinue of Henry, Duke of Hereford.

1399 Henry, now Duke of Lancaster, deposed Richard II and became king.

1400 Quarrel with Grey of Ruthin. The Rebellion begins. Henry IV's 1st invasion of Wales.

1401 Owain's victory at Nant Hyddgen, attacks on Abbey Cwm Hir and New Radnor, and defeats at Welshpool and Caernarfon. Henry IV's 2nd invasion of Wales.

1402 Capture of Grey. Battle of Pilleth. Invasion of Glamorgan and Gwent. Henry IV's 3rd invasion of Wales with three armies.

1403 Owain's successes in south Wales. Henry IV's victory at Shrewsbury over Hotspur. His 4th invasion of Wales, recapture of Carmarthen. Failure to defeat Owain or to protect border shires against Welsh raids.

1404 Owain took Cardiff, Aberystwyth and Harlech, held Parliament at Machynlleth, treated with the Scots, French and Avignon pope.

1405   The Tripartite Treaty. Welsh defeats at Grosmont and Pwll Melyn.

1406-09 The king crushed Scrope's Rebellion. Franco-Welsh march to Worcester. Henry IV's 5th invasion of Wales. Owain's power declined: loss of French and Scots support (French civil war, capture of James I by English). Defeat and death of Northumberland. Fall of Aberystwyth and Harlech: death of Mortimer there, capture of his family and Owain's. Defeat of Owain's raid into Shropshire, his military power broken.

1412   Capture and ransoming of Dafydd Gam, the last known aggressive act by Owain Glyn Dŵr.

1412-15 Amnesty offered to all rebels by Henry V. Disappearance of Owain Glyn Dŵr, probably living secretly with Alice and John Scudamore in Kentchurch/Golden Valley area, where he probably died on 20/21 September, 1415.

1416-17 Maredudd ab Owain received his pardon, but there was no news of Owain Glyn Dŵr.

The Pedigree and Progeny of Owain Glyn Dŵr

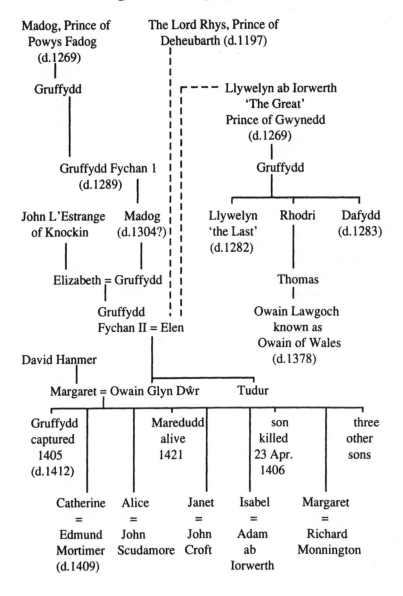

Mortimer of Wigmore; Plantagenet, York and Lancaster

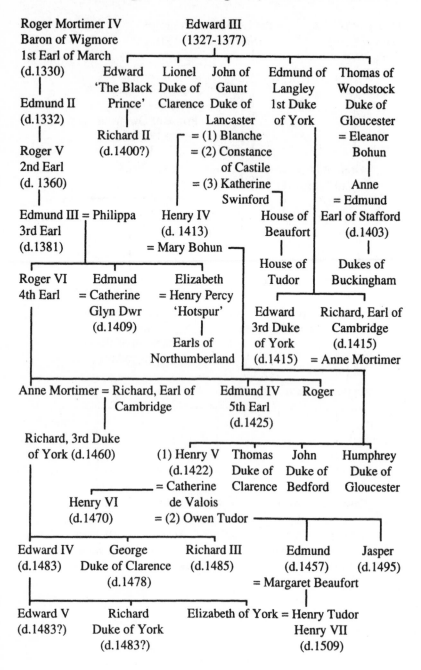

FOOTNOTES

Chapter One

1. Caradog is the Welsh form of Caratacus, familiarly but wrongly known as Caractacus; in the same way, Boudicca is erroneously called Boadicea.
2. M. Prestwich, *Edward I* (London, 1988), 207-16; R.R. Davies, *Conquest, Coexistence and Change: Wales 1053-1415* (Oxford. 1987), 338-39. 3. ibid., 362, 392-400, especially Maps 10 and 11.
4. ibid., chapter 15.
5. Prestwich, 348-59.
6. Carole Rawcliffe, *The Staffords, earls of Stafford and dukes of Buckingham 1394-1521* (Cambridge, 1978), 14-15; Anthony Goodman, *John of Gaunt* (London, 1992), 310-11, 400 (Map 2).
7. Quoted from John Buchan, title page to *The Blanket of the Dark*.
8. Goodman, 310.
9. Davies, 399-05, 439; T.B. Pugh, *Henry V and the Southampton Plot of 1415* (Southampton, 1988), 32-33.
10. ibid., 34; Davies, 371-73, 412-13, 421-22.
11. Pugh, 31; Davies, 411, 417-19, 430.
12. ibid., 398-99, 10-11; Glanmor Williams, *Owain Glyndŵr* (Cardiff, 1993), 10-11.
13. ibid., 398, 439-40; G. Williams, *Owain Glyndŵr* 9-10; Pugh. 34-35.
14. A well-known situation which offers some comparison is that, in 1642, Puritans such as John Pym and John Hampden, Oliver Cromwell and Robert Harley of Brampton Bryan felt that the policies of King Charles I had left them with no alternative but armed resistance. Owain Glyn Dŵr's Rising had nothing to do with religion, which was perhaps the main cause of the Great Civil War; but both rebellions had this in common: a conviction that the king could not be trusted.

Chapter Two

1. *Henry IV, Part I*, Act III, Scene 1.
2. J.E. Lloyd, *Owen Glendower* (Oxford, 1931), 52; *Ann.Hen.IV*, 349; Thomas Walsingham, *Historia Anglicana* (London,1863), ii, 254. See Ch.6, note 4.
3. Davies, 353.
4. John Buchan, *Augustus* (London, 1937), 8; E.V. Rieu, *Odyssey* (Penguin Classics, 1945), Book 11, 175-76.
5. Christopher Morris, 'Shakespeare's Politics', *The Historical Journal*, viii, 3 (1965), 293-308, esp. 294-97. For an epilogue on Tudor misrule, see K.B. McFarlane, *England in the Fifteenth Century* (London, 1981), 43.

6. *Henry IV, Part I*, Act I, Scene 1; Act III, Scene 1; Joan Rees, 'Shakespeare's Welshmen', *Literature and Nationalism*, ed. Vincent Newey and Ann Thompson (Liverpool, 1991).

7. *The History of the Kings of Britain* (London, 1966), 174; Mary E. Giffin, 'Cadwalader, Arthur and Brutus in the Wigmore Manuscript', *Speculum*, 16 (1941), 109-10. See Ch. 6 below, n. 7, for *The Brut* (History of Britain).

8. J.Y.W. Lloyd, *History of Powys Fadog* (London, 1887), i, 194-98; Lloyd, 8-17, explains Fychan ('lesser'): 'Such forms as Gruffydd ap Gruffydd or Rhys ap Rhys were obnoxious to the Welsh ear; the invariable rule was to use instead the epithet Fychan, which has no reference to stature.' (p.9, n.3); R.A. Griffiths, *The Making of the Tudor Dynasty* (Gloucester, 1985), 16-18; G. Williams, *Owain Glyndŵr* (Cardiff, 1993), 12-13.

9. Davies, 438, 448-49, also 'Owain Glyn Dŵr and the Welsh Squirearchy', *TCS* (1968), ii,150-69; G. Williams, *Owain Glyndŵr*, 11.

10. *Powys Fadog*, i, 194-98; Lloyd, 8-17. See Table 1 below, 'The Pedigree of Owain Glyn Dŵr'.

11. Thomas Pennant, *A Tour in Wales* (London, 1778; this edn. 1784), i, 326; *Powys Fadog*, vi, 1-2; Lloyd, 18-19, who rejects Trefgarn Owain near St. David's as Owain's birthplace; G. Williams, *Owain Glyndŵr*, 14.

12. R. Ian Jack, 'New light on the early days of Owain Glyndŵr', *BBCS* 21 (1964-66) 163-65; Lloyd, 16-17; G. Williams, *Owain Glyndŵr*, 14-16. The author thanks Mr. C.O.M. Bedingfield, Q.C., for his suggestion that Owain was probably a royal ward, and Professor Williams for his comment that Arundel was most likely to have held the wardship, as he was dominant in the area and knew Owain's family.

13. ibid., 14-17; Walsingham, ii 246; *Ann.Hen.IV*, 333; Lloyd, 24-25; T.A. Jones, *Without my Wig* (Liverpool, 1945), 36; Mr. Bedingfield kindly gave me details of medieval legal training.

14. *Henry IV, Part II*, Act III, Scene 2.

15. A.E. Goodman, 'Owain Glyndŵr before 1400', *WHR*, 5 (1970-1), 67; Lloyd, 21-22; Thomas Ellis, *Memoirs of Owen Glendowr*, appendix to *A History of the Island of Anglesey*, probably by John Thomas of Beaumaris, (London, 1st ed. 1775, this ed. 1853), 70-74 (Gruffydd Llwyd's poem); G. Williams, *Owain Glyndŵr*, 15-16. See below, Appendix 4, 'Bastard Feudalism'.

16. Pennant, i, 328; Lloyd, 23; T.A. Jones, 36-38; G. Williams, *Owain Glyndŵr*, 15-16;

17. Goodman, *Owain*, 68; for Cadzand, *The Great Chronicle of London*, ed. A.H. Thomas & I.D. Thornley (London, 1938), 46.

18. *Eulogium Historiarum*, Continuation of, ed. F.R. Haydon (London,

1858-63), iii, 388; Walsingham, ii, 246: *Ann.Hen.IV*, 333; Ellis, 57;
Pennant, i, 327; John Webb, 'A Brief Account of Owen Glyndwr'
(HCL, MS.A.6391/1, 1833), 39; Goodman, *Owain*, 69.

19. C.L. Kingsford, *English Historical Literature in the Fifteenth Century*
(Oxford, 1913), 12-21.

20. Ellis, 57; J.R.S. Phillips, 'When did Owain Glyn Dŵr die?', *BBCS* 4
(1970-72), 59-77, goes very thoroughly into Owain's Welsh sources;
Lloyd, 147-158, 'Welsh Sources for the History of the Glyn Dŵr
Movement'.

21. *Powys Fadog*, 1, 211-15; Lloyd, 26-7; G. Williams, *Owain Glyndŵr*,
17-18; Iain Skydmore, *Owain Glyndŵr* (Swansea, 1978), 19-21; *DNB*,
1313.

Chapter Three

1. M. McKisack, *The Fourteenth Century* (Oxford, 1959), chs. 13-15;
Davies, 439-40.

2. K.B. McFarlane, *Lancastrian Kings and Lollard Knights* (Oxford,
1972), 17-19; Goodman, chapter 6 passim.

3. McKisack, 462-78; *Richard II*, Act 3, Scene 1.

4. McFarlane, 35-39. See Appendix 4 below.

5. McKisack, 478-98.

6. *Richard II,* Act IV, Scene 1.

7. *The Chronicle of Adam of Usk*, ed. E.M. Thompson (London, 1904;
paperback edn. Felinfach, 1990), 34-35; Pugh, 75-77; Dugdale,
Monasticon VI, i, 354.

8. E.F. Jacob, *The Fifteenth Century* (Oxford, 1961), 3-4, 10-17.

9. Davies, 442-43.

10. Jacob, 9-10.

11. J.M.W. Bean, 'Henry IV and the Percies', *History*, 44 (1959), 212-27;
McFarlane, 72-75; Pugh, 13-16.

12. G. Williams, *Owain Glyndŵr*, 22; Simon Walker, *The Lancastrian
Affinity 1360-1399* (Oxford, 1990), Appendix 1: Annuitants of John of
Gaunt; Original Letters II, i, 14 (Beaumaris and Denbigh).

13. Christopher Allmand, *Henry V* (London, 1992), 12-13; McFarlane,
104-105, 115, 120-22; for Richard II's reburial, extracts given in *Issues
of the Exchequer*, ed. F. Devon (London, 1837), show costs of up to
£110 2s.4d, though a note says that there were others.

14. Allmand, 58; McFarlane, 123-24; Morris, 'Shakespeare's Politics',
301-302; E.M.W. Tillyard, *Shakespeare's History Plays*
(Harmondsworth, 1962), 119, 123-24; P. Saccio, *Shakespeare's English
Kings* (Oxford, 1977), 61-62.

15. Allmand, 33-35, 93-95, 124-25; Rhidian Griffiths, (a) 'Prince Henry,
Wales and the Royal Exchequer', *BBCS* 32 (1985). 202-205, and (b)

'Prince Henry's War: armies, garrisons and supply during the Glyndŵr Rebellion', *BBCS* 34 (1987), 165-73.
16. *Henry V*, Act IV, Scenes 6 and 7; *Henry IV, Part II*, Act IV, Scene 3.
17. *Anglo-Norman Letters*, ed. M.D. Legge (Oxford, 1941), no. 223; *Henry V*, Act III, Scene 6, and Act IV, Scenes 1 and 7.
18. *Henry V*, Act 2, Scene 2; Allmand, 436. The connection between Falstaff and Oldcastle may seem far-fetched, but Shakespeare hints at it: 'Falstaff shall die of a sweat, unless already a' be killed with your hard opinions; for Oldcastle died a martyr, and this is not the man.' (Epilogue to *Henry IV, Part II*; see also Tillyard, 123-24).

Chapter Four

1. *CPR*, ii, 234; Usk, 112.
2. *Historia Vitae et Regni Ricardi II* a Monacho quodam de Evesham, ed. T. Hearne (Oxford, 1729); *Incerti Scriptoris Chronicon Angliae*, ed. J.A. Giles (London, 1848).
3. *Eulogium*, iii, 388; Walsingham, ii, 246; Pennant, i, 333. The *Eulogium* was a Latin chronicle, whose original part ends in 1366 and was probably written at Malmesbury Abbey. The Continuation was written by many different authors up to 1413. See Chapter 2 above, note 17.
4. Evesham, 171, who is followed by Giles, 20-21; Goodman, 'Owain before 1400', 70.
5. McFarlane, 145-46.
6. Lloyd, 149-50 (*Ann.OGD*), 29-32.
7. Usk, 78; Evesham, 171; Ellis, 57-58.
8. Ellis, 58; Pennant, 339; *Powys Fadog*, vi, 309-10, the destruction of Oswestry was recorded in a seventeenth-century document, Harleian MS 1981; Lloyd,32, n.3, 149.
9. Hardynge, *Chronicle*, ed. H. Ellis (1812), 358.
10. For Shrewsbury, see Rymer, viii, 160; Lloyd, 32-34; Griffiths, 21. See Chapter 2 above, n.8: Maredudd ap Tudur, their brother, was ancestor of the Tudor dynasty.
11. *CPR*, i, 386, in *Powys Fadog*, i, 200-201; Pennant, i, 340.
12. *RP*, iii, 508-509; *Original Letters*, II, 8-9; Lloyd, 35-36; Davies, 437.
13. R.A. Griffiths, 'Some Partisans of Owain Glyndŵr at Oxford', *BBCS*, 20 (1962-4), 282-92; Usk, 15, 17-18. Adam claimed that he had been indicted as 'the chief leader and abettor of the Welsh'; he also saw the army of the Appellants march through before the battle of Radcot Bridge.
14. Goodman, 62-63, 310-11.
15. Lloyd, 35-36; *PPC*, ii, 55, 59-60.
16. *DNB*, 1308, quoting *Powys Fadog*, i, 220 (Iolo Goch).
17. Usk, 96; *Original Letters* II, i. 13-14; Lloyd, 37; Allmand, 36-37; Rhidian Griffiths, 'Prince Henry's War', 167-69.

18. Usk, 96; Royal Letters, i, 69-72; Lloyd, 37-38; Rhidian Griffiths, 'Prince Henry and the Exchequer', 202, 207.
19. *PPC*, i, 150-51; Lloyd, 38-39.
20. *PPC*, i, 151-52.
21. Usk, 96; Rhidian Griffiths, 'Prince Henry and the Exchequer', 202; Lloyd, 37-39;
22. *PPC*, ii, 54-56; *PPC*, i, 133-35; Lloyd, 39-41; *Henry IV, Part II*, Act 3, Scene 2; Rhidian Griffiths, 'Prince Henry's War', 165-66.
23. Davies, *Welsh Squirearchy*, 159.
24. *PPC*, i, 151-53.
25. *Anglo-Norman Letters and Petitions*, ed. M.D. Legge (Oxford, 1941), no. 226; Lloyd, 42.

Chapter Five

1. Lloyd, 150-51 (*Ann.OGD*).
2. Ellis, 58.
3. *Inventory of Ancient Monuments in Wales, Montgomeryshire* [1911], no. 921; Lloyd, 39, n.3; Pennant, i, 343-44; Thomas Thomas, *Owen Glendower* (Haverfordwest, 1822), 75-76; *Powys Fadog*, i, 202; The Stones are the Standing Stones at map reference 783897 on OS Sheet 135 (1:50,000); one of them is visible with binoculars from Maes y Nant, where the tarmac ends. It is a mile to the Stones; Afon Hengwm and Afon Hyddgen can be hard to ford, but there is a footbridge further up Afon Hengwm. (Hill walkers in Wales must often marvel at the vast cairns which crown so many peaks: Snowdon, the Carneddau, Cader Idris and Plynlimon for instance. There are three huge stone beacons on the remote summit of Drygarn Fawr, above the Claerwen valley in Radnorshire. Why were they built, and when?)
4. *The Itinerary of John Leland* (Oxford, 1779), vol. 4; Pennant, i, 343; Thomas, 72-75; Jonathan Williams, *History of Radnor* (Brecon, 1905), 51; *Powys Fadog*, i, 202; W.H. Howse, *Radnorshire* (Hereford, 1949), 43, and 'New Radnor Castle' (*Rad.Soc.Trans.*, xxviii, 1958), 24-25; *Illustrated London News*, 4 Oct. 1845, 223-24; CPR, i, 120. See Ch.6, n.5 and Ch.7, ns.1-3 and 13 below.
5. Glanmor Williams, *Renewal and Reformation: Wales c.1415-1642* (Oxford, 1987), 19.
6. J.H. Parry, *The Register of Robert Mascall, Bishop of Hereford 1404-1415* (Hereford, 1916), 20-22. See Appendix 3 below.
7. *Anglo-Norman Letters*, no. 236; Rhidian Griffiths, 'Prince Henry and the Exchequer', 208: other payments of £1,000 from the Exchequer were made on 30 August and 21 November.
8. Usk, 107; Leland, v, 4; Pennant, i, 343; Thomas, 73; Williams, Radnor, 51. Pennant and Thomas say that Montgomery Castle was stormed.

9. Usk, 107; *Anglo-Norman Letters*, nos. 227, 235 and 237; Pennant, i, 344; Thomas, 76; Lloyd, 40-44.

10. Usk, 107; Evesham, 174-75.

11. *PPC*, i, 173-79; Usk, 108 (Charlton). *Anglo-Norman Letters*, no.237, King to Prince, 14 Nov.1401, for the appointment of the Bishop of St. David's as surveyor; see Appendix 1 below for castles.

12. Usk, 107-108; *PPC*, ii, 64; *Original Letters* II, i, 14; Evesham, 174-75; Lloyd, 44-45; *DNB*, 1309.

13. *PPC*, i, 175, and ii, 59-60; *Anglo-Norman Letters*, no. 244. 14. ibid.; *PPC*, i, 177-78; *Original Letters* II, i.

14; Lloyd, 45-46.

15. *PPC*, i, 178; *Anglo-Norman Letters*, nos. 215 and 228.

16. Usk, 101 (Dunbar), 108-12; Jacob, 34-36.

17. F.M. Stenton, *Anglo-Saxon England* (Oxford, 1971), 575; Davies, 243.

18. Bower, *Johannis de Fordun Scotichronicon* (Edinburgh, 1759), ii, 457-58 ('the Alban people' are the Scots); Usk, 108-12; *DNB*, 1309; Lloyd, 47.

19. Usk, 108-09.

20. *DNB*, 463-64; Usk, 75-76; *Eulogium*, iii, 389; Walsingham, ii, 248; *Ann.Hen.IV*, 338.

21. *Ann.Hen.IV*, 338-39; Eulogium, iii, 389; Usk, 117; Lloyd, 48-9; and 151 (*Ann.OGD*); Hardyng, 358; Ellis confuses this with Burnell's victory in 1400 (58); see also Evesham, 177 and Giles 26.

Chapter Six

1. *Ann.Hen.IV*, 340; Walsingham, ii, 249-50.

2. *Eulogium*, iii, 389-94; Jacob, 94-96.

3. Lloyd, 50; Allmand, 21.

4. B.P. Evans, 'The Family of Mortimer' (University of Wales, unpublished Ph.D. Thesis, 1934), 330.

5. Evesham, 179; *Eulogium*, iii, 398.

6. Lloyd, 151 for Gruffydd Hiraethog (*Ann.OGD*).

7. *The Brut*, ed. F.W.D. Brie, (London, 1908-9), ii, 393. Brutus is hard to avoid in medieval England, giving his name to Britain, to the Britons, and even to this chronicle (Allmand, 414); Elizabeth Dunn, 'Owain Glyndŵr and Radnorshire' (*Trans.Rad.Soc.*, vol.xxxvii, 1967), 27-35; Frank Noble, 'Bleddfa', (ibid.), 60-63; Mascall, 20-22; Lord Rennell of Rodd, *Valley on the March* (Oxford, 1958), 228; *CPR*, ii, 120-21; See Ch.5 above, note 10, Ch.7 below, notes 1-3 and 16, and Appendix 3. 'Maelienydd' can be found on OS sheet 148 at SO 710130; Glyndŵr's Way can be seen on this sheet and also on 147, where the mountain road through Staylittle appears as a more practical military route, though less attractive for hikers.

8. Evesham, 178; Giles, 27; *Ann.Hen.IV*, 341; Walsingham, ii, 250; Usk, 116; *The Brut*, ii, 393; Dugdale, *Monasticon VI*, i, 354; Usk, 116; Lloyd, 151 (*Ann.OGD*); *Eulogium*, iii, 394 and Hardyng, 358-59, note the defeat and capture of Mortimer, but give no further details; see Pugh, 36 for the stratagem to trap Mortimer.

9. *Domesday Book* (Herefordshire), ed. F. and C. Thorn (Chichester, 1983), 9.13 (Pilleth), 24.3. See above for references: The Monk of Evesham, Giles and Leland give Pylale, but Gruffydd Hiraethog prefers Pilale. His chronicle was the main source used by Vaughan and Ellis, who misspells it Pilate. *The Brut* calls it Pymaren (ii, 393); Leland mentions 'a Chapel of owr Lady of Pylale' (but not the battle) and gives the course of the Lugg to Leominster (v, 12); W. Wynne-Jones, *A Guide to Pilleth Church* (1989), 5. See OS Sheet 148, 256683.

10. Walsingham, ii, 258. For the statute of the Confessor, see John Price, *Historical Account of Leominster* (Ludlow, 1795), 18, and Jonathan Williams, *Leominster Guide* (Leominster, 1808), 52-54.

11. Giles, 27.

12. C.J. Robinson, *Castles of Herefordshire* (Hereford, 1869), 104-105 and 132-33 (Devereux); 135-36 (Whitney); 88-89 (Kinard de la Bere); 40-41, (Clanvowe); Robinson, *Manors of Herefordshire* (Hereford 1873), 217; Lloyd, 50, Thomas Clanvowe. See W.H. Howse, *Radnorshire*, (Hereford, 1949), 43, and Appendix 2 below; Mcfarlane, 230-32, Appendix B, (Clanvowe's possessions). See Appendix 5 below, 'Sir John Clanvowe and Lollard Doctrine'. Kinnersley is at present still inhabited and is open to the public during the summer.

13. *Ann.Hen.IV*, 341.

14. Evesham, 178 (Rees Gytch or Gethin); Lloyd, 66-67 (Owain's captains).

15. Goodman, 364.

16. For the Manor Road see Rennell, 85-88.

17. I am most grateful to Mr. Peter Hood of Pilleth Court for his advice on local topography, details about drainage, and other points such as the probable loss of Green-Price records during the war, when Norton Manor was occupied by troops (conversation, 12 March 1994).

18. Noble, 61; Hatfield, *Knighton*, 14-15.

19. Dugdale, VI, i, 354; *The Brut*, ii, 393; Evesham, 172; Giles, 27.

20. Perhaps this is roughly the same as Alfred Burne's theory of 'Inherent Military Probability'; see *The Crécy War* (London 1955), 12.

21. J. Williams, *Radnor*, 311-12.

22. Walsingham, ii, 250; *Eulogium*, iii, 398; *Ann.Hen.IV*, 341; Evesham, 178; Giles, 27; Usk, 116-17; Lloyd, 151 (*Ann.OGD*); Ellis, 59.

23. Walsingham, ii, 178; Evesham, 178; Pennant, i, 352-53.

24. Evan Williams, 'On the Church, etc., at Pilleth', *Archaeologia*

Cambrensis, ii (1847), 330; Howse, 43-44. Written evidence about Sir Richard's activities is lacking, but the wellingtonias are mute witnesses. Three can be seen from the road, one of which conceals a fourth tree.

25. John Lodge, *History of the County of Hereford* (1793); John Price, *Leominster*, 16-28; John Duncumb, *County of Hereford*, i (Hereford 1804); N.C. Reeves, 'Five Leominster Historians', (*Wool.Trans.* xlv (i), 1985), 284-95; J. Williams, *Radnor*, 51; see Ch.4, n.10 and Ch.5, n.7; for Thomas Thomas, see Chapter 5, note 3.

26. *Henry IV, Part I*, Act I, Scene 3; Williams, *Leominster*, 52-55 and 66, *Radnor*, 51-52; Price, 19; Duncumb, i, 86-87.

27. J. Williams, *Leominster*, 53-73; Duncumb, i, 87; Price, 20; Regarding Williams' orations, I am indebted to Professor Glanmor Williams for this interesting point: 'Theophilus Evans, grandfather of Theophilus Jones, the Breconshire historian, had made such eve-of-battle speeches very popular in Wales in his book, *Drych y Prif Oesoedd* (1716, 2nd edn. 1740).' See G.F. Townsend, *Town of Leominster* (1862), 38. Price also believed that the Welsh troops fought at Mortimer's Cross: see Geoffrey Hodges, *Ludford Bridge and Mortimer's Cross* (Logaston, 1989), 57-58, in which Price and Williams are confused).

28. Price, 24; Duncumb, 87; J. Williams, *Leominster*, 52-53, 73-74, quoting Thomas Blount of Orleton (1618-79), MS. 'History of Herefordshire', Vol. 2. It is a topography in alphabetical order; Vol. 2 begins at L. The original is in Hereford City Library (f LC 942.44/AC). The Hereford Record Office has a copy, ref. B 56/12, dating from about 1800. The warrant is in French; 'bests et herbez' is translated 'beasts and forage', which implies military stores. (Williams translates it 'cattle and sheep'). Lingein or Lingain are both used in the MS; they are medieval ways of spelling Lingen; Robinson, *Castles*, 94, and *Manors*, 220-21, for biographical details of Thomas Blount; the first volume of the Blount MS. was lost in the eighteenth century. The City Library has some extracts in the Walter Pilley Collection [(P.C.181) 091.42]; the Hereford Cathedral Library has more extracts in John Webb: 'An Account taken out of Mr. Blount's Manuscript of Herefordshire' (6391/1), including 'A Brief Account of Owen Glendwr', based on Ellis. There is a modern description of the collection in Theo Bongaerts, *The Correspondence of Thomas Blount* (Amsterdam, 1978). A pure guess is that Janin de Brompton, recipient of Lingein's warrant, could be John Harley of Brampton Bryan.

29. *The Brut*, 362-63; *Original Letters*, II, 1, 9; Pennant, i, 347; see Ch. 10 and Table 1, 'The Pedigree of Owain Glyn Dŵr' below; *Henry IV, Part I*, Act III, Scene 1; see Lloyd's summary, 49, note 2.

30. *PPC*, i, 185; *CPR*, i, 137-39.

31. Mascall, 20-22, and Appendix 3 below.

32. *CPR*, ii, 120; see Appendix 1, and Chapter 8 below, notes 23-25.
33. Pennant, i, 387-88; *Ann.Hen IV*, 341; Hardynge, 358-59. Walsingham does not mention Mortimer's collusion with Owain in his own chronicle; it could have been been introduced into the *Annals* by one of his editors.

Chapter Seven
1. Lloyd, 54 and 151-52 (*Ann.OGD*).
2. Usk, 177-78; Lloyd, 54; for Stafford revenues, see Pugh, 38 and 46.
3. *Ann.Hen.IV*, 343; *CPR*, ii, 137-40.
4. Shakespeare, *Henry IV, Part I*, Act III, Scene 1. (In Ch.12, 'Owain Glyn Dŵr's Place in History', a comparison is made with Rommel).
5. ibid; *RP*, iii, 487; Lloyd, 57, n.2; *Ann.Hen.IV*, 349; Usk, 177-78; *CPR*, ii, 121 (Merbury).
6. *RP*, iii, 508-509.
7. *RP*, iii, 487; *Ann.Hen.IV*, 349.
8. *CPR*, ii, 170, 471, and ii, 52, 94 (Clanvowe). See Appendix 2 below.
9. *Ann.Hen.IV*, 341; *Eulogium*, iii, 396; *Henry IV, Part I*, Act I, Scene 3.
10. Pugh, *Southampton Plot*, 61-62, 79-80, 88-102, 122-36; Allmand, 74-77; *Henry V, Act 2*, Scene 2.
11. Usk, 116-17; *Original Letters II*, i, 24-6; *Ann.Hen.IV*, 349; *Eulogium*, iii, 398, and 389-90 for the alleged survival of Richard II; Lloyd cites Issue Roll of 1 Henry V, Michaelmas, 22 February 1414 for Catherine's name, though the extract given by Devon in *Issues of the Exchequer* (p.332) does not include this. For the marriages of Owain's daughters see Ch.11 below. See also Evans, Mortimers, 332-33.
12. The appointment took effect on 1 April. Lloyd, 60-62; *Original Letters II*, i, 13-14 for details of castles; Rhidian Griffiths, 'Prince Henry and the Exchequer', 204-08; Allmand, 23.
13. *Original Letters II*, 10-13; *PPC*, ii, 61-63; Lloyd, 60-62.
14. *CPR*, i, 280.
15. *Original Letters II*, i, 13-14.
16. *Royal Letters*, 138-40, 146-51; *Original Letters II*, i, 19-20; Lloyd, 63-66, esp. 66, n.4.
17. C.A.J. Armstrong, *England, France and Burgundy in the Fifteenth Century* (London, 1983), 114, 119; *PPC*, i, 185-86; Lloyd, 65, n.1.
18. *Original Letters II*, i, 14-19; *Royal Letters*, 141-48; *CPR*, ii, 91, 293 (commissions to Kingston); Lloyd, 65-69.
19. *PPC*, i, 206-207; *Anglo-Norman Letters*, no. 293.
20. *Original Letters II*, i, 15-16, 21-23; *DNB*, 1310; Lloyd, 66 and 68-69: 240 'spers' means spearmen, probably on foot (Orig.Lett.16). The official letters list numbers of 'lances' and 'archers', a 'lance' meaning a mounted man-at-arms; the word can mean not only the man-at-arms,

but also his armed servants, of whom there might be four or more.
21. *Ann.Hen.IV*, 344-47; *Eulogium*, iii, 396; Davies, *English Chronicle*, 27: this English vernacular chronicle, based on *The Brut*, follows the Latin account of this incident in the *Eulogium*. Pugh, 11, 15.
22. Walsingham, ii, 255-58; *Ann.Hen.IV*, 368; *Eulogium*, iii, 396-98; Giles, 33; *Henry IV, Part I*, Act V, 1 & 5; McFarlane, 73-75; *CPR*, i, 293 (heads and quarters of rebels).
23. *CPR*, ii, 294; Allmand, 26; Rhidian Griffiths, 'Prince Henry and the Exchequer', 203.
24. *Royal Letters*, 152-54; in contemporary English the word 'disease' meant literally 'not at ease'. For Abergavenny revenues see Pugh, 46.
25. *Royal Letters*, 155-59.
26. Usk, 124-25.
27. *CCR*, ii, 185.
28. Rymer, viii, 328-29; *CCR*, ii, 111; Thomas, 75; Williams, *Radnor*, 51; *Powys Fadog*, i, 202.
29. *CPR*, i, 354, 215 and 487; see Appendix 2 below.
30. Lloyd, 75-76; *DNB*, 1311.
31. *CPR*, i, 295-97.
32. *Royal Letters*, 160-2. Davies, *Welsh Squirearchy*, 159.
33. *Original Letters* II, i, 14, 30-38; *PPC*, i, 221; Lloyd, 77-81.
34. Bower, vol. ii, 455.

Chapter Eight
1. *PPC*, i, 265-67; Lloyd, 77, 81; Glanmor Williams, *Owain GlynDŵr*, 36; Jacob, 53.
2. *PPC*, ii, 77-78; Lloyd, 86-87.
3. *CPR*, ii, 192. In April 1406 the abbey was given the advowson of the church of Rushbury, in Hereford diocese between Craven Arms and Church Stretton. This form of patronage was held by many monasteries, making it possible to appoint a vicar (or substitute for a rector), and enjoy any glebe land which might go with the church, together usually with the great tithes of the parish.
4. *PPC*, i, 223-25.
5. Allmand, 27; *PPC*, i, 229-32; *CPR*, ii, 50, 53.
6. *Eulogium*, iii, 401; Lloyd, 152 (*Ann.OGD*).
7. *PPC*, i, 236.
8. *Anglo-Norman Letters*, nos. 293 & 296; *PPC*, i, 232; Rhidian Griffiths, 'Prince Henry and the Exchequer', 209.
9. Lloyd, 67, especially n.5 for many details including the pictorial life of the Earl of Warwick, 68, 152 (*Ann.OGD*); *PPC*, i, 230; Pennant, i, 368 (Ellis ap Richard). For Campston, see OS Sheet 162 (1:50 000), SO 365226.

10. Jacob, 67-72; see n.15 below.
11. Lloyd, 115-18.
12. *Religieux de Saint-Denys, Chronique du*, ed. L. Bellaguet (Paris, 1841) iii, 165-67; T. Mathews, *Welsh Records in Paris* (Carmarthen, 1910), 23-31, and Rymer, viii, 356, for the documents.
13. *DNB*, 1311-12; Usk, 127. The Parliament House at Machynlleth is open to the public. *The Inventory of Ancient Monuments in Wales, Montgomeryshire* [1911], 746, dates it to the late 15th or early 16th century, but it could well be on the site of an older building used for Owain's Parliament.
14. *Original Letters* II, i, 43.
15. G. Williams, *Owain Glyndŵr*, 46-48; *Ann.Hen.IV*, 415-16. See Chapter 10 below, n.2.
16. Ellis, 59-60; Bower, ii, 452; Pennant, i, 348 and 359-61; Davies, 453; Thomas, 108-11; See below: n.23-25 for Pwll Melyn, and Chapter 11, n.2.
17. Enguerrand de Monstrelet, *Chronicles*, ed. Thomas Johnes (Hafod, 1810), i, 44-45; Rymer, viii, 357; *CPR*, i, 310; *Chronique Normande de Pierre Cochon* (Rouen, 1870), 209.
18. ibid., 209-10; Saint-Denys, iii, 166-67, 222-25; Monstrelet, i, 44-45; Lloyd, 88-89.
19. *PPC*, ii, 68-69; *PPC*, i, 246-47.
20. *Ann.Hen.IV*, 398-99; *CPR*, i, 204-205; *PPC*, i, 252; *Southampton Plot* 11, 78-79.
21. *Original Letters* II, i, 27-28; Lloyd, 93-95.
22. Lloyd., 95, esp. n.1.; G. Williams, *Owain Glyndŵr*, 39-40; O.S. Sheet 138, 1:50 000, SO 792885; Richard Williams, 'GlynDŵr's Checkpoint Charlie', *Country Quest* (June 1992), 27-28, 34.
23. *PPC*, i, 248-50; *Original Letters* II, i, 39-41. See Appendix 1 below.
24. Lloyd, 98 and 152 (*Ann.OGD*); *Ann.Hen.IV*, 399-400; Usk, 152-3, who incorrectly translates the abbey as Llanthony; Bower, ii, 452. Before he died, Gruffydd endured six years of imprisonment in various castles, including Nottingham. Bower is wrong in calling Oldcastle Lord Cobham, as he did not acquire that title till 1409, when he married the heiress.
25. Bower, ii, 456-7.
26. Ellis, 61.
27. Lloyd, 99, esp. n.4., and Appendix III, 157-8.

Chapter Nine

1. *Ann.Hen.IV*, 403-406; Jacob, 58-62; Pugh, 18-19; Allmand, 30. Adam of Usk goes further when noting Henry's death in 1413: 'he had been tormented for five years by a rotting of the flesh, by a drying up of the

eyes, and by a rupture of the intestines' p.168.

2. St. Denys, iii, 323; Cochon, 214; Monstrelet, i, 51; *Ann.Hen.IV*, 415:
   Choix de Pièces Inédits (Paris, 1863-64) i, 270-71, 299; Bower, 455. Of
   all these contemporary sources, only St. Denys and Monstrelet give
   much detail, in that order of reliability; see Lloyd, 101-102, especially
   his notes; Pennant, i, 373-74; Thomas, 135-39; G. Williams, *Owain
   Glyndŵr*, 41.
3. Rymer, viii, 406-407; *CCR*, ii, 527-28.
4. St. Denys, iii, 325-27; Monstrelet, i, 51; *Ann.Hen.IV*, 415; Pennant,
   373-74. I am grateful to Mr. Roger Worsley for help in finding Picton:
   see OS Sheet 157 (1:50 000), SM 008134.
5. Monstrelet, i, 51; T. Nash, *History of Worcestershire* (London, 1782),
   ii, 466; Pennant, i, 375-77.
6. Nash, 465; V. Green, *History of Worcester* (London, 1796), i. 326;
   Lloyd, 104, ns. 1 and 2; OS Sheet 138 or 150 (1:50 000) S0 750645
   (Woodbury). See also John Webb, 'A Brief Account of Owen
   GlenDŵr', (Hereford Cathedral Library, MS. A.6391/1) p.23.
7. Monstrelet, i, 51; St. Denys, iii, 325; Pennant, i, 375-77; Richard
   Williams, 'But was it war?', *Country Quest* (September, 1993), 36-37;
   on OS Sheet 138 or 150, SO 754657 is about the centre of the area
   suggested.
8. Roy Palmer, *The Folklore of Hereford and Worcester* (Logaston,
   1992), 144, 210-11.
9. *Anglo-Norman Letters*, no.334; *Richard II*, II, 1.
10.*Victoria County History of Hereford*, i, 218 and n.23, for Ivington.
11. *Ann.Hen.IV*, 415; Monstrelet, i, 51; St. Denys, iii, 329; Cochon, 214.
12. Lloyd, 106-07.
13. *Ann.Hen.IV*, 419, gives 28 ships, and Walsingham, ii, 273, gives 38;
    otherwise the two accounts are similar. See *Pièces Inédits*, i, 299-300,
    and Lloyd, 126-27.

Chapter Ten

1. *CCR*, ii, 460; Pennant, i, 379; Lloyd, 105-106.
2. R.A. Griffiths, 'Some Secret Supporters of Owain Glyn Dŵr?', *BIHR*,
   37 (1964), 77-100; *Ann.Hen.IV*, 415-16; Walsingham, 244.
3. Lloyd, 119-21.
4. ibid., 152 (Ann.OGD), 126-29; Usk, 153-54.
5. Jacob, 64. At the end of Henry VIII's reign, the infant Mary Queen of
   Scots was also sent to the safety of the French court.
6. Rymer, viii, 436-37; Lloyd, 129; Allmand, 40.
7. Ellis, 68-69.
8. Lloyd, 131; Davies, *Welsh Squirearchy*, 158. John Talbot, who was
   now Lord Furnival in the right of his wife, later became the most

illustrious English soldier in Lancastrian France; created Earl of Shrewsbury, he was killed in 1453 at Castillon, the last battle of the Hundred Years' War.

9. Rymer, viii, 497-99.
10. Lloyd, 153 (*Ann.OGD*).
11. *RP*, iii, 611-12; *Henry V*, Act 4, Scene 3; Allmand, 32, 96. York was one of the very few English captains to die at Agincourt, perhaps from a heart attack; he is said to have been very fat, though not by Shakespeare.
12. Allmand, 312-13.
13. *PPC*, i, 302-303 (France); Rymer, viii, 499-500 (Brittany); Francoise Autrand, *Charles VI* (Paris, 1986), 349-60. Hugh Mortimer was chamberlain to Prince Henry and an experienced diplomat; he was probably a distant cousin of the Earl of March.
14. Walsingham, ii, 277-78; Usk, 154-55; Jacob, 64-65; Lloyd, 133-35.
15. ibid., 153 (*Ann.OGD*); Rymer, viii, 547.
16. Lloyd, 136-37; *PPC*, ii, 339-41, which also quotes a poem, probably by the contemporary writer John Lydgate, about the siege of Harfleur, in which 'Messenger', 'King's Daughter' and 'London' are guns taking part in a grim game of tennis. It shows that the famous story of the insulting French gift of tennis balls to Henry V has an early origin (*Henry V*, Act 1, Scene 2). The metal of burst guns was accounted for. No doubt the new 'Messenger' and 'King's Daughter' at Harfleur were recast from the metal of the original.
17. Usk, 167-68; *Issues of the Exchequer*, 321, 326-27; Lloyd, 136-38; Jacob, 65. The Issue Rolls do not name Mortimer's wife, so it is not clear where Lloyd gets her name of Catherine. Mr. Richard Williams kindly gave me a photograph of the Montgomery effigy.
18. Rymer, viii, 611-12; *CPR*, ii, 414, 469.
19. Usk, 126, 165-67: 'like another Job, I gathered to myself servants, and books, and garments, and household goods, wherefore blessed be God for ever and ever!'; Lloyd, 138-39.
20. Usk, 166; Lloyd, 153-54 (*Ann.OGD*), 138, 141-42.

Chapter Eleven
1. McFarlane, 108-12; Allmand, 40-58; *Henry IV, Part II*, IV, 4; Pugh, 24-26.
2. Rhidian Griffiths, 'Prince Henry's War', 173; Rymer, viii, 753; Thomas, 108-111; Pennant, 360; Davies, 453, for the amount of the ransom; Hodges, *Ludford Bridge and Mortimer's Cross*, Genealogical Table 3.
3. *Issues of the Exchequer*, 332; Prestwich, 502-03 (Menteith); Buchan, Montrose (Oxford, 1957), 381-84; Lloyd, 142-43.

4. Lloyd, 142; Usk, 167-8.
5. Ellis, 62-63; Phillips, *When did Owain Glyn Dŵr die?*, 60.
6. ibid., 71; Rymer, ix, 283; Lloyd, 143-44; Davies, *Welsh Squirearchy*, 159.
7. Usk, 167, 183; a report that he died in the tenth year of Henry IV has no support in other sources, English or Welsh (Hardynge, 365).
8. Lloyd, 154, (*Ann.OGD*); Ellis, 62; Phillips, 72.
9. Lloyd, 143-44; Rymer, ix, 283 and 330-31; Phillips, 67-72: there is a third piece of evidence, a document dated 'the sixth year after the revolt of Owain GlynDŵr' 1421, if that event ended in 1415, but not specifically for his death. 'Lastly, there is an englyn of uncertain date which states quite clearly that Owain GlynDŵr rose in revolt in 1400 and died fifteen years later in 1415.'
10. John Webb, *Owen GlenDŵr* (HCL, MS. A.6391/1), 39, citing Rymer (notes 2, 6 and 9 above) for Talbot's commissions of pardon to Owain and Maredudd. Webb traces the tradition that Owain died on 20 September at Monnington-on-Wye to Browne Willis, *A Survey of the Cathedral Church of Bangor* (London, 1721); Thomas Carte repeats it in his *General History of England* (London, 1750), ii, 670; it can be traced to Ellis, 63; see Phillips, 59, 63-5. The modern spelling of 'Monnington' is used in this book, both for the family and for the two places of this name.
11. Kingsford, 51-67, and *The Life of Henry V* (Oxford, 1911), 10, 191, edn. of Tito Livio, *Gesta Henrici Quinti*; *Mirror for Magistrates*, 128-30.
12. Pennant, 393-95; Price, 27-28; J. Williams, 75; Lloyd, 144; Phillips, 60, 62; OS Sheet 149 (1:50 000) SO 474504 (Lawton's Hope Farm), SO 480360 (Haywood); Sheet 162 SO 530280 (Harewood). Harewood (formerly a Templar manor) and Dinmore belonged to the Dinmore Commandery of the Knights of St. John of Jerusalem. See also Robinson, *Manors*, 97-98, 130-32, 135, 144-47.
13. Rymer, ix, 330; Ellis, 65; *Powys Fadog*, i, 214-17; Lloyd, 144-45; O.G.S Croft, *The House of Croft of Croft Castle* (Hereford, 1949), 28-31. The names of Owain's daughters vary. Only Ellis calls Alice Elizabeth, but he calls Monnington's wife Margaret; Croft, quoting Llyfr Baglan, calls her Anne; Lord Grey's mythical marriage to one daughter has been explained in Chapter 6, p.12, note 28.
14. *RP*, *Henry VI*, iv, 140-41; Robinson, *Castles*, 33; Croft, 30-32; Glanmor Williams, *Wales 1415-1642*, 13.
15. Croft, 31; see Eilert Ekwall, *The Concise Oxford Dictionary of English Place Names* (Oxford, 4th ed., 1960), 331, 449, for Monnington in Straddel. Monnington Court is on OS Sheet 149, SO 382368, and four miles south of Monnington-on-Wye, itself two

miles upstream from Byford; see Lewis Byford (Lewis ab Ieuan).

16. Croft, 34: Sir John Lloyd to Owen Croft, (letter), 1931.

17. Lloyd, 1-2; Phillips, 61-62.

18. Croft, 34-35.

19. G. Williams, *Wales 1415-1642*, 26, 106, 114, 116, 128. 153, 157.

20. Croft, 34-35; See Palmer, 33, 35-37.

Chapter Twelve

1. Davies, 453-56; Rhidian Griffiths, 'Prince Henry and the Exchequer', 211-13, and 'Prince Henry's War', 165-73.

2. G. Williams, *Wales 1415-1642*, Chapter 1, esp. 12, 14-16, 20, 24-25, 28; *Henry IV, Part I*, Act 3, Scene 1.

3. Rhidian Griffiths, *Prince Henry's War*, 172.

4. Phillips, 61; G. Williams, *Owain Glyndŵr*, 60.

5. *Henry V*, Act 4, Scene 1.

6. Hodges, *Ludford Bridge and Mortimer's Cross* (Logaston, 1989).

7. Desmond Young, *Rommel* (London, 1955 ed.), 23, 149-50. After the war the author met Fritz Bayerlein, one of Rommel's finest officers, who gave many examples of Rommel's Fingerspitzengefuhl (fingertip feeling), 'that innate sense of what the enemy was about to do.' No wonder his soldiers thought he bore a charmed life. One example was when he and Bayerlein were observing a battle. Rommel insisted on moving 200 yards to a flank, as he was sure the British were about to shell the place where they were. Bayerlein agreed, they moved, and within five minutes Rommel was proved right.

8. *Original Letters* II, i, 43.

9. Thomas Ellis, 63.

10. G. Williams, 48.

Appendix 1

1. *PPC*, i, 173-9.

2. *CCR*, ii, 111 and Rymer, viii, 328-9 (King to Bishop of St. David's, at Worcester, 8 Sept. 1403). See J.E. Lloyd, *Owen Glendower*, 73-4. See Ch. 6 above, note 18, for castles in north-west Herefordshire and Radnorshire.

3. *PPC*, i, 251-53.

4. Rhidian Griffiths, 'Prince Henry and the Royal Exchequer', 210; *CPR*, ii, 120; Ch. 6 above, note 30.

Appendix 2

1. *CPR*, i, 354. See also Chapter 7, note 19 above.

2. *CPR*, i, 170 and 471, and ii, 52.

3. *CPR*, ii, 94.

Appendix 4
1. David Crouch, William Marshal (Harlow, 1990), 135-42; K.B.
   McFarlane, *England in the Fifteenth Century* (London, 1981), 'Bastard
   Feudalism', 25: a pioneer work on this subject.
2. N. Pronay and J. Cox, *The Crowland Chronicle Continuations 1459-
   1486* (London, 1986), 133.
3. Livery also meant the tax paid when an heir entered into his estates.

Appendix 5
1. V.J. Scattergood, *The Works of Sir John Clanvowe* (Cambridge, 1975),
   9, 18-27, 68-69 (quotation from 'The Two Ways'); another name for
   'The Cuckoo and the Nightingale' is 'The Boke of Cupide'; K.B.
   McFarlane, *Lancastrian Kings and Lollard Knights*, 165-66, 177, 201-
   06 (Sir John Clanvowe's life); See *Ann.Hen.IV*, 395 (Salisbury).

Abbreviations

Ann.Hen.IV	Annals of Henry IV (London, 1866)
Ann.OGD	Annals of Owain Glyn Dŵr
BBCS	Bulletin of the Board of Celtic Studies
BIHR	Bulletin of the Institute of Historical Research
CCR	Calendar of Close Rolls
CPR	Calendar of Patent Rolls
DNB	Dictionary of National Biography
HCL	Hereford Cathedral Library
NLW	National Library of Wales
OS	Ordnance Survey
PPC	Proceedings and Ordinances of the Privy Council of England
Rad.Soc.Trans.	Transactions of the Radnorshire Society
WHR	The Welsh History Review
Wool.Trans	Transactions of the Woolhope Naturalists' Field Club

Select Bibliography

Adam of Usk *Chronicon* ed. & trans. E.M. Thompson (London, 1904; Llannerch paperback edition)

Allday, D. Helen *Insurrection in Wales* (Lavenham, 1981)

Allmand, Christopher *Henry V* (London, 1992)

Anglo-Norman Letters and Petitions from All Souls Ms. 182 ed. M.D. Legge (Anglo-Norman Text Society, 1941)

Annals of Henry IV. See Walsingham

Archaeologia Cambrensis (Vol ii, 1847)

Autrand, Francoise *Charles VI* (Paris, 1986)

Bean, J.M.W. 'Henry IV and the Percies', *History*, Vol xliv, no 152 (1959), 212-27

Blount, Thomas (1618-79) 'MS. History of Herefordshire', Vol ii, original at Hereford City Library (f.LC 942.44/AC), late 18th century copy at Hereford Record Office (B 56/12)

Nongaerts, Theo ed. *The Correspondence of Thomas Blunt* (Amsterdam, 1978)

Bower, Walter *Johannis de Fordon Scotichronicon cum supplementis et continuatione Walteri Boweri* ed. Walter Goodall (Edinburgh, 1759, Vol. ii)

Burne, Alfred *The Crécy War* (London, 1955)

Calendar of Close Rolls, Henry IV

Calendar of Patent Rolls, Henry IV

Camden, William *Britannia* ed. Edmund Gibson 1697 (London, 4th ed.,1772)

Choix de Pièces Inédites relatives au règne de Charles VI ed. L. Douet d'Arcq (Paris, 1863), Vol. i.

Cochon, Pierre *Chronique Normande de Pierre Cochon* ed. C. de Roubillard de Beaurepaire (Rouen, 1870)

Davies, J.S. *An English Chronicle of the Reigns of Richard II, Henry IV, Henry V and Henry VI* (Camden Society, old series, vol. lxiv, 1856)

Davies, R.R. *Conquest, Coexistence and Change: Wales 1063-1415* (Oxford, 1987)
       'Owain Glyn Dŵr and the Welsh Squirearchy' (*Transactions of the Honourable Society of Cymmrodonin* [1968], ii, 150-169)

Dictionary of National Biography

Dugdale, W. ed. *Monasticon Anglicanum* (London, 2nd. ed., 1817-30, Vol. i)

Duncumb, John *History of the County of Hereford* (Hereford, 1804, Vol. i)

Dunn, Elizabeth 'Owain GlynDŵr and Radnorshire' (*Transactions of the Radnorshire Society*, Vol. xxxvii, [1967], 27-35)

Ellis, T. *Memoirs of Owen Glendowr* printed as a supplement (pp. 57-74) to *A History of the Island of Anglesey* (London, 1775; this edition 1853)

Eulogium Historiarum ed. F.S. Haydon (London, 1858-63, Vol. iii)

Evesham. See *Historia Vitae et Regni Ricardi II, a Monacho de Evesham*

Evans, B.P. 'The Family of Mortimer' (University of Wales, unpublished Ph.D. Thesis, 1934)

Giffin, Mary E. 'Cadwalader, Arthur and Brutus in the Wigmore Manuscript' (*Speculum*, Vol xvi [1941], 109-120)

Giles, J.A. *Incerti Scriptoris Chronicon de regnis Henrici IV, Henrici V, et Henrici VI* (London, 2nd. ed., 1848)

Goodman, Anthony *John of Gaunt: the Exercise of Princely Power in Fourteenth Century Europe* (London, 1992)

'Owain GlynDŵr before 1400' (*Welsh History
Review* 5, [1970-71], 60-77)

Griffiths, R.A. *The Making of the Tudor Dynasty* (Gloucester,
1985)

'Some Partisans of Owain Glyn Dŵr at Oxford'
(*Bulletin of the Board of Celtic Studies* 20
[1962-4], 282-92)

'Some Secret Supporters of Owain Glyn Dŵr?'
(*Bulletin of the Institute of Historical Research* 37
[1964], 77-100)

Griffiths, Rhidian 'Prince Henry, Wales and the Royal Exchequer'
Bulletin of the Board of Celtic Studies 32
(1985), 202-15

'Prince Henry's War: armies, garrisons and
supply during the GlynDŵr Rebellion' *Bulletin
of Celtic Studies* 34 (1987), 165-73

Hardyng, John *Chronicle* ed. H. Ellis (London, 1812)
Historical Monuments Commission *Inventory of Ancient
Monuments in Wales* (London, 1911)
*Historia Vitae et Regni Ricardi II, a Monacho quodam de Evesham
consignata* ed. T. Hearne (Oxford, 1729)
Hodges, Geoffrey *Ludford Bridge and Mortimer's Cross*
(Logaston, 1989)
Howse, W.H. *Radnorshire* (Hereford, 1949)
'New Radnor Castle' (*Transactions of the
Radnorshire Society*, Vol. xxviii, [1958], 24-6)

Issues of the Exchequer ed. F. Devon (London, 1837)

Jack, R.I. 'New light on the early days of Owain Glyn Dŵr'
Bulletin of the Board of Celtic Studies 21 (1964-6), 163-66
Jacob, E.F. *The Fifteenth Century* (Oxford, 1961)
Jones, T.A. *Without my Wig* (Liverpool, 2nd ed., 1945)

Kingsford, C.L. *English Historical Literature in the Fifteenth
Century* (Oxford, 1913)

Leland, John The Itinerary of ed. Thomas Hearne (Oxford, 3rd. ed., [1779], Vols. iv and v)

Lloyd, J.E. *Owen Glendower* (Oxford, 1931)

Lloyd, J.Y.W. *History of Powys Fadog* (London, 1881, 6 volumes)

Lodge, John *History of the County of Hereford* (Hereford, 1793)

McFarlane, K.B. *England in the Fifteenth Century* (London, 1986)
        Lancastrian Kings and Lollard Knights (Oxford, 1972)

McKissak, May *The Fourteenth Century* (Oxford, 1959)

Mascall, Robert. See Parry, J.H.

Monmouth, Geoffrey of *The History of the Kings of Britain* (London: Penguin Books, 1966)

Monstrelet *Chronicles of Enguerrand de* ed. Thomas Johne (Hafod, 1810)

Morris, Christopher 'Shakespeare's Politics' *The Historical Journal*, viii, 3 (1965), 293-308

Nash, T. *History of Worcestershire* (London, 1782, Vol. ii)

Noble, Frank 'Excavations at Bleddfa Church, and associated problems of the history of the lordship of Bleddfa' *(Transactions of the Radnorshire Society*, Vol. xxxiii, [1963], 57-63)

Original Letters illustrative of English History ed. H. Ellis (1827, Series II, Vol. i)

Palmer, Roy *The Folklore of Hereford & Worcester* (Logaston, 1992)

Parry, J.H. *The Register of Robert Mascall, Bishop of Hereford 1404-1416* (Hereford, 1916)

Pennant, Thomas *A Tour in Wales* (London, 1784 edition, 3 volumes)

Phillips, J.R.S. 'When did Owain Glyn Dŵr Die?' *Bulletin of the Board of Celtic Studies* 24 (1970-72), 59-77

Pilley, Walter a collection from Blount's MS. (Hereford City Library, [P.C.181] 091.42)

Powys Fadog See under Lloyd, J.Y.W.

Prestwich, Michael *Edward I* (London, 1988)

Price, John *Historical Account of Leominster* (Ludlow, 1795)

Priestley, E.J. *The Battle of Shrewsbury 1403* (Shrewsbury, 1979)

Proceedings and Ordinances of the Privy Council of England ed.
N.H. Nicolas, (London, 1834, Vols. i and ii)

Pronay, Nicholas, and John Cox *The Crowland Chronicle
Continuations 1459-1486* (London, 1986)

Pugh, T.B. *Henry V and the Southampton Plot* (Gloucester, 1988)

Rawcliffe, Carole *The Staffords, Earls of Stafford and Dukes of
Buckingham, 1394-1521* (Cambridge, 1978)

Rees, Joan *Shakespeare's Welshmen* ed. Vincent Newey and Ann
Thompson (*Literature and Nationalism*, Liverpool, 1991)

Reeves, N.C. 'Five Leominster Historians' (*Transactions of the
Woolhope Naturalists Field Club*, Vol. xlv, 1985, 284-95)

Religieux de St. Denys, Chronique du, ed. L. Bellinguet (Paris
1839-1852, Vol. iii)

Rennell of Rodd, Lord *Valley on the March* (London, 1958)

Robinson, C.J. *Castles of Herefordshire* (Hereford, 1869)
Mansions and Manors of Herefordshire (Hereford,
1873)

Royal and Historical Letters during the reign of Henry the Fourth
ed. F.C. Hingeston (London, 1860)

Rymer, T. ed., *Foedera, conventiones, literae, etc.* (The Hague,
1739-44)

Saccio, Peter *Shakespeare's English Kings* (Oxford, 1977)

Scattergood, V.J. ed. *The Works of Sir John Clanvowe* (London,
1975)

Shakespeare, William *King Richard II*
King Henry IV, Parts I and II
King Henry V

Skidmore, Ian *Owain GlynDŵr, Prince of Wales* (Swansea, 1978)

Thomas, A.H., and I.D. Thornley *The Great Chronicle of London*
(London, 1st ed. 1938, microprint ed. 1983)

Thomas, Thomas *Memoir of Owen Glendower* (Haverfordwest, 1822)

Tillyard, E.M.W. *Shakespeare's History Plays* (Harmondsworth, 1962)

Townsend, G.F. *Town and Borough of Leominster* (Leominster, 1862)

Usk. See Adam of Usk

Walker, Simon *The Lancastrian Affinity 1360-1399* (Oxford, 1990)

Walsingham, Thomas *Historia Anglicana* ed. H.T. Riley (London, 1863-4, Vol. ii)
     Annals of Richard II and Henry IV ed. H.T. Riley (London, 1866)

Webb, John 'A Brief Account of Owen GlenDŵr' in 'An Account taken out of Mr. Blount's Manuscript of Herefordshire' (Hereford Cathedral Library, MS. 6391/1, 1833)

Wigmore Chronicle See Dugdale, W. *Monasticon*

Williams, Evan 'On the Church, etc. at Pilleth' *Archaelogica Cambrensis* Vol. ii (1847) 329-32

Williams, Glanmor *Owain GlynDŵr* (Cardiff, 1993)
     Renewal and Reformation: Wales 1415-1642 (Oxford, 1993)

Williams, Jonathan *A Leominster Guide* (Leominster, 1808)
     History of the County of Radnor (Brecon, 1905)

Williams, Richard 'GlynDŵr's Checkpoint Charlie' (*Country Quest*, June 1992, 26-7, 34)
     'But was it war?' (*Country Quest*, September 1993, 36-7)

Wynne-Jones, Walford *A Guide to Pilleth Church* (1989)

INDEX

Abberley Hill 134
Abbey Cwm Hir 53, 169
Aberdovey 144
Abergavenny 4, 89, 90, 105, 117, 142, 176, 177
Aberystwyth 2, 8, 45, 55, 56, 94, 95, 101, 108, 110, 113, 118, 119, 146-50, 175, 177
Ackhill 73
Aconbury 113
Adam ab Iorwerth 162
Agincourt 33, 35, 36, 116, 135, 147, 154, 157, 171
Alburbury 182
Alfred the Great 171
Ambrosius 16
Angelsey 2, 4, 23, 32, 42, 58, 95, 109, 128, 145, 146
Anhuniog 146, 149
Aquitaine 47, 48, 122
Arc, Joan of 171
Archenfield 54, 113, 182
Arthur 16, 133, 159
Arundel, Archbishop 23, 33, 101, 114, 123, 137, 142, 147, 157
Arundel, Richard, Earl 18, 19
Arundel, Richard the younger Earl 19, 21, 22
Arudndel, Thomas, Earl 23, 27, 28, 31, 33, 90, 104, 111, 122, 131, 150, 151
Ashton 182
Auchinleck, General 172
Audley, Lord 98, 99, 194, 146, 163
Avalon 159

Avignon 117, 143, 144
Ayencourt 78, 140
Aylesbury 63

Bacton 182
Bala 155
Baldock, Walter de 63
Bangor 9, 10, 42, 117, 123, 144, 149, 156
Bardolf, Lord 123, 129, 144, 148
Barmouth 151
Barons Cross 83
Bastard Feudlaism 183-6
Bath 144
Baugé 162
Bayldon, Reginald of 109
Beauchamp, Earls of Warwick See Warwick
Beauchamp, William Lord Abergavenny 105
Beaufort, Edmund 162
Beaufort, Henry, Bishop of Winchester 153
Beaufort, John, Earl of Somerset 43, 58, 95, 107, 162
Beaufort, Thomas, Earl of Dorset 106, 153
Beaumaris 2, 32, 42, 45, 95, 96, 114, 128, 142, 145
Bedell, John 107
Bedford, John Duke of 35
Beguildy 75
Belay, Le Begué de 139
Benedict XIII 144, 151
Bere, Sir Kinaird de la 70, 79
Berkeley, Lord 104, 138
Berkhamsted 100
Berkshire 142

Berwick-on-Tweed 21, 46
Beryn Hills 67, 165
Bishops Castle 4, 181, 182
Black Death 8, 184
Black Prince 10, 19, 25, 63
Bleddfa 67, 69, 75
Bodenham, John 97, 145
Bohun, Joan de 33, 101, 136, 138
Bohun, Mary de 28
Bolingbroke, Henry 7, 8, 22, 26-9, 31, 33, 65, 91, 98, 162
Bosworth 70, 100, 172
Boudicca 2, 12, 83
Bourbon, Jaques de, Count of la Marche 117, 121, 122, 130
Bower, Walter 60, 110, 120, 126, 127
Bramham Moor 148-9
Brampton Bryan 55, 176
Brecknockshire 120
Brecon 4, 8, 17, 56, 97, 99, 107-8, 126, 137, 142, 175, 177
Bredwardine Church 155, 182
Brest 121
Bridgnorth 124
Bristol 104, 108, 110, 170
Brittany 37, 108, 116, 121, 130, 131, 148, 167
Brampton Bryan 75
Bromfield 7
Bruce, Robert 53, 171
Brut, the 102, 159
Brutus 16, 59, 110, 124
Bryn Glas (Pilleth) 76, 78-81
Buchan, John 12, 155
Bucknell 182
Buildwas 112
Builth 2, 4, 8, 12, 56, 97, 108, 175

Burford 73
Burgundy, Duke of 116, 148
Burnell, Hugh 41, 57, 104, 148
Butler, William 154
Byford, Lewis 117, 123, 129, 144, 148
Bytham 136
Byton 86, 182
Byton Hand 73

Cader Idris 43, 49
Cadwaladir Fendigaid 16
Cadzand 22
Caerleon 4, 6, 57, 90, 102, 103, 127, 133, 176
Caernarfon 2, 4, 8, 43, 57, 58, 95, 96, 108, 109, 110, 114
Caerphilly 176
Calais 31, 47, 85, 154, 162, 165
Cambridge 43
Cambridge, Richard Earl of 36, 113, 115
Camden, William 134
Campston Hill 115
Canon Pyon 161, 164
Canterbury 63
Caradog 2, 12, 72
Cardiff 89, 90, 108, 113, 142, 176
Cardigan 4, 17, 51, 52, 56, 95, 108, 110, 133, 175, 177
Cardigan Bay 96
Cardiganshire 100, 147, 149
Carew, Lord 96, 102, 110, 146
Carmarthen 4, 17, 48, 50, 56, 95-6, 99-102, 107, 132-4, 137, 175, 177
Carmarthenshire 98, 118, 142-4
Carreg Cennen 7, 99, 108, 143, 162, 176

Carrog 18
Casgob 69, 73
Castell Foel-allt 73, 78
Castile 26, 31, 32
Caxton, William 173
Cedewain 6
Cefnllys 67, 176
Cemaes 163
Cent, Sion 166
Ceredigion 144
Charles V 17, 116
Charles VI 116, 143
Charlton, Edward 56, 104, 144, 151
Charlton, John 49-51, 55, 56
Chaucer, Geoffrey 21, 26, 187
Cheapside 145
Cheltenham 122
Chepstow 4, 7, 90
Cheshire 27, 104, 114, 144
Chester 2, 4, 21, 64, 90, 95, 96, 109, 110, 152, 157, 168, 170
Chesterton 124
Chirk 4, 7
Cirencester 57, 143
Clanvowe, Sir John 70, 142, 166, 187-9
Clanvowe, Sir Thomas 70, 79, 93, 179-80
Clarence, Lionel, Duke of 6, 30
Clarence, Thomas, Duke of 59, 153
Clarendon, Sir Roger of 63
Claudius, Emperor 2, 12
Clifford 4, 107, 108, 179, 182
Clun 4, 7, 54, 182
Clyro 176
Cochon, Pierre 121, 130, 132
Coety Castle 141

Codnor, Lord Grey of 90, 126, 145, 177
Cokayn, John 143
Coke, Thomas 107
Combe 73
Coneway, Owen 44
Conwy 2, 8, 45-7, 55, 58, 95-6, 109-10, 114
Cornewall, Sir John 33, 73
Cornewall, Richard, Lord Fanhope 73
Court, Francis 140, 146
Courtenay, Richard 146
Craig y Dorth 115
Crécy 97, 116, 135
Crew, Sir Ranulfe 7
Cricieth 8, 95
Crickhowell 6, 176
Croft Ambrey 83
Croft Castle 163, 164, 171
Croft, Sir John 162
Croft, Owen 163, 164, 166
Crowland 142
Curteys, William 64
Cusop 70, 179, 182
Cwm-Aran 67
Cwm Llannerch 71
Cyffin, Hywell 41, 43
Cymer Abbey 155
Cynllaith 162
Cynllaith Owain 18

Danbury 63
Dartmouth 121
David I 97
Davies, Prof. Rees 48, 120
Davies, Richard 169
Dda, Hywell 118
Dee, River 170
Denbigh 4, 6, 8, 41, 60, 64, 66, 114
Despensers 7, 47
Despenser, Sir Hugh le 58
Despenser, Lady 122, 123
Devereux, Sir Walter 70
Devon 121

Dinas Bran 19
Dinefwr Castle 98, 100
Dinmore Manor 161
Dolgellau 67, 75, 117, 121, 155
Dorstone 176, 182
Douglas, Earl of 58, 91, 103
Dryden, John 143
Dublin 59, 128
Dunbar, George 58
Duncumb 82, 84
Durham, Bishop of 148
Dwnn, Henry 48, 98, 108, 109, 157
Dyffryn Clwyd 38
Dyfrdwy 17

Eardisley 176, 182
Ednyfed ap Tudur 157
Edward I 2-4, 16, 17, 30, 42, 45, 71, 183
Edward II 8, 9, 70, 185
Edward III 6, 16, 18, 25, 30, 37, 97, 106, 116, 187
Edward IV 65, 172, 185
Edward V 65
Edward VI 186
Edward the Confessor 59, 68, 69
Eleanor, Duchess of Gloucester 102
Elen, mother of Glyn Dŵr 17, 19
Elfael 7
Elizabeth I 171, 186
Ellis ap Richard 116
Ellis, Thomas 23, 41, 51, 84, 120, 127, 159, 160, 161, 173
Erpingham, Sir Thomas 33, 58, 148
d'Espagne, Jean 108, 110
Essex 142
Essex, Earl of 14
Evesham Abbey 48

Evesham, Monk of 38, 39, 41, 48, 56, 65, 68, 72, 76, 79, 80, 105, 176
Ewyas Harold 4, 176
Ewyas Lacy 144
Exeter 144

Fairford, John 98, 99, 100, 102
Falmouth 122
Falstaff 20, 34, 35, 48
Fastolfe, Sir John 34
Ferrers, Lord 70
Ferriby, William de 35
Ffinnant, Crach 41
Flanders 163
Flint 2, 4, 8, 21, 41, 95, 114, 119
France 27, 41, 42, 59, 65, 89, 108-10, 121, 129-40, 144, 145, 148, 153, 167, 168, 173, 183
Franciscans 42
Friars Minor 114

Gam, Dafydd 36, 120, 121, 126, 154, 155, 171
Gam, Gwladys 155
Gascoigne, Chief Justice 34, 154
Gaunt, John of 7, 8, 23, 25-32, 35, 43, 44, 48, 58, 98, 125, 184
Gavelkind 17, 18
Geneville 6
Giles (Chronicle) 68, 72, 76, 79, 104
Glamorgan 4, 7, 67, 89, 125, 126, 128, 133, 141
Glasbury 107, 179
Glaslyn 96
Glen Trool 53

Gloucester, Thomas,   26, 28, 31
   Duke of
Gloucestershire   86, 141
Glyn Dyfrdwy   23, 38, 41, 162
Glyn Dŵr, Alice   99, 143, 162
Glyn Dŵr, Catherine   150, 162
Glyn Dŵr, Gruffydd   125, 127, 162
Glyn Dŵr, Isabel   162
Glyn Dŵr, Janet   162, 164
Glyn Dŵr, Maredudd   156, 160, 162
Glyn Dŵr, Margaret   150, 162
   (wife)
Glyn Dŵr, Margaret   162-4
   (daughter)
Glyn Dŵr, Owain   2, 6, 7, 10, 11-
24, 25, 27, 33,
34, 37-44, 46-
50, 51-62, 64-8,
71-86, 89, 91,
92, 94-9, 102,
104, 107, 109,
110, 111-28,
129, 133, 134,
137, 138, 140,
141-152, 153-
66, 167-74, 175,
184
Glyn Dŵr, Tudur   21, 22, 41, 50,
127
Goch, Iolo   24, 44
Godwinson, Harold   2
Golden Valley   163
Goodman, Dr.   21
Goodrich   176
Gower   7, 102, 144
Great Schism   117, 144
Great Witley   134, 135, 137
Green-Price, Sir   81
   Richard
Grey, Lord   34, 37, 38, 40,
58, 60, 61, 64,
66, 86, 87, 92,
107, 119, 151,
167, 184
Grey, Sir Thomas   36

Greyndor, John   86, 87, 94, 125,
126, 146, 178
Griffiths, Prof. Ralph   141, 142, 143
Griffiths, Dr. Rhidian   47, 154, 168, 171
Grosmont   7, 115, 125, 127,
130
Grosvenor, Sir Robert   21
Gruffydd, Elis   165, 170
Gruffydd Fychan I   17
Gruffydd Fychan II   17, 18, 19
Gruffydd ap Llewelyn   59
Gruffydd ap Madog   17, 18
Gruffydd Thomas   147
Gwent   67, 90, 116, 119,
125, 126, 132
Gwilym ap Tudur   42, 44, 45-7
Gwrtheyrnion   6
Gwynedd   109, 118, 125,
147
Gwynionydd   19

Hales, Sir Robert   26
Hall, Edward   13, 84, 161
Hangest, Jean de   132, 138, 140
Hanmer, Sir David   10, 20, 39, 171
Hanmer, Gruffydd   41, 43
Hanmer, Margaret   20, 24
Hanmer, Philip   41, 43
Hanseatic League   47
Hardynge, John   41, 61
Harewood Forest   161, 164
Harfleur   121
Harlech   2, 8, 45, 55, 57,
58, 87, 94, 95,
96, 108, 109,
110, 113, 118,
119, 146, 149,
150
Harley, Brian   55
Harwarden   41
Hatfield, William   75
Havard, Jenkin   98, 100, 102
Haverfordwest   131, 132
Hay   4, 8, 177
Haywood Forest   161, 164

Hendy-gwyn-ar-daf	118	Herefordshire (cont.)	147, 148, 154,
Henry I	16		157, 161, 166,
Henry II	16		169, 176, 179,
Henry III	30		181, 182, 187
Henry IV	1, 30-2, 36, 37,	Hergest	70
	39, 40, 41, 43,	Heuse, Sieur de la	130
	45, 46, 47, 50,	Hindwell	71
	56, 58, 63, 64,	Hiraethog, Gruffydd	40, 51, 79, 89,
	66, 73, 85, 87,		113, 115, 125,
	90, 93, 97, 99,		126, 144, 147,
	101, 103, 107,		149, 152, 159
	111, 116, 118,	Holbeach	142
	120, 122, 129,	Holinshead, Raphael	13
	131, 133, 134,	Holt	41, 90
	135, 137, 138,	Homildon Hill	91, 103
	141, 144, 151,	Hopkin ap Thomas	102, 126
	153, 167, 169,	Hotspur, Harry	11, 14, 15, 16,
	170, 173, 175,		28, 29, 32, 33,
	180		45-7, 49, 60, 64,
Henry IV, Part I	1, 11		65, 82, 91, 93,
Henry V	33, 34, 35, 83,		102, 103, 104,
	154, 156, 160,		123, 135, 167,
	165, 171, 172,		173
	174, 188	Hugueville, Sieur de	130
Henry VI	83, 184, 185	Humphrey, Duke of	160
Henry, Prince of Wales	32, 33, 37, 45,	Gloucester	
	55, 57, 58, 83,	Humphreys, Humphrey	156
	87, 90, 94, 95,	Hundred Years War	42, 71, 135, 139,
	104, 111, 112,		169
	114, 115, 118,	Huntingdon	142, 143
	119, 120, 124,	Huntington	4, 7, 72, 107,
	140, 145, 146,		142, 176
	149, 153, 161,	Huss, John	171, 185
	167, 168, 172	Hyddgen, Battle of	51-62, 66
Hentland	182	Hywell y Fwyall, Sir	9
Hereford	55, 56, 85, 86,		
	87, 90, 98, 105,	Ireland	22, 29, 31, 33,
	107, 108, 113,		47, 131, 148
	115, 129, 134,	Isabelle of France	116
	138, 141, 144,	Iscennen	99
	151, 161, 164,	Iscoed Uch Hirwen	19
	168, 177	Ivington	83, 137
Hereford, Earls of	120, 124		
Herefordshire	1, 6, 69, 82, 101,	Jack, Dr. R. Ian	18
	107, 113, 145,	James I	145

James of St. George, Master 2
Jenkin ap Llewelyn 100
Jenkin ap Rhys 146
Jerusalem 28
Jevan Goz, Sir David ap 59
Jevan ap Meredith 119
Joan, Queen 102
John, King 59, 136
John IV, Duke of Brittany 116

Kenderchurch 182
Kentchurch 163, 164, 165
Kidwelly 4, 7, 48, 98, 99, 102, 108, 143
Kingsland 86
Kingston, Richard 100, 105, 113
Kingstone 181
Kington 54, 182
Kinnersley Castle 70
Kinsham 73
Kinver 124
Knighton 68, 72, 74-6, 83
Knucklas 67

Lacy 6
Lancaster, duchy of 6, 28, 106
Lancaster, Edmund, 1st Earl of 30
Lands End 122
Langland, William 26
Langley 33
Laugharne 102, 176
Launde 63, 142
Lawton's Hope 161, 164
Lear, King 16
Leicester 63, 101, 134
Leland, John 53, 55, 87, 168
Leogra 124
Leominster 54, 83, 85, 86, 115, 136, 137, 161, 182
L'Estrange, Elizabeth 18

L'Estrange, John 18
L'Estrange, Sir Richard 151
Lewis ab Ieuan 117
Lichfield 144
Lincolnshire 142
Lingein, Richard de 83, 84
Lingen 73
Little Malvern 115
Livio, Tito 160
Llanbadarn 95, 96, 175
Llandaff 9, 56, 106, 151
Llandeilo 98
Llandovery 56, 98, 99, 137, 163, 175, 176
Llanfaes 42, 169
Llangarron 182
Llangunllo 75
Llanidloes 67, 75
Llanrhaeadr-ym-Mochnant 165
Llanrothal 182
Llantarnam 126, 127, 133
Llanthony 113
Llawhaden 176
Llewelyn Bren 3
Llewelyn ap Iowerth 17, 30, 59
Llewelyn ap Gruffydd 12, 17
Llewelyn ap Howel 154
Lloyd, Sir John 159, 164
Llwyd, Gruffydd 21, 24
Lodge, Rev. John 81
Lollards 26, 64, 70, 142, 166, 187-9
London 19, 95, 104, 152
London, Tower of 126
Lords Appellant 22, 26, 28
Ludford Bridge 78
Ludlow 4, 6, 68, 69, 71, 73, 75, 78, 85, 86, 171
Lugg, River 72, 73, 74, 76
Lydbury North 181, 182
Lyonshall 54, 70, 86, 107, 176, 182

Macleod, Neil, of Assynt 155

Machynlleth 75, 118, 120, 144, 154

Madley 142, 182

Maelienydd 6, 67, 69, 71, 75, 79, 86

Maidstone, William 123

Malban, William 149

Manorbier 176

March, Edmund, 3rd Earl of 6, 38

March, Roger, 4th Earl of 30, 31

Maredudd ap Tudor 17

Mark Castle 162

Martley 136

Mascall, Robert 181

Massy, John de 45

Mawddach 96

Mawddwy 43

Mawddwy, William of 18

Menteith, John of 155

Merbury, Nicholas 91

Mercia 124

Merciless Parliament 27

Merlin 16, 102, 133

Merioneth 4

Mersey, River 124

Middleton, Robert 151

Milan, Duke of 61

Mile End 26

Milford Haven 130, 138

Moccas 182

Mone, Guy de 175

Monnington, Ralph 98, 99, 163

Monnington, Richard or Roger 163

Monnington in Straddle 163, 164, 165

Monnington on Wye 160, 161, 163, 164

Monnow, River 163

Monmouth 4, 7, 36, 102, 115, 125, 134

Monmouth (cont.) 143, 182

Monmouth, Geoffrey of 16, 59, 60, 61, 102

Monstrelet 121, 130, 134, 138, 139, 153

Montgomery 4, 6, 55, 56, 142, 151, 182

Morgannwg 125

Morris, Christopher 14

Mortimer, Sir Edmund 1, 12, 14, 15, 16, 32, 33, 54, 58, 65-87, 89, 92, 94, 150, 162, 167, 173

Mortimer, Edmund, last Earl of March 31, 33, 36, 60, 65, 94, 122, 123

Mortimer, Hugh 148

Mortimer, Roger (brother of last Earl) 65, 122

Mortimers, the 6, 12, 29, 30, 141

Mortimer's Cross 70, 76, 83, 172

Mowbray, Thomas, Earl Marshall 123, 129

Mowbray, Thomas, Earl of Nottingham 28, 29, 31

Myndd Epynt 8

Narberth 6

Nash, Dr. 133, 134, 136

Nefyn 169

Netherlands 151

Neville, Ralph, Earl of Westmorland 33, 148

New Radnor 53, 54, 169, 176, 182

Newcastle Emlyn 100, 101, 177

Newcastle upon Tyne 104

Newent 141

Newport 90, 108, 119, 142, 176

Newport, William 125

Newtown 67

Neville's Cross 97

Nicholls, Benedict 149

Nicopolis 116

Noble, Frank 75
Normandy 59, 130
Northampton 41
Northumberland, Earl 16, 31, 57, 58,
of 91, 93, 103, 123,
129, 144, 148,
167, 173
Norton 73, 86
Norway 59

Oates, Titus 143
Ocle Pychard 179
Offa 2
Offa's Dyke 124
Ogmore 7
Oke, John 141, 143
Old Radnor 54, 182
Oldcastle, Sir John 34, 36, 126, 146,
166, 175, 188
Oriennau Meigiawn 124
Orléans, Duke of 116, 129, 140,
144, 148
Oswestry 4, 7, 18, 19, 41,
114, 122
Otterburn 91
Overton-on-Dee 169
Oxford 43, 44, 146
Oxford, Robert de 22, 27
Vere, Earl of
Owain Lawgoch 17, 44, 120
Owen, William 128

Painscastle 56
Parliament 92, 99, 118, 147,
162, 174
Paris 117, 144
Pastons 34
Pay, Henry 138
Peasants Revolt 25, 31
Pembridge 82, 83, 86
Pembroke 4, 51, 52, 96,
140, 145
Pembrokeshire 99, 108, 131,
137, 140, 156,
163,

Penclawdd 115
Pennal 144
Pennant, Thomas 18, 23, 53, 80,
82, 84, 87, 92,
131, 134, 136,
161, 176
Peterchurch 182
Pevensey 123
Philip II 59, 136
Phillips, Dr. 157, 159, 165,
170
Picton Castle 132
Pilleth, Battle of 1, 12, 54, 63-88,
89, 93, 100, 107,
137, 179, 180
Plantagenet 27, 30, 37
Plymouth 121, 122, 137
Plynlimon 51, 55, 56
Poitiers 135
Ponfald 125
Pontefract 29, 106, 131
Pontesbury 54, 182
Popish Plot, The 143, 186
Powel, David 120
Powys 4, 114
Powys Fadog 16, 17, 18, 84
Prague 28
Presteigne 54, 67, 72, 83,
86, 94, 100, 182
Price, John 82, 84
Pulle, Sir John de 64
Pulverbatch 182
Pwll Melyn 120, 125, 128,
130

Radcot Bridge 22, 27
Radnor 4, 6, 67, 71, 89,
94, 107, 125,
126, 142, 177
Ramsey 142, 143
Rees, Prof. Joan 14
Rhys Ddu (the Black) 146, 147, 149
Rhys Gethin 71, 80
Rhys ap Gruffydd, Sir 9
Rhys ap Tudur 42, 44, 45-7,

Rhys ap Tudur   152, 157
  (cont.)
Rhys, Prince of   17
  Deheubarth
Rhuddlan   2, 8, 41, 95, 114
Richard I   1, 6, 10, 21, 22,
Richard II   25, 26, 27, 29-
                       33, 42, 43, 48,
                       63, 65, 93, 101,
                       111, 116, 129,
                       137, 140, 141,
                       148, 155, 180,
                       185, 187
Richard II   14, 23, 137
Richard III   65, 70, 185
Richard ap Gruffydd   146, 151
Richards Castle   73
Rieux, Marshal de   130, 131, 132
Risbury   83
Robert III   58, 145
Rodd   73
Rome   38, 60, 117, 143,
                       144
Rommel   172
Ross   134
Ruthin   8, 41, 61, 83,
                       159, 161

St. Albans   23, 143
St. Asaph   9, 10
St. Clears   102, 132, 133
St. Davids   9, 56, 144
St. Denys, Monk of   117, 121, 130,
                       131, 132, 133,
                       138, 139
St. Dubricius   182
St. Edmunds Abbey   142
St. Malo   121
St. Pol de Leon   138, 151
St. Swithins Church   150
St. Weonards   182
Sais, Sir Degory   9, 20, 21, 171
Saltash   121
Scarisbec, Henry of   110
Scipio Africanus   173

Scotland   3, 21, 31, 40, 41,
                       42, 58, 59, 89,
                       103, 167, 168,
                       173, 174, 183
Scrope, Henry of   36
  Masham
Scrope, Richard,   129, 134
  Archbishop of York
Scrope, Richard, Lord 21
Scrope, Stephen   128
Scudamore, Sir John   99, 142, 143,
                       162, 163
Scudamore, Philip   152
Scudamore, Philpot   143
Seine, River   117
Sele, Hywel   121
Severn estuary   106
Shakespeare, William   1, 13, 14-6, 23,
                       27, 29, 32-6, 80,
                       82, 84, 93, 104,
                       123, 147, 169
Shallow, Justice   20, 48
Shobdon   73
Shrawardine   182
Shrewsbury   42, 55, 86, 90,
                       95, 113, 148,
                       151, 152, 168
Shrewsbury, Battle of 15, 72, 82, 89,
                       103, 105, 129,
                       148
Shropshire   1, 6, 82, 86, 111,
                       112, 140, 144,
                       147, 148, 169,
                       181
Six Ashes   124
Skenfrith   7
Smithfield   26
Snodhill   176, 182
Snowdonia   61, 87, 109, 128,
                       155, 156
Somerset, John   See Beaufort
  Beaufort Earl of
Southampton Plot   36
Spain   108, 122, 167
Stafford, Earl of   72, 90

Stanley, Sir John	119	Tupsley	181
Stanley, Sir William	64	Tywi valley	107
Stapleton	72, 73, 107, 176		
Stewart, Robert, Duke	145	Ulchelwyr	9, 17, 19, 48
of Albany		Ulster	6
Stowe	182	Uthr Pendragon	16, 57
Strata Florida	56, 127, 155,	Usk	4, 6, 47, 57, 59,
	169		90, 125, 144,
Sudbury, Archbishop	26		152, 157, 176
Swineshead, John	142	Usk, Adam of	8, 30, 38, 41, 44,
Swynford, Katherine	43		45, 55, 60, 68,
Sycarth	18, 19, 23-4, 173		79, 90, 94, 106,
			118, 125, 148,
Tacitus	83		150, 151, 155,
Talbot, Gilbert, Lord	149, 157, 159,		156, 157, 159,
Furnival	165		160, 164, 171
Talbot, John	146, 149		
Teifi valley	100	Valle, Sieur de la	135
Teme, River	74, 75, 134, 137	Vaughan, Howel	94
Tenbury	134, 137	Vaughan, Robert	23, 159, 160
Tenby	132	Vaughan, Roger	154, 155
Teutonic Knights	28	Venables, William	109
Tewkesbury	172	Venice	28
Thetford	142	Vercingetorix	12
Thomas, Thomas	82	Veyse, John	142, 143
Thorney	142	Vienna	28
Three Castles, The	143	Vikings	59
Tiptoft, John	154	Vilna	28
Titley	182	Vowchurch	182
Townsend, George	83		
Trefnant, John	10, 19	Wakefield	100
Trefor, John	10, 39, 43, 117,	Wallace, William	155, 171
	123, 129	Wallingford	47, 49, 50
Trent, River	123, 124	Walsingham, Thomas	20, 22, 23, 38,
Tretower	176		40, 78, 79, 80,
Trevenant, John	65		87, 104, 125,
Trie, Jean de	138		130, 133, 138,
Trie, Patrouillart de	131, 135		143
Tripartite Indenture	15, 123, 144	Walter ap Lhwyd	155
Trothy valley	115	Walter, Miles	105
Trumpington, Thomas	155	Wapley Hill	83
of		Wars of the Roses	30, 155, 172, 184
Tudor, Henry	131, 170, 185	Warwick, Richard	27, 28, 31, 90,
Tudor, Jasper	131, 172	Beauchamp, Earl of	105, 113, 115,
Tudor, Owen	17, 172		146

227

Washbourne, Sir John 136
Waterton, Sir Hugh 98, 99, 136
Watling Street 124
Webb, John 160
Wede, John 150
Wellington, Duke of 173
Welshpool 41, 55, 56, 57, 58, 114
Wentnor 182
Weobley 54, 70, 182
Westminster 20
Wetsbury 182
White Castle 7
Whitmore, David 119
Whitney, Sir Robert 70, 179-80
Whitney-on-Wye 70, 182
Whitton 72
Wichenford 136
Wigmore 4, 6, 69, 71, 73, 75, 83, 90, 171, 182, 183
Wigmore, Monk of 68, 76
Wigmore, Robert 100, 107
Willis, Browne 160
Windsor Castle 122
Winforton 182
William I 42
William ap Thomas 155
Williams, Evan 80
Williams, Rev. Jonathan 77, 82, 83, 84
Woburn 142
Wolfscastle 156
Wolverhampton 124
Woodbury Hill 134-7
Worcester 47, 48, 50, 56, 107, 113, 115, 124, 133, 134, 135, 137, 144, 168
Worcester, Thomas Percy, Earl of 31, 33, 56, 57, 58, 96, 103, 104, 175
Wrekin 124
Wyclif, John 26, 64, 187, 188

Yale 7
Yazor 70
York, Edmund, Ist Duke of 26
York, Edward, Duke of 101, 107, 111, 122, 123, 147
York, Richard of (brother of Edward) 113, 115
York, Richard, Duke of 100, 115
Yorkshire 148
Young, Gruffydd 117, 144, 149
Young, Richard 121
Ystrad Tywi 144